HATE SPEECH, PORNOGRAPHY, AND THE RADICAL ATTACK ON FREE SPEECH DOCTRINE

James Weinstein

Arizona State University

D0061204

Westview
PRESS

A Member of the Perseus Books Group

Copyright © 1999 by Westview Press, A Member of the Perseus Books Group

Published in 1999 in the United States of America by Westview Press, 5500 Central Avenue, Boulder, Colorado 80301-2877, and in the United Kingdom by Westview Press, 12 Hid's Copse Road, Cumnor Hill, Oxford OX2 9JJ

Find us on the World Wide Web at www.westviewpress.com

Library of Congress Cataloging-in-Publication Data
Weinstein, James, 1926–
 Hate speech, pornography, and the radical attack on free speech
doctrine / James Weinstein.
    p. cm.
 Includes bibliographical references and index.
 ISBN 0–8133–2708–3 (hardcover). —ISBN 0–8133–2709–1
(pbk.)
    1. Freedom of speech—United States.   2. Hate speech—United
States.   3. Pornography—United States.   I. Title.
KF4772.W45   1999
342.73'0853—dc21   99–34285
                                                                                                   CIP

The paper used in this publication meets the requirements of the American National Standard for Permanence of Paper for Printed Library Materials Z39.48-1984.

10   9   8   7   6   5   4   3   2   1

Hate Speech, Pornography, and the Radical Attack on Free Speech Doctrine

THIS BOOK IS DEDICATED TO
THE MEMORY OF MY MENTORS
KENNETH S. GOLDSTEIN, IRVING HILL,
AND EDWARD B. IRVING JR.

CONTENTS

ACKNOWLEDGMENTS

I am indebted to many people for their help on this book: Paul Bender, Keith Hunsaker, David Kaye, Jeffrie Murphy, Robert Post, Eugene Volokh, Leo Wiegman, and an anonymous "political scientist in a major northeast university" provided helpful suggestions and comments; Mary Sigler and Phyllis New supplied invaluable research assistance; reference librarian Alison Ewing unfailingly located every source material I requested; copy editor Alice Colwell cast her eagle eye on the manuscript; and Kay Winn and Fran Scott rendered much-needed secretarial assistance.

James Weinstein

HATE SPEECH, PORNOGRAPHY, AND THE RADICAL ATTACK ON FREE SPEECH DOCTRINE

1

INTRODUCTION

A recent Supreme Court decision declares: "[I]t is a central tenet of the First Amendment that the government must remain neutral in the marketplace of ideas."[1] Such claims are red flags to radical theorists, who deny that neutrality exists in the political world that legal rules inhabit. Radical legal theorists, like their kindred spirits in philosophy, history, and literature, view such assertions as just so much rhetoric disguising what is in fact some oppressive value choice imposed by elites on the less powerful.

Radical legal critics, especially adherents of "outsider jurisprudence" and critical race theory, have good reason to be suspicious of neutrality claims. American legal history is replete with what can now be recognized as outright oppression of racial minorities dressed up as the inevitable result of the application of some neutral principle. In the notorious case of *Plessy v. Ferguson,* the United States Supreme Court upheld a Louisiana law requiring "equal but separate" accommodations for "white" and "colored" railroad passengers.[2] The Court brushed aside the claim that despite its formal neutrality in the treatment of white and black, the law was nonetheless based on racist notions of black inferiority. "[T]he assumption that the enforced separation of the two races stamps the colored race with a badge of inferiority," the Court explained, "is not by reason of anything found in the act, but solely because the colored race chooses to put that construction upon it."

The *Plessy* travesty was made possible by a brand of jurisprudence that had its heyday in the late nineteenth century and was so ubiquitous that it had no name but today is referred to, usually derisively, as "legal formalism." Formalist judges believed, or at least acted as if they did, that cases could be decided by mechanical application of legal rules. A key feature of this jurisprudence is its claim that it leaves no room for value choices by judges, whose role was to "find" the law, not "make" it.[3] This formalist mythology was exploded in the 1920s and 1930s by the legal realists, who demonstrated the large extent to which value choice did, and in fact must, enter into judicial decisions. Like Jeremy Bentham's exposé of natural law jurisprudence a century earlier, legal realists showed that the value choices disguised by formalism often served economically powerful interests at the expense of those less well-off.

Under the intellectual influence of the realists (as well as the experience of the Great Depression), Supreme Court doctrine became less formal and abstract and more attuned to context and pragmatics, at least so far as economic matters were concerned. The 1930s and 1940s saw the demise of almost all formalist doctrine relating to commercial matters. It was not until 1954, however, that the Court declared in *Brown v. Board of Education* that segregation in public education is "inherently unequal."[4] As late as 1967, the State of Virginia still argued that its antimiscegenation law did not discriminate against blacks because it punished equally white and black participants in interracial marriages. This time the Supreme Court recognized the racist purpose of the law and invalidated it as a violation of the Equal Protection Clause of the Fourteenth Amendment.[5] But short-lived indeed would be the Court's realism, especially with respect to race. By the 1980s, formalism, which had never completely disappeared, was again flowering.

Current Supreme Court jurisprudence is marked by various "tests" that often serve to obscure value choice and by invocation of false symmetries. The Court in *Brown v. Board of Education* invoked no formal tests to assess whether black children were being deprived of equal protection of the laws but instead forthrightly declared that segregation "generates a feeling of inferiority as to their status in the community that may affect their hearts and minds in a way unlikely ever to be undone." Today, in contrast, the Court subjects racial classifications to "strict scrutiny," a test that requires both that the classification be designed to advance a "compelling governmental interest" and that the means chosen to advance that goal be "necessary" to achieving it. By focusing on racial classifications in the abstract rather than on the history of racial oppression in this country, the Court was able to assimilate race-conscious affirmative action programs into the same juridical category as the racial segregation involved in *Plessy* and *Brown*.[6] Formal neutrality and false symmetry thus triumph once again. By treating all racial classifications the same, modern formalist doctrine succeeds in obscuring the moral difference between remedial programs designed to *include* minorities in areas in which they have historically been denied access and the racist schemes of *exclusion* that made these remedies necessary in the first place.

No wonder critical race theorists are suspicious of modern free speech doctrine, one of the most formalistic areas of the law and one that claims to be assuring "neutrality" in the marketplace of ideas. *Words That Wound,* a collection of essays by critical race theorists Mari Matsuda, Charles Lawrence, Richard Delgado, and Kimberlè Crenshaw, boldly challenges this claim of neutrality. The authors explain how racist speech is used to intimidate, degrade, and silence people of color and thus is an important part of the mechanism by which minorities are subordinated. When minorities seek legal protection from verbal assault, they are told that laws against racist speech turn on the speaker's viewpoint and thus violate the key neutrality command of the First Amendment. But the claim that free speech doctrine is so pristinely neutral is, according to these critics, a lie. To the contrary, free speech doctrine is, in their view, biased against minorities: When powerful forces in society complain that speech is impairing their interests, courts readily find exceptions to free speech principles and allow regulation, as in the case of commercial and industrial speech and libel. But when minorities complain that racist speech interferes with their educational and employment opportunities or causes severe emotional injury, these harms are discounted or ignored and no exception is forthcoming. On a deeper level, radical critics complain that the whole idea of a "neutral" marketplace of ideas is a fantasy. They point out that access to the means of communication that form opinion in this country is so expensive as to be prohibitive to marginalized people and, in any event, is controlled by forces that have no interest in giving voice to their ideas.

Radical feminist legal scholars make similar claims, and they, too, have good reason to be suspicious. If late-nineteenth-century jurisprudence obscured racial oppression, it made gender oppression invisible. Closely allied to the formalist claims of neutrality are claims that certain results are dictated by the "nature of things." It was nature that formalist judges invoked to uphold the legal exclusion of women from important roles in civil life and to confine them in the domestic sphere. In 1872 the Court upheld a law forbidding women to practice law.[7] "The natural and proper timidity and delicacy which belongs to the female sex," declared Justice Joseph Bradley in a concurring opinion, "evidently unfits it for many of the occupations of civil life." "[T]he nature of things," he continued, "indicates the domestic sphere as that which properly belongs to the domain and functions of womanhood."

As long as it took for the Court to acknowledge racial segregation as a tool of racial oppression, it took even longer before gender-based laws were invalidated as discrimination against women. A few years before *Brown* was decided, the Court upheld a state law that forbade a woman from obtaining a bartender's license unless she was the wife or daughter of a male owner of a licensed liquor establishment.[8] The Court accepted the state's argument that the "protecting oversight" of husbands or fathers was necessary to minimize hazards to which "barmaids" would be subject, and it refused even to consider the possibility that "the real impulse behind this legislation was an unchivalrous desire of male bartenders to try to monopolize the calling."

Not until 1971 did the Supreme Court find that a law that discriminated against women violated the Equal Protection Clause: It held unconstitutional an Idaho law that gave preference to men over women in the appointment of administrators of estates.[9] But despite this limited and belated recognition in this and subsequent cases that unfair and oppressive discrimination against women did indeed exist, doctrinal formalism would once again obscure this reality. Three years later the Court ruled that a state's insurance system that excluded pregnancy and childbirth from disability coverage did not discriminate against women.[10] Classifications based on pregnancy, concluded the Court, do not discriminate on the basis of gender but between "pregnant women and nonpregnant persons." Similarly, the Court found that a state law granting a lifetime employment preference in the state civil service for veterans— over 98 percent of whom were male—did not constitute gender discrimination.[11] Given this long-standing and often invisible bias against women in American constitutional doctrine, radical feminists have good reason to suspect that free speech doctrine is in reality far from neutral when it comes to women's interests.

Current free speech doctrine is in some ways a traditional institution. Its intellectual origins trace back to the works of seventeenth-century poet John Milton and nineteenth-century philosopher John Stuart Mill; its legal roots are in the decisions of early-nineteenth-century jurists Oliver Wendell Holmes Jr. and Louis Brandeis. Adherents to traditional institutions usually do not welcome radical critique. For this reason, it is not surprising that many supporters of free speech doctrine dismiss radical critics as dangerous heretics or, taking a page from Emperor Julian's book, ignore them altogether, hoping that they will go away. Yet on a deeper level this reaction is surprising, even paradoxical. At least where other institutions are concerned, free speech doctrine recognizes the value of radical critique as an antidote to intellectual stultification, keeping good ideas from becoming stale dogma. As Mill explained more than a century ago, even if "opinion be in error, it may, and very commonly does, contain a portion of truth; and since the general or prevailing opinion on any subject is rarely or never the whole truth, it is only by collision of adverse opinions that the remainder of the truth has any chance of being supplied."[12]

Adherents of traditional free speech doctrine, however, have typically reacted to attacks on the fundamental precepts of the doctrine more like high priests defending religious faith than heirs of the intellectual skeptics who laid the foundation of the principle they so vigorously defend. It is ironic indeed that many radicals are more attuned than are some of the most vociferous free speech traditionalists to Mill's and Holmes's most important legacy to free speech doctrine: that in the world of human affairs *all* truth—including truth about free speech—is only provisional.

Mill's point that even erroneous opinion contains "a portion of the truth" accurately describes radical critique of free speech doctrine. As I explain at length in this book, in asserting that free speech has not on the whole been an ally of the oppressed, the radicals are "in error." They are thus unwise to call for revision of free speech doctrine to permit government greater latitude to suppress speech that it finds obnoxious or even dangerous. Experience in this country and elsewhere shows that it is radical speech that government is most eager to suppress. That leftist radicals writing in a society that has long been and continues to be hostile to their ideology would want to weaken the principle that government may not suppress expression because of hostility to its viewpoint seems odd, to say the least. The main thrust of radical critique is, moreover, theoretically shaky. As a means of attacking claims of neutrality, they employ an epistemology that denies all eternal verities. Yet at the same time they establish current notions of racial and gender equality as an unquestionable, transcendent truth. This is a deep inconsistency that the radical critics do not even attempt to explain.

Despite the hyperbole and unwarranted condemnation of the core of traditional free speech theory, radical critique nonetheless serves to alert us to the danger of uncritical and mechanical application of free speech doctrine. There have, in fact, been free speech decisions that discount injury to minorities. For example, two state supreme courts, supported by academic commentary, recently invoked the First Amendment to invalidate laws that enhance punishment for racially motivated crimes, including violent crimes such as battery, arson, and murder.[13] The rationale of these cases called into question not just the federal criminal civil rights laws that have been on the books for more than a century but the modern civil rights laws, such as Title VII, as well. Fortunately, the United States Supreme Court in 1993 put a stop to this engine of destruction.[14]

A year earlier, however, the Supreme Court itself succumbed to the allure of formalism and false symmetry. In a case involving the burning of a cross on a black family's lawn, the Court, in an opinion by arch formalist Antonin Scalia, concluded that face-to-face racial verbal assaults are no more alarming to the victim than are nonracial "fighting words."[15] Accordingly, the Court concluded that although government can forbid the use of all "fighting words," the First Amendment's neutrality principle forbids singling out racist verbal assaults for prohibition. Surely, in this country at this time, racial epithets, let alone burning a cross on a black family's lawn, are much more likely to cause alarm or start a fight than is calling someone a "bastard," a "son of a bitch," or most any other epithet one could think of. This is not to say that the invalidation of the poorly crafted law at issue in that case was wrong. What is troubling is Scalia's inability to recognize that the legacy of racial terrorism in this country makes placing a burning cross on a black family's lawn in the dead of night more harmful than other types of verbal assaults. Does the First Amendment's neutrality principle really prevent recognition of the special harms attendant to racist "fighting words"? As we shall see, this question is much more difficult than Scalia cares to recognize.

The burden of this book is to demonstrate that the ultimate radical claim that First Amendment doctrine is rotten to its core (or that it does not have a core) cannot be sustained. At the same time, I show that around the edges free speech doctrine has failed adequately to account for injury suffered by women and minorities.

Before one can assess the claim that traditional doctrine is biased against women and minorities, one needs familiarity with this doctrine. I thus devote Part 1 of this book to acquainting the reader with the basics of American free speech doctrine. This part comprises three chapters: In Chapter 2 I identify the reasons free speech is valued in a democratic society and trace the history of free speech doctrine in the United States; in Chapter 3 I then sketch the salient features of current doctrine. Chapter 4 offers a discussion of why under current doctrine hate speech laws and laws prohibiting pornography demeaning to women are unconstitutional.

The second part of the book is a description of and response to the radical attack on modern free speech doctrine: In Chapter 5 I investigate the radical charge that modern free speech doctrine is in the service of the rich and powerful and selectively discriminates against the interests of women and minorities. I go on in the next chapter to demonstrate that the relationship between free speech and equality is far more complex and ambivalent than either the radical critics or many liberal defenders acknowledge.

Part 3 goes beyond what the law is to what it should be. I ask if doctrine should be modified so as to permit broad hate speech and pornography restrictions. Answering this question requires an assessment of the costs and benefits of hate speech and pornography regulation: In Chapter 7 I discuss whether banning this speech would be an effective remedy for the various harms hate speech and pornography are said to cause. In the next chapter, I assess the impact that modifying doctrine to permit such regulation would have on free speech in this society. In Chapter 9 I inquire whether there is a principled justification for banning hate speech and pornography that is sufficiently narrow so as not to imperil core free speech values. In Chapter 10 I offer some conclusions about the wisdom of the various proposals to ban hate speech and pornography in this country.

In the Appendix I discuss in detail the scientific studies of the harm caused by pornography, the Attorney General's Commission on Pornography's evaluation of these studies, and various criticisms of the commission's conclusions.

PART ONE

Modern Free Speech Doctrine

Legal doctrine—the body of rules governing an area of law—can be difficult to comprehend for several different reasons. Doctrine often involves rarified abstractions having little connection with anything tangible, as is the case, for example, with the rules governing the jurisdiction of federal courts. Others areas are difficult to master because of the sheer number of detailed and technical rules. Some areas are confusing because the law is in flux, with many conflicting precedents. Finally, as in other so-called learned disciplines, jargon often impedes laypeople's access to legal doctrine.

To some extent, free speech doctrine is beset with all these problems. But the primary reason that free speech doctrine is difficult is the same reason that basic problems of moral philosophy are difficult. Free speech problems often present basic questions of human conduct that people have been wrestling with for a very long time and that are answerable only through deep normative judgments. Personally, I find these normative questions far more perplexing than the technical abstrusities with which law professors often deal. The good news for the nonlawyer, however, is that the basically normative nature of free speech problems makes them far more accessible than, say, tax, copyright, or jurisdictional questions. Still, there is an important technical side to free speech doctrine that cannot be disregarded. Free speech doctrine is not merely a philosopher's code but a system of real-world rules constructed by judges in light of experience and professional judgment.

The following two chapters review basic free speech doctrine with one predominant aim: providing the reader with sufficient background to evaluate the various claims and charges that radicals have made about doctrine. Constitutional law scholarship in general and free speech scholarship in particular are marked by an unhelpful tendency to confuse the descriptive—what the law *is*—with the normative—what the law *should be.* In the following pages, I endeavor to separate as much as possible descriptive from normative analysis. Although I cannot render a purely value-neutral description, I nonetheless try to give a fair summary of free speech doctrine so that the reader may become an informed participant in the debate about this doctrine.

2

THEORY AND HISTORY

The goal of free speech doctrine can be easily stated: forbidding government from suppressing speech that must be permitted in a free and democratic society while allowing it to punish speech that causes harm that government may legitimately prevent. Accomplishing this goal is not so easy. Clearly, there is some expression, such as advocacy of law or policy reform through peaceful, democratic means, that must be protected against government suppression. Just as surely government must not be constitutionally inhibited from prohibiting speech such as perjury, bribery, or solicitation to murder. But what about speech that advocates social change through violence or other forms of law violation or that defames public officials? Or political protests that use offensive phrases like "fuck the draft" or inflammatory symbols such as flag burning? Or sexually explicit speech whose primary purpose and effect is sexual arousal?

In order to decide hard cases like these, we must have a fairly clear vision of why the Constitution limits the government's power to suppress speech. To this end, in the first section of this chapter I attempt to identify the various values underlying American free speech doctrine. Like all law, though, free speech doctrine is not just a product of theory but of experience and pragmatic judgment as well. As we shall see, early attempts to construct constitutional rules to separate protected from suppressible speech did not adequately account for the tendency of legislators, prosecutors, and even judges to confuse offensive critique of government policies with speech that actually impedes the government's ability to carry out its legitimate functions. I therefore review in some detail what are now seen as failed attempts to construct free speech doctrine that correctly strikes the balance between the individual's right to critique society and the government's ability to accomplish its proper goals.

WHY PROTECT SPEECH?

Three basic values are most commonly cited as underlying the free speech principle: democratic self-governance; search for truth in the marketplace of ideas; and noninstrumental values such as individual autonomy, self-fulfillment, and self-expression.[1]

Democratic Self-Governance

The connection between free speech and democracy is manifest. As the ultimate source of political authority, the people must be able to talk to one another about the performance of governmental officials and the policies these officials implement. If government could punish speech with which it disagrees, then the public opinion that influences official decisionmaking and ultimately determines whether governmental officials will stay in power would reflect not the will of the people but the will of the government officials. The Supreme Court has thus explained that "the First Amendment was fashioned to assure unfettered interchange of ideas for the bringing about of political and social changes desired by the people."[2]

It is sometimes alleged that a constitutional right to free speech *inhibits* democracy to the extent that it permits courts to void laws the people desire. For instance, Frederick Schauer argues that "[a]ny distinct restraint on majority power, such as a principle of freedom of speech, is by its nature anti-democratic, anti-majoritarian."[3] But democracy is something more than static majoritarianism. At minimum, it must also include the right of the minority to try to persuade the majority to change its mind. Preventing a current majority from suppressing the discourse that allows for the creation of new majorities thus promotes rather than inhibits democracy.

Some have argued that democratic self-governance is the only value underlying the free speech principle.[4] But although democracy is undeniably a core value, it is difficult to explain the full expanse of the free speech principle as it operates in this country exclusively in such terms. For instance, the expression of many, if not most, scientific and mathematical ideas have no direct connection with democratic self-governance; even more so, abstract art and symphonic music would seem to have little connection with the speech by which we govern ourselves. Yet under modern doctrine all these forms of expression are afforded rigorous protection against government suppression. Accordingly, unless the concept of democratic self-governance is stretched beyond all recognition,[5] we must look to other values as well.

Truth Discovery in the Marketplace of Ideas

First invoked by John Milton in the seventeenth century, the truth discovery rationale for free speech was fully developed in the middle of the nineteenth century by John Stuart Mill in his influential essay *On Liberty*.[6] In the early-twentieth century, Justice Oliver Wendell Holmes wrote that "[t]he ultimate good desired is better reached by free trade in ideas" and "that the best test of truth is the power of thought to get itself accepted in the competition of the market."[7] Several decades later, a majority of the Court invoked the search for truth in excluding face-to-face insults, defamation, and obscenity from First Amendment protection. Such utterances, the Court explained, are "no essential part of any exposition of ideas" and only of "slight" value as "a step to truth."[8] As we shall see, the Court would later discover that even these forlorn categories of expression could not be neatly excised from the body of speech that did involve "the exposition of ideas" and search for "the truth." Still, the Court's perception retains validity: Face-to-face, personal insults; lies that damage an individual's reputation; and explicit depictions of sex intended merely to arouse seem far afield from truth seeking in the marketplace of ideas.

To the modern ear, the concept of the search for "truth" may sound quaint (and to the postmodern ear, perhaps even absurd). Justice Felix Frankfurter recast this rationale in somewhat more contemporary terms when he spoke of the "progress of civilization" that occurs in the continual process by which beliefs that "once held sway as official truth" are displaced by new ideas.[9] But whether conceptualized as the search for truth or as an indispensable mechanism of cultural progress, this rationale, unlike the democratic self-governance justification, "carries beyond the political realm" to "the building of the whole culture [including] all of the areas of human learning and knowledge."[10] Whether its ultimate goal be truth or progress, the marketplace-of-ideas rationale has considerable descriptive power. It explains, for instance, far more readily than does the self-governance rationale the broad scope of expression protected under modern free speech doctrine. And the Supreme Court continues frequently to invoke the metaphor.[11]

Noninstrumental Values

Both the democratic self-governance and marketplace-of-ideas rationales justify free speech *instrumentally,* that is, in terms of the good it produces for society as a whole. Neither is deeply rooted in some moral conception of the relationship between the individual and the state. This is particularly true of the marketplace-of-ideas rationale, which bears no obvious connection to any moral view about the way government must treat individuals. (As we shall see, it is somewhat easier to posit a moral, individual-focused basis for democracy.) There are several problems, however, with viewing free speech as purely instrumental to accomplishing some social good.

First, instrumentally based rights tend to be more fragile than morally based ones; they are vulnerable to being overridden in a specific instance or even extinguished altogether if the utilitarian calculus suggests that society would be better off without them. In contrast, rights that are justified in terms of moral rights of individuals as well as benefiting society as a whole tend to be sturdier than those justified by only one of these rationales. In addition, despite the claims of some commentators, free speech doctrine has always treated free speech as an *individual* right, not just as an interest assigned to individuals as a strategic means for promoting the common good.[12] Finally, there is the strong intuition, shared not just by lawyers and judges but by the American public as well, that regardless of any societal good accomplished by expression, people in this country have a basic right to speak their minds unless the government has a good reason for stopping them.

It is in part to explain this intuition that the Court and commentators have looked beyond instrumental justifications for free speech to try to ground free speech in individual interests, such as self-expression, self-fulfillment, and autonomy. But any broad conception of such interests as basic values underlying the constitutional protection of speech creates more problems than it solves. Just as the self-governance and marketplace-of-ideas rationales explain too little, these rationales explain too much.

Virtually all speech (and most conduct) can be seen as promoting self-expression, self-fulfillment, or individual autonomy. Blasting music late at night in a residential neighborhood might for some be the height of self-expression; for others it might be angrily "cursing out" anyone who displeases them, such as the judge who refuses to dismiss a parking ticket. For some, threatening to kill a hated enemy might be quite self-fulfilling, as might inciting a crowd to riot. Two business competitors agreeing to fix prices are exercising their autonomy, as is a psychiatrist who decides that she should counsel her chronically depressed patients to commit suicide. The laws currently in place that prevent this expression would not, however, seem to implicate core free speech values.[13] Thus whatever role some broad conception of self-expression, self-fulfillment, or autonomy might play in free speech doctrine, they would not seem to be central values. More important for our purposes, these values do not inform us which speech government may readily regulate and which it must refrain from suppressing.[14]

There is, however, a more limited sense in which autonomy can be seen as playing a major role in free speech jurisprudence. In an insightful article, Thomas Scanlon neatly avoids the problem of autonomy's explaining too much by concentrating not on the speaker's rights but on *the listener's interests*. He posits that deeply embedded in free speech doctrine is the premise that people are "equal, autonomous, rational agents" and that each person "see[s] himself as sovereign in deciding what to believe and in weighing competing reasons for action." Accordingly, "an autonomous person cannot accept without independent consideration the judgment of others as to what he should believe or what he should do."[15] Scanlon focuses on whether the government's *reasons* or *justifications* for suppressing speech are contrary to this basic presumption of an autonomous and rational audience. He thus excludes as a legitimate justification the government's controlling information "to assure that [people] will maintain certain beliefs." As eloquently stated by another prominent philosopher:

> [M]orally responsible people insist on making up their own minds about what is good and bad in life or in politics, or what is true and false in matters of justice or faith. Government insults its citizens, and denies their moral responsibility, when it decrees that they cannot be trusted to hear opinions that might persuade them to dangerous or offensive convictions. We retain our dignity, as individuals, only by insisting that no one—no official and no majority—has the right to withhold opinion from us on the ground that we are not fit to hear and consider it.[16]

Scanlon's autonomy theory provides an important supplement to the democratic self-government and marketplace-of-ideas rationales. Unlike the democratic self-governance theory, it is not limited to political speech. And unlike the marketplace-of-ideas rationale, whose scope it approximates, it is firmly rooted in the rights of individuals rather than in some prediction of consequences for society as a whole. To my mind, this theory best explains our strong intuition, as well as the doctrinal practice, of valuing free speech as an end as well as a means. Additionally, the focus on the state's justification for regulating expression rather than on the nature of the speech explains why even nonideational art is protected. As has often been observed, authoritarian governments routinely prohibit even nonideational art on the supposition that regardless of the artist's intent, certain types of art will have a corrupting influence or lead people to question authority.[17]

One shortcoming of Scanlon's theory, however, is that its focus on the right of individuals to *receive* information to effectuate autonomous choice does little to explain the right of individuals to *convey* messages. Into the breach steps Ronald Dworkin, who generates a theory of speech protection using essentially the same first-order political principle

Scanlon employs. But where Scanlon emphasizes the "autonomous" aspect of the foundational principle that government must treat each individual as "equal, autonomous, rational agents," Dworkin emphasizes the "equal." To Dworkin, government violates the basic command of equal treatment when "it disqualifies some people from [expressing their views] on the ground that their convictions make them unworthy."[18] Democracy in this view is valued not just because it leads to stability, wealth, peace, and good order but because it is the only form of government that does not insult the dignity of some members of society by treating others as more valuable or worthy of respect. Just as denying some people the right to vote because the government disagrees with whom or what they intend to vote for is contrary to the basic equality principle on which democracy is founded, so, too, is denying some people the chance to shape public opinion because the government finds their ideas to be wrong or offensive. Dworkin thus supplies a moral, noninstrumental reason for the democratic self-governance rationale for free speech, thereby firmly grounding it as an individual right.[19]

THE LESSONS OF HISTORY

Radical critics claim that free speech doctrine is ahistorical in that it does not account for the legacy of this country's long-standing racist institutions, such as slavery and apartheid. There is much to this charge. But radical critics are also guilty of ahistoricism, for they ignore or trivialize the fact that current doctrine is largely a product of the failure of early cases to protect against governmental suppression of radical ideology at turbulent times in our nation's history.

The Espionage Act Cases, Advocacy of Illegal Activity, and the "Clear and Present Danger" Test

In light of the values underlying free speech doctrine, especially the core value of democratic self-governance, speech that simultaneously advocates political change and violation of existing laws has presented a most difficult challenge for free speech doctrine. This problem was acutely raised by opposition to U.S. involvement in World War I that urged resistance to the draft or harshly criticized conscription in ways that could be interpreted as advocating refusal to serve. Similar problems would arise later in the century when members of the American Communist Party combined critique of the deficiencies of capitalism with advocacy of the violent overthrow of the American government.

The First Amendment's majestic command—"Congress shall make no law abridging the freedom of speech"—was added to the Constitution by the Bill of Rights in 1791. But it was not until 1919, in *Schenck v. United States*, that the Supreme Court decided its first important free speech case.[20] The case arose when Charles Schenck, the general secretary of the Philadelphia Socialist Party, mailed pamphlets to military conscripts condemning the draft implemented during World War I. The pamphlets described conscription as "despotism in its worst form and a monstrous wrong against humanity in the interest of Wall Street's chosen few," asserted that the draft was a violation of the Thirteenth Amendment's prohibition against slavery, and urged conscripts to assert their rights. Schenck was convicted of violating the Espionage Act of 1917, which among other things made it a crime to "willfully cause or attempt to cause insubordination, disloyalty, mutiny, or refusal of duty, in the military or naval forces of the United States."

Affirming the conviction for a unanimous Court, Justice Oliver Wendell Holmes pronounced the famous "clear and present danger" test. Government may legitimately suppress speech, he wrote, that creates "a clear and present danger" of "substantive evils that Congress has a right to prevent." Holmes reasoned that because both the "tendency" of the speech and its "intent" were to obstruct recruitment, sufficient danger had been shown to warrant its suppression.[21] In the abstract, the "clear and present danger" test may have seemed a logical way to strike the proper balance between dissidents' right to protest and the government's legitimate power to prevent serious law violation. But as Holmes had written many years before, "the life of the law has not been logic; it has been experience."[22] Experience would soon reveal the shortcoming of this test in protecting free expression in a democratic society.

In *Frohwerk v. United States*, decided just a week after *Schenck*, the defendant was sentenced to ten years' imprisonment under the Espionage Act for publishing two articles in a German-language newspaper critical of U.S. involvement in World War I.[23] In the first article, the author declared such involvement to be a "monumental and inexcusable mistake" resulting from the influence of "the great trusts" and spoke of the "unconquerable spirit" of the German nation. In the second article, the defendant deplored the draft riots but, according to Holmes, "in language that might be taken to convey an innuendo of a different sort." The writer stated further that although draft resistance is technically "wrong" and "ill-advised," the resister is "more sinned against than sinning"; who, he asked, "will pronounce a verdict of guilty upon him if he stops reasoning and follows the first impulse of nature: self-preservation"? Holmes conceded that, unlike in *Schenck*, the defendant made no special effort to reach men subject to the draft. Nonetheless, noting that "the circulation of the paper [might have been] in quarters where a little breath would be enough to kindle a flame," he upheld the conviction.

Debs v. United States, decided the same day as *Frohwerk,* affirmed the Espionage Act conviction of Eugene Debs, the leader of the Socialist Party and frequent presidential candidate.[24] Debs was sentenced to twenty years in prison for a speech he delivered at a state Socialist convention in which he praised the courage of three antiwar protestors convicted of aiding and abetting draft resistance, reminded young men that they were "fit for something better than slavery and cannon fodder," sneered at the advice to cultivate war gardens, and blamed the high price of coal on the "plutocrats." Holmes held that these comments, together with the Socialist Party's antiwar proclamation, which called for "continuous, active, and public opposition to the war, through demonstration, mass petitions, and all other means within our power," warranted the jury's finding that the intent of Debs's speech was to obstruct the draft. If this was its intent, Holmes continued, such would be its "probable effect," thereby creating a sufficient danger to justify punishment.[25]

As originally enacted, the Espionage Act was designed to prevent specific interference with the war effort, such as insubordination in the armed forces or obstruction of recruitment. In 1918, however, the act was amended to strike broadly at disloyal speech. Among other speech prohibitions, it made criminal during wartime "disloyal, profane, scurrilous or abusive language about the form of government of the United States" or "any language intended to bring the form of government of the United States . . . into contempt, scorn, contumely or disrepute," even statements intended to hinder the sale of U.S. bonds. In addition, the 1918 amendments made it a crime to "urge" curtailment of the production of materials necessary to the prosecution of the war with intent to hinder its prosecution. Soon after these amendments were enacted, Jacob Abrams and several anarchist colleagues distributed a circular protesting the expeditionary forces that the Allies had sent to Russia in an attempt to put down the Bolshevik revolution. One of the pamphlets, entitled "The Hypocrisy of the United States," asserted that "[the president] is too much of a coward to come out openly and say: 'We capitalistic nations cannot afford to have a proletarian republic in Russia,'" that "there is only one enemy of the workers of the world and that is capitalism," and called upon the workers to "Awake! Rise! Put down your enemy and mine." Another leaflet proclaimed, "Workers in the ammunition factories, you are producing bullets, bayonets, cannon, to murder not only the Germans, but also your dearest, best, who are in Russia and are fighting for freedom." The leaflet concluded by calling for a general strike.

Abrams and his associates were convicted on several counts under the 1918 amendments, including using "disloyal, scurrilous and abusive language about the form of Government of the United States" and language "intended to bring the form of Government of the United States into contempt, scorn, contumely and disrepute," as well as for inciting resistance to the war effort and for urging curtailment of munitions production. In *Abrams v. United States,* the Supreme Court affirmed the convictions.[26] The Court, however, rested its affirmance solely on the counts relating to inciting resistance and urging curtailment of munitions production, citing *Schenck* and *Frohwerk* as foreclosing any First Amendment challenge. Since the twenty-year sentences the defendants were given did not exceed what might have been imposed under any single count, the Court decided it did not have to rule on the validity of the convictions on the counts relating to abusive speech about the form of government or to decide whether the defendants' abusive statements against the president would qualify as "about the form of Government of the United States." Remarkably, nary a word of concern is uttered about whether punishment for abusive speech against government institutions is consistent with free speech in a democratic society.

This time, however, Holmes dissented, finding that the publishing of "a silly leaflet" by "poor and puny anonymities" did not create an immediate danger of disrupting munitions manufacturing. Holmes's *Abrams* dissent, which newly appointed justice Louis D. Brandeis joined, remains one of the most eloquent and moving defenses of free speech:

> [W]hen men have realized that time has upset many fighting faiths, they may come to believe even more than they believe the very foundations of their own conduct that the ultimate good desired is better reached by the free trade in ideas—that the best test of truth is the power of the thought to get itself accepted in the competition of the market, and that truth is the only ground upon which their wishes safely can be carried out. That at any rate is the theory of our Constitution. It is an experiment, as all life is an experiment. Every year if not every day we have to wage our salvation upon some prophecy based upon imperfect knowledge. While that experiment is part of our system I think that we should be eternally vigilant against attempts to check the expression of opinions that we loathe and believe to be fraught with death, unless they so imminently threaten immediate interference with the lawful and pressing purposes of the law that an immediate check is required to save the country.

Holmes believed that Abrams and his codefendants were being made to suffer "not for what the indictment alleges but for the creed they avow." But were not Schenck and Debs also punished for the creed they avowed, or was there not at least that distinct possibility? And wasn't it likely that Frohwerk was punished for his pro-German sentiments? Although still insisting that these earlier cases had been "rightly decided," Holmes had evidently traveled a long distance in his thinking about free speech in the few short months since *Schenck.*

Two years earlier, in *Masses Publishing Co. v. Patten*, Learned Hand, then a young federal district court judge, took a different approach to defining the limits of free speech.[27] Interpreting the Espionage Act in light of the background constitutional principles of a society "dependent upon the free expression of opinion as the ultimate source of authority," Hand held that only speech that directly counseled or advised breaking the law violated the Espionage Act. The postmaster general had declared the radical magazine *The Masses* unmailable because it contained cartoons and poems critical of the draft that "tended to produce a violation" of the Espionage Act. Hand recognized that the challenged material, like all political agitation, might "by the passions it arouses or the convictions it engenders" stimulate violation of the law. But because the material did not directly counsel or advise law violation, it was not, in his view, punishable.

Under Hand's "direct incitement" test, the speech involved in *Schenck, Frohwerk, Debs,* and possibly even *Abrams* would have been protected. But the test was much too far ahead of its time to survive. The Court of Appeals quickly disapproved it, ruling that because "the natural and reasonable effect" of the material was to "encourage resistance to a law" and was intended "to persuade resistance," the postmaster had acted properly in refusing to mail the magazine.[28] As we shall see, Hand's approach would be vindicated, but not for nearly half a century.[29]

From the standpoint of history and experience, we can now discern that the main problem with the Supreme Court's initial attempt to formulate free speech doctrine is that it was, as Hand predicted, unreliable "in practical administration" adequately to protect unpopular opinion.[30] It did not require that the speaker expressly advocate law violation but permitted the use of innuendo. In addition, the test required ad hoc and often speculative judgments about whether the speech in question was likely to cause harm and whether this harm was imminent. As Hand observed in private correspondence,

> Once you admit that the matter is one of degree, ... you give to Tomdickandharry D.J. [district judge] so much latitude that the jig is at once up. [Even] the Nine Elder Statesmen have not shown themselves wholly immune from the "herd instinct" and what seems "immediate and direct" today may seem very remote next year even though the circumstances surrounding the utterance be unchanged. I own I should prefer a qualitative formula, hard, conventional, difficult to evade.[31]

Under the "clear and present danger" test as it was applied in the Espionage Act cases, it is likely that speakers were imprisoned not for actually causing imminent harm to some vital governmental interest, such as procurement of men and munitions to support a war effort, but for expressing unpopular ideas, such as the condemnation of capitalism or support for the Bolshevik revolution. Although it may fairly be doubted that the speakers caused imminent danger in these cases, there can be no doubt that their radical ideas, often expressed in a rude and caustic manner, both frightened and infuriated those who were to judge them. By the time the Espionage Act prosecutions ran their course, more than 2,000 people would be convicted.[32] From the standpoint of adequate constitutional protection for opinion that challenged the status quo, the situation was to get even worse.

The "Red Scare" Cases

At least theoretically, one of the speech-protective elements of the "clear and present danger" test as practiced in the Espionage Act cases was that it was the judiciary (supposedly less immune to the "herd instinct" than the legislature) that was to assess the imminence of the alleged danger. However, in a 1925 decision, *Gitlow v. New York*, the Court held that a legislative finding of danger "must be given great weight" by the courts. The Court readily deferred to the judgment of the New York legislature that any speech advocating the forceful overthrow of organized government was per se dangerous, regardless of circumstances.[33] It affirmed the conviction of a defendant charged with publishing a newspaper that advocated "mass industrial revolts" and "revolutionary mass action" for purposes of establishing a "revolutionary dictatorship of the proletariat." (The silver lining in this dark cloud was that the Court for the first time held that the free speech provision of the First Amendment applied to the states by virtue of the Fourteenth Amendment's Due Process Clause.)[34]

Two years later, in *Whitney v. California*, the Court reviewed a conviction under a California law that made it a crime to be a member of an organization that advocated force or violence as a means to "a change in industrial ownership" or any "political change."[35] The defendant in that case was personally opposed to violence as a means of political change and had supported a resolution, ultimately defeated, proposing achievement of the party's ends through the traditional political process. Nevertheless, the Court affirmed her conviction, stating her free speech challenge was "nothing more than an effort to review the weight of the evidence." In a concurring opinion joined by Holmes, Brandeis wrote that "even advocacy of [law] violation . . . is not a justification for denying free speech where the advocacy falls short of incitement and there is nothing to indicate that the advocacy would be immediately acted on."[36] Nearly fifty years later, the Court would adopt something quite like this formulation. In the meantime doctrine remained inadequately protective of dissident speech.

A smattering of cases during the 1930s showed that there was some limit to the government's ability to suppress speech based on the claim that it might lead to lawlessness. For instance, the Court reversed the conviction of a black Communist Party organizer sentenced for violating a Georgia law criminalizing any "attempt to incite insurrection."[37] The attempted "insurrection" consisted of possession of a document that called for "equal rights for the Negroes and self-determination of the Black Belt." Yet even here the Court's vote to reverse the conviction was by the narrowest of margins (5–4). Moreover, the majority opinion was an ad hoc denunciation of an obviously outrageous infringement of civil liberties, offering little in the way of general speech-protective principles.

The sorry state of free speech doctrine in the United States soon became apparent. In 1940 Congress passed the Smith Act, which made it a crime for anyone to "advocate, abet, advise, or teach the duty, necessity, desirability or propriety of overthrowing or destroying any government in the United States by force or violence." The law also made it criminal to "become a member" of "any society, group, or assembly of persons who teach, advocate, or encourage" such violent overthrow. In 1948, high-ranking officials of the American Communist Party were convicted of violating this law. It was Learned Hand, by then a Court of Appeals judge, who in *Dennis v. United States* wrote the opinion affirming the convictions.[38] Candidly admitting the confused state of the "clear and present danger" test, a standard he had never much liked, Hand nevertheless struggled scrupulously to find a formula that described the current state of the law. He proposed the following: "In each case [courts] must ask whether the gravity of the 'evil,' discounted by its improbability, justifies such invasion of free speech as is necessary to avoid the danger."

The Supreme Court upheld Judge Hand's affirmance of the convictions.[39] There was no majority opinion. A plurality of four justices, in an opinion by Chief Justice Fred Vinson, purported to adopt Hand's test. Acknowledging that there was no evidence that the speech in question presented an imminent likelihood of violent overthrow of the U.S. government, Vinson declared that "an attempt to overthrow the Government by force, even though doomed from the outset . . . is a sufficient evil for Congress to prevent." But there also was no evidence that the advocacy was likely to cause an imminent *attempt* at violent overthrow. Nevertheless, Vinson thought that the proof at trial that the defendants intended to attempt to overthrow the government "as speedily as circumstances would permit" presented a sufficiently grave and imminent danger. An obscure and remote danger was thus judicially transfigured into a "clear and present" one.

In a concurring opinion, Justice Felix Frankfurter charged the Vinson plurality with not fairly applying any recognizable form of the "clear and present danger" test. He nevertheless voted to affirm the judgment on the ground that the "primary responsibility for adjusting the interests" between free speech and public safety in a case like this lay with Congress. Frankfurter candidly admitted, however, that "in sustaining the convictions before us we can hardly escape restriction on the interchange of ideas." He noted that advocacy of violent overthrow of the government is often "coupled with . . . criticism of defects in our society" and that punishing such advocacy will inevitably "also silence critics who do not advocate overthrow but fear that their criticism may be so construed." He therefore branded as "self-delusion" the position that affirmance of these convictions would not add "to the risks run by loyal citizens who honestly believe in some of the reforms these defendants advance."[40] It would take the Warren Court to finally put some teeth into the protection afforded dissident speech.

Advocacy of Illegal Activity and the Warren Court

As we have seen, perhaps the major failure of free speech doctrine during World War I was that it permitted ambiguous statements by war critics to be construed as advocating criminal activity. Well aware of this defect, the Warren Court made sure that this would not happen in cases involving critics of the Vietnam War. In 1966 the Georgia House of Representatives refused to seat Julian Bond, a young, black civil rights activist duly elected to the house, on account of antiwar statements he had made. Bond had endorsed a statement by the Student Nonviolent Coordinating Committee (SNCC) that declared: "We are in sympathy with, and support, the men in this country who are unwilling to respond to a military draft." Bond added that he was a pacifist and was "eager and anxious to encourage people not to participate" in the Vietnam War, and that although he did "not advocate that people should break laws" he "admired the courage" of people who burned their draft cards.

In an opinion by Chief Justice Earl Warren, the Supreme Court unanimously held that neither the SNCC declaration nor Bond's own statements could be used by the State of Georgia to refuse to seat Bond.[41] These statements were, the Court explained, "at worst unclear" as to whether illegal means should be used to avoid the draft and thus were protected by the First Amendment. Based on this case, a federal Court of Appeals reversed the conviction of Dr. Benjamin Spock for conspiring to counsel registrants to violate the draft law.[42] Spock had stated that he hoped that the frequent stating of his antiwar views, which included signing a document calling for draft resistance, would give young men "courage to take active steps in draft resistance."

In 1969, during the height of the Vietnam War, the Court similarly extended First Amendment protection to a young man who, at an antiwar rally, declared, "If they ever make me carry a rifle, the first man I want to get in my sights is LBJ. They are not going to make me kill my black brothers." In reversing the conviction under a law prohibiting threats to kill the president, the Court acknowledged that a true threat to kill was not protected by the First Amendment but cautioned that "[w]hat is a threat must be distinguished from what is constitutionally protected speech." Sensitive to "the profound national commitment to the principle that debate on public issues should be uninhibited, robust, and wide-open," the Court interpreted the federal statute as not outlawing "political hyperbole" such as the defendant's speech.[43]

Later that year, the Court was finally ready to state a new, more speech-protective test for determining when advocacy of law violation could be punished consistent with the First Amendment. *Brandenburg v. Ohio* involved a Ku Klux Klan leader who had uttered derogatory remarks against blacks and Jews and warned: "We're not a revengent organization, but if our President, our Congress, our Supreme Court, continues to suppress the white, Caucasian race, it's possible there might have to be some revengeance taken."[44] Based solely on this speech, the Klan leader was convicted under an Ohio law forbidding "advocat[ing] the duty, necessity, or propriety of crime, sabotage, violence, or unlawful methods of terrorism as a means of accomplishing industrial or political reform." The Supreme Court reversed the conviction, holding that the First Amendment does not permit government to punish "advocacy of the use of force or of law violation except where such advocacy is directed to inciting or producing imminent lawless action and is likely to incite or produce such action."[45]

As an astute commentator has observed, the *Brandenburg* test combines "the most protective ingredients of [Learned Hand's] *Masses* incitement emphasis with the most useful elements of the clear and present danger heritage."[46] No longer could critics of government policy be punished for the "innuendo" or the dangerous "tendency" of their speech. Indeed, as a prophylactic measure to make sure that dissidents are not punished by hostile juries merely for the "creed they avow," *Brandenburg* extends First Amendment protection to express advocacy of illegal activity; it is only when this advocacy crosses over into "incitement"—a call to immediate action—that it can be punished, and then only if it causes "a clear and present danger" of law violation (or as that hoary test is rephrased in *Brandenburg*, when the speech is "likely to . . . produce imminent lawless action"). Free speech doctrine, then, had come a long way from the days of *Debs, Whitney,* and *Dennis*.

Subsequent cases would confirm, moreover, that *Brandenburg* worked well in action, not just on paper. For instance, in *Hess v. Indiana* more than 100 anti–Vietnam War protestors blocked a street until the police finally arrested some protestors and moved the others to the curb. Hess was arrested for yelling, "We'll take the fucking street later [or again]."[47] The Supreme Court reversed the conviction: "At best . . . the statement could be taken as counsel for present moderation; at worst, it amounted to nothing more than advocacy of illegal action at some indefinite future time. . . . [Thus] those words could not be punished by the State on the ground that they had a tendency to lead to violence."

The *Brandenburg* incitement test was to prove useful not just for antiwar dissidents but, together with other Warren Court free speech cases to be discussed later, for civil rights protestors as well. For example, in 1966 the National Association for the Advancement of Colored People (NAACP) called a boycott of white merchants in Claiborne, Mississippi, who discriminated against blacks. Although conducted largely through legal means, the boycott did involve some sporadic violence. The merchants sued for civil damages in state court and recovered a judgment of $1.2 million against the NAACP and several other defendants, including civil rights activist Charles Evers. The Mississippi Supreme Court affirmed the award.[48] The Mississippi courts found that a speech by Evers stating that boycott violators would be "disciplined" was not expression protected by the First Amendment. In reversing the large civil judgment, the U.S. Supreme Court disagreed:

> While many of the comments in Evers' speeches might have contemplated "discipline" in the permissible form of social ostracism, it cannot be denied that references to the possibility that necks would be broken implicitly conveyed a sterner message. . . . This Court has made clear, however, that mere *advocacy* of the use of force or violence does not remove speech from the protection of the First Amendment. . . . [The] emotionally charged rhetoric of Charles Evers' speech did not transcend the bounds of protected speech set forth in Brandenburg [because almost all] acts of violence . . . occurred weeks or months after [the speech].

Long and painful was the path from *Schenck* to *Brandenburg*. In retrospect, there is consensus that the "clear and present danger" test as applied in the Espionage Act cases was sorely inadequate to protect speech in a society in which the people hold the ultimate responsibility for determining social policy. There is more debate about whether the suppression of communist speech was also inconsistent with our ideals of a liberal democracy. But the weight of history seems to be with Justice William Douglas's conclusion that the communist threat, too, though "often loud," was "puny" and made serious only by "judges so wedded to the status quo that critical analysis made them nervous."[49] There is also consensus that under the *Brandenburg* test dissident speech was much better protected in the turbulent years of the civil rights and anti–Vietnam War movements.

What doctrinal lessons, then, can be learned from this history? We have already discussed the problem of speculation and ad hoc predictions about harm and its imminency required under the "clear and present danger" test. Another important lesson is the danger of abstractions. Like the people on the Lord High Executioner's little list, there appear to be certain types of speech that never would be missed. As a matter of abstract theory, one could make a strong argument that excising from public discourse speech advocating criminal activity as a means of destroying democratic institutions is not only consistent with but positively promotes the commitment to democratic self-governance underlying free speech. Fifty years of experience with the "clear and present danger" test, however, revealed that banishing even a narrow class of seemingly worthless and particularly dangerous speech from the body of political discourse is difficult to do without jeopardizing other speech as well.

Speech "Outside" the Scope of the First Amendment

The "clear and present danger" test was not the only instance of an attempt to draw a line between legitimate discourse and worthless speech that failed in practice. In the abstract, it would seem that face-to-face verbal assaults ("fighting words"), false statements injurious to reputation (defamation), and sexually oriented material intended solely for sexual arousal (obscenity) could be prohibited without unduly impairing legitimate public discourse. Or so the Court thought in 1942 when it declared:

> There are certain well-defined and narrowly limited classes of speech, the prevention and punishment of which has never been thought to raise any Constitutional problem. These include the lewd and obscene, the profane, the libelous, and the insulting or fighting words. . . . It has been well observed that such utterances are no essential part of any exposition of ideas, and are of such slight social value as a step to truth that any benefit that may be derived from them is clearly outweighed by the social interest in order and morality.

Fighting Words. This exercise in abstractly separating useful from useless speech came in *Chaplinsky v. New Hampshire*.[50] The case upheld the conviction of a Jehovah's Witness, who in an argument with a law enforcement official referred to him as a "God damned racketeer" and "a damned Fascist." The Court found that use of such "fighting words" "by their very utterance inflict injury" and, in addition, "are likely to provoke the average person to retaliation," thereby causing a breach of the peace. The Court concluded that "[r]esort to epithets or personal abuse is not in any proper sense communication of information or opinion safeguarded by the Constitution." By the 1960s, however, a troubling pattern had emerged: Law enforcement officials were using the fighting-words exception to selectively prosecute antiwar and civil rights protestors. In response, the Court reversed every fighting-words conviction that came before it during this turbulent era.[51] Although it has not formally overruled the fighting-words doctrine, the Court has yet to affirm another conviction for the use of fighting words in the more than fifty years since *Chaplinsky*.

Defamation. In *Chaplinsky* the Court also declared libel to be without First Amendment protection.[52] In the abstract, this ruling seems unobjectionable, for what is there possibly worth protecting in a factual assertion that is not only false but also injurious to someone's good name? Like face-to-face verbal assaults, such scurrilous statements would seem to be "no essential part of any exposition of ideas" nor "a step to truth." But experience revealed that libelous statements were often inextricably bound up with the exposition of ideas and that allowing government free rein to suppress libel also gave it the power to suppress unpopular points of view.

In 1960 an Alabama jury awarded a police commissioner $500,000 in damages against the *New York Times* and several civil rights activists, finding that an advertisement carried by the paper in support of the protests led by Dr. Martin Luther King Jr. was libelous. The finding was based on several false statements contained in the advertisement, such as the charge that King had been arrested seven times by the Montgomery police for his protest activities, when in fact he had been arrested only four times. Finally recognizing that *Chaplinsky's* categorical exclusion of libel from the realm of First Amendment protection had imperiled public discourse, the Court in *New York Times v. Sullivan* held that "libel can claim no talismanic immunity from constitutional limitations."[53] Writing for the Court in this landmark 1964 decision, Justice William Brennan formulated a principle that has guided free speech decisions ever since: "[W]e consider this case against the background of a national commitment to the principle that debate on public issues should be uninhibited, robust, and wide-open, and that it may well include vehement, caustic, and sometimes unpleasantly sharp attacks on government and public officials."

To protect public discourse from being unduly restricted by defamation actions, the Court held that public officials can recover for defamatory statements concerning their conduct in office only if they can prove by clear and convincing evidence that the defendant made the statement with "malice," that is, knowledge of its falsity or with reckless disregard for whether the statement was true or not.[54] Because the police commissioner could not show that the factual misstatements in the advertisement were made either with knowledge of their falsity or with reckless disregard for the truth, the Court reversed the judgment.

Commercial Speech.   In 1942, the same year it decided Chaplinsky, the Supreme Court decided a case that cast commercial speech—speech that does no more than propose a commercial transaction—outside the protection of the First Amendment.[55] If any category of speech were so distinct from the marketplace of ideas that it could be regulated without inhibiting robust public discourse, it would seem to be commercial speech. But cases involving advertisements by abortion providers and civil rights lawyers revealed that even commercial advertising cannot be neatly separated from public discourse.[56] In the 1970s the Court began extending some First Amendment protection to commercial advertising, and in 1980 it devised an elaborate four-part test to govern challenges to regulation of commercial speech.[57] The upshot of this test is to require that government show that the regulation is a reasonable means of accomplishing a legitimate objective. Unlike the Brandenburg incitement test or the *New York Times* malice test, which were designed to be exceedingly difficult to meet, the commercial speech test provides considerable leeway for regulation, and the Court has on several occasions upheld prohibitions on commercial speech under this test.[58]

Obscenity.   The doctrinal direction since the late 1960s, then, has been distinctly away from Chaplinsky's categorical exclusion methodology and toward a more refined examination of the free speech interest and governmental purposes involved in the regulation of these various types of speech. Of the several varieties of expression that Chaplinsky declared to be outside the bounds of First Amendment protection, only obscenity still remains unprotected. But even with regard to obscenity the Court has endeavored to prevent regulation of sexually explicit speech from inhibiting public discourse.

A 1959 decision, *Roth v. United States,* confirmed that obscenity fell outside the protection of the First Amendment.[59] Because it upheld governmental power to ban obscenity, *Roth* is most often viewed by liberals as a speech-repressive decision. Often overlooked is that in confirming this traditional understanding of the First Amendment, *Roth* strictly confined the category of obscenity. Writing for the Court, Justice Brennan explained that "[t]he portrayal of sex in art, literature and scientific works is not itself sufficient reason to deny material the constitutional protection of freedom of speech and press." Rather, to be legally obscene material must "appeal to the prurient interest" and be "utterly without redeeming social importance." In other words, it must constitute what today would be called "hard-core" pornography. To assure that serious art and literature were adequately "safeguard[ed]," the Court specifically rejected a test for obscenity then in use that allowed material to be judged by the effect of an isolated passage upon particularly susceptible persons. *Roth* insisted that the work be judged instead "as a whole" and under "contemporary community standards."

Before *Roth* narrowed the category of what could be constitutionally suppressed as obscene, government often used the obscenity laws to prohibit important works of art, including Theodore Dreiser's *American Tragedy*, D. H. Lawrence's *Lady Chatterley's Lover*, and Henry Miller's *Tropic of Cancer* and *Tropic of Capricorn*.[60] Obscenity laws were also used in unsuccessful attempts to suppress educational material such as sex education pamphlets and *Life* magazine's "Birth of a Baby."[61]

The current constitutional definition of obscenity, announced in 1973 in *Miller v. California*, also limits obscenity to "hard-core" pornography so as to protect serious artistic and literary expression.[62] To be legally obscene and thus without First Amendment protection, the material must, taken as a whole, "appeal to the prurient interest," describe "ultimate sexual acts" in a "patently offensive way," and lack "serious literary, artistic, political, or scientific value."[63]

Despite the Court's efforts to protect art, literature, and the expression of ideas by confining the material that may be banned as obscene, recent developments have again proved the danger of categorically excluding speech from First Amendment protection. Obscenity laws have been used to prosecute a museum for showing Robert Mapplethorpe's homoerotic art and to convict a record dealer for selling a recording by the black rap group 2 Live Crew. The jury acquitted the museum curator because it assumed that photographs displayed in a prominent museum must have some serious artistic value.[64] In contrast, the 2 Live Crew album, which did not have the imprimatur of a socially acceptable museum, was held obscene by a federal judge who turned a deaf ear to expert opinion that the record contained artistic value when viewed within the context of the black urban experience.[65] (This ruling was eventually reversed by a federal appellate court.)[66]

Assessment of the Categorical Exclusion Approach.   The lesson to be learned from the now discredited and largely abandoned Chaplinsky categorical exclusion approach is much the same lesson learned from the failure of the original "clear and present danger" test: What appears in the abstract to be a reasonable accommodation between free speech and legitimate or even compelling governmental interests often turns out in practice to have a far greater impact on free expression than anticipated. Moreover, the victims of such overreaching enforcement are often those whose speech the authorities find particularly unsettling—such as antiwar protestors, civil rights activists, or black rap artists.

This is not to say that the categorical exclusion of certain types of speech will inevitably lead to the suppression of unpopular ideas or otherwise impair robust public discourse.[67] Perjury, bribery, and solicitation of criminal acts have always been considered categorically unworthy of any First Amendment protection, yet their exclusion has not interfered with democratic self-governance or any other purpose served by the constitutional protection of speech. Whether á given categorical exclusion will result in impairment of core free speech values depends primarily on pragmatic considerations. These considerations include the breadth of the exclusion, the overlap of the excluded category with categories of speech essential to public discourse, the specificity with which the excluded category can be defined, and the discretion invested in law enforcement officials to decide which speakers to arrest and prosecute.

Since the 1960s the distinct trend has been toward eliminating categories of unprotected speech or drastically reducing their scope. There is, however, one modern decision that defies this trend. In 1982 the Court held in *New York v. Ferber* that child pornography (photographs of children engaging in sexual acts) is categorically without First Amendment protection.[68] Because the Court carefully confined the category of child pornography, it is possible that this exclusion, like the exclusion of bribery and perjury and unlike the exclusion of libel and fighting words, will not significantly impair public discourse or artistic expression.

3

AN OVERVIEW OF MODERN
FREE SPEECH DOCTRINE

In the previous chapter, I explored several basic rules governing several key areas of free speech doctrine, such as advocacy of illegal activity, fighting words, defamation, and commercial speech. But because the focus of that discussion was historical, emphasizing how the lessons from the past shape today's rules, I made no attempt to explain how these rules relate to each other or to survey the entire landscape of free speech doctrine. In this chapter, therefore, I canvass the basic rules and investigate how (or if) they form a coherent framework. I begin by discussing what is encompassed within the meaning of "speech" as that term is used in First Amendment case law. The bulk of the chapter, however, is dedicated to examining the rule against *content discrimination*. We will discover that despite some loose language in several Supreme Court decisions suggesting that all content-based regulations are presumptively unconstitutional, this is not the case. Rather, some types of content regulation are viewed suspiciously, whereas others raise no serious constitutional problems at all. I conclude the chapter by suggesting a way to make sense of this curious pattern.

THE BASIC TAXONOMY

The text of the First Amendment refers to "speech" and "the press." To prevent the purpose of the First Amendment from being stifled by cramped literalism, however, the amendment has been read more generally to protect "expression." Thus communication that is literally neither speech nor the press—such as photographs, films, paintings, and dance—is protected. But "expression" is an extremely capacious concept.

Indeed, in some sense all voluntary human activity is expressive, including some of the most harmful things that human beings do. Terrorist bombings, political assassinations, genocide, and rape can all be highly expressive activities. For First Amendment protection to be meaningful, it cannot extend to all human activity. At some basic level, then, free speech doctrine must distinguish between activity eligible for First Amendment protection ("speech" or "expression") and that which is not ("conduct").

To this end, free speech case law divides the universe of human activity into four categories: (1) protected speech, (2) unprotected speech, (3) expressive conduct, and (4) nonexpressive conduct. As the terminology suggests, the basic dichotomy is between "speech" and "conduct." "Speech" is any activity that makes use of a conventional mode or medium of communication. For example, talking, singing, dancing, parading, broadcasting, filmmaking and distribution, musical composition and performance, painting, sculpture, and displaying objects in a museum would all be considered speech for First Amendment purposes.[1] "Conduct" is residually defined as all other human activity. Without further refinement, however, such a stark division would place on the "speech" side of the line activity that obviously should not be afforded constitutional immunity (such as perjury or solicitation of murder), while at the same time defining as "conduct" activity whose sole function is expressive (such as flag burning as a form of political protest). To mitigate the rigidity of this basic dichotomy, the Court has subdivided "speech" into "protected" and "unprotected" speech and "conduct" into "expressive" and "nonexpressive" conduct.

"Protected" and "Unprotected" Speech

As we have seen, a hallmark of the First Amendment jurisprudence of the 1940s and 1950s was that certain large categories of expression—including "fighting words," libel, obscenity, and commercial speech—were cast outside the realm of First Amendment protection. So long as the state could demonstrate that speech fits within one of these constitutionally forlorn categories of expression, it could ban the speech without any need to make a particularized showing that the speech in question is harmful. Although the categorical exclusion approach has been largely discredited, the Court has not entirely renounced it. Obscenity (and arguably "fighting words") remains categorically bereft of First Amendment protection, as do perjury, bribery, some forms of libel, criminal solicitation, threats, and child pornography.[2]

"Protected speech" is the residual category here, comprising all expression in a conventional medium that does not fall into a category of unprotected speech. Not all protected speech is protected equally, however. For instance, the First Amendment imposes greater obstacles to the regulation of a political editorial in the newspaper than to regulation of workplace conversation. Later in this chapter we will explore in some detail the general topic of differential treatment of protected speech. At this point, however, in light of our particular focus on pornography regulation, I want to highlight a particularly stark example of such differential treatment.

Protected but "Lower-Value" Speech?

Although sexually explicit material that does not meet the *Miller* standard for obscenity is protected speech in that it cannot be banned, several Supreme Court decisions suggest this material is not entitled to full First Amendment protection. In *Young v. American Mini Theatres*, Justice John Paul Stevens, writing for a plurality of the Court, opined that while "the First Amendment will not tolerate the total suppression of erotic materials that have some arguably artistic value, it is manifest that society's interest in protecting this type of expression is of a wholly different, and lesser, magnitude than the interest in untrammeled political debate."[3] The Court in *Young* allowed a city to apply special zoning requirements to prevent "adult" movie theaters and bookstores from locating within 1,000 feet of any two other "regulated uses" (which included "adult" bookstores and theaters as well as pool halls, bars, and cabarets). A majority of the Court has never expressly endorsed the view that nonobscene, sexually explicit material is "low-value" speech.[4] But the Court's holding in *Young*, as well as its subsequent decision in *Renton v. Playtime Theatres*, which allowed a city to concentrate "adult" theaters in a certain area of town, show that sexually explicit, nonobscene speech is in fact treated as "lower-value" expression.[5]

"Expressive" and "Nonexpressive" Conduct

"Expressive conduct" is activity that does not utilize any conventionally recognized form of communication but is nevertheless sufficiently communicative to be entitled to First Amendment protection. To qualify as expressive conduct, activity must "inten[d] to convey a particularized message" under circumstances in which "the likelihood [is] great that the message would be understood by those who viewed it."[6] Examples of activity deemed "expressive conduct" include draft card burning, flag burning, displaying a red flag, wearing a black armband, and nude dancing.

Activity qualifying as "expressive conduct" is entitled to First Amendment protection, but the degree of protection depends enormously on the state's justification for regulating the activity. If the state is unable to offer a reason "unrelated to the suppression of free expression," then the regulation will be treated as a content-based regulation of protected speech and invalidated unless the government can show some extremely weighty reason for the regulation.[7] If, in contrast, the government presents a justification that is "unrelated to the suppression of free expression," the regulation will likely be upheld.[8] The expressive conduct cases thus underscore an important feature of modern free speech jurisprudence: concern with regulatory *purpose*.[9] We will encounter this theme often in the pages to come.

"Nonexpressive conduct" is that large, residual realm of human activity that qualifies as neither protected or unprotected speech, nor as expressive conduct. It includes everything from changing the oil in one's car to robbing a bank. Government may regulate nonexpressive conduct without hindrance from the First Amendment so long as it can offer some legitimate reason for the regulation. Thus the state may punish racially motivated assaults more harshly than other assaults on the theory that bias crimes inflict more emotional injury on the victim and are more disruptive to the community; it may not, however, increase the penalty to punish the defendant for holding racist beliefs.[10] Once again, we see the central role governmental purpose plays in modern free speech doctrine.

Regulating Protected Speech: The Search for a Basic Rule

Now that we have mapped the basic structure of free speech doctrine and explored some of the values underlying that structure, we are in a position to tackle one of the most difficult questions in all of free speech doctrine: Under what circumstances may government regulate expression protected by the First Amendment?

It is sometimes assumed that if speech does not fall within one of the categories of unprotected speech, it is immune from government regulation unless it creates "a clear and present danger" of some harm government may legitimately prevent. But there are numerous instances where government can regulate speech on grounds far short of a clear and present danger of harm. For instance, government may insist, without showing such language creates an imminent danger, that students and teachers in classrooms at public universities, as well as workers in government agencies, not use profanity. Similarly, regulations of commercial and industrial speech, such as laws against misleading advertising, often seek to prevent harm that is neither clear nor present. The reason the "clear and present danger" test does not serve well as a basic rule governing the regulation of protected speech is that it was not developed for this purpose. Rather, this test was devised to determine when *political advocacy* that encourages *law violation* loses its constitutional immunity. Transformed and strengthened in *Brandenburg v. Ohio,* the current test for when advocacy of law violation may be constitutionally punished is a cornerstone of modern free speech jurisprudence. Nonetheless, it has little direct application outside the realm of advocacy of law violation.

The Court has suggested another rule as a basic standard for determining whether a regulation of protected speech comports with the First Amendment. "[A]bove all else," the Court declared in a 1972 decision, "the First Amendment means that government has no power to restrict expression because of its message, its ideas, its subject matter, or its content."[11] By the 1990s the Court purported to operationalize this policy into a rule that "[c]ontent-based regulations are presumptively invalid."[12] We shall discover that this rule against content discrimination is not nearly so broad as it purports to be. Still, it is an extremely important feature of modern free speech doctrine.

The Distinction Between Content-Based and Content-Neutral Regulations

Older free speech decisions tended to focus on the nature of the speech in question. Thus the Espionage Act and Smith Act cases asked whether the defendants' speech created a "clear and present danger" of some grave harm, just as the Court in *Chaplinsky* inquired whether the speech in question was "communication of information or opinion safeguarded by the Constitution."[13] A singular characteristic of recent free speech jurisprudence, in contrast, is its focus on the *nature of the regulation.* The key question in most of the free speech decisions since the 1970s has been whether the regulation is content based or content neutral.

The Court's hostility to content-based laws is manifest. "Regulations which permit the Government to discriminate on the basis of the content of the message," the Court declared in a 1984 decision, "cannot be tolerated under the First Amendment."[14] As we shall see, this statement is too broad, for some content-based restrictions are routinely and uncontroversially permitted under the First Amendment. A more accurate statement is that *in certain contexts* content-based restrictions will almost always be invalidated. (We will later try to determine in which contexts this strong rule against content discrimination operates.) A broad statement about content discrimination that is almost always true, however, is that *only* content-based restrictions are likely to be invalidated; content-neutral laws, in contrast, are almost always upheld.

Given the importance of the distinction between content-based and content-neutral regulations, it is crucial to understand what is meant by these terms. Content-based laws are ones in which the government seeks to regulate expression because of the message it conveys.[15] A law prohibiting anyone from criticizing the government's drug policy would be content based. Content-neutral laws ordinarily regulate the "time, place or manner" of speech without reference to or concern with its message.[16] An ordinance prohibiting the use of loudspeakers in residential neighborhoods after 10:00 P.M. would be content neutral.

Content-based regulations come in different varieties, some worse than others from a First Amendment standpoint. As the Court explained in a recent decision, "viewpoint discrimination" is an "egregious" form of content regulation.[17] Viewpoint discrimination occurs when the regulation is based on the "specific motivating ideology or the opinion or perspective of the speaker." A law prohibiting anyone from stating that abortion is murder is viewpoint discriminatory, as is a law that forbade anyone from expressing the view that blacks are genetically inferior to whites. Because viewpoint-discriminatory regulations are considered to be fundamentally contrary to basic free speech norms, patently viewpoint-based regulations are infrequent. A rare example of a plainly viewpoint-based regulation can be found in *Kingsley International Pictures Corp. v. Regents*.[18] In this 1959 case, the New York film board denied a license to *Lady Chatterley's Lover* on the grounds that it presented adultery "as being right and desirable" in certain situations. In finding the denial of the license unconstitutional, the Court explained that "the First Amendment's basic guarantee is of freedom to advocate ideas" and that the denial of the license "thus struck at the very heart of constitutionally protected liberty."

Viewpoint discrimination does not, however, exhaust the universe of content-based regulation. For instance, a law that prohibited any discussion of abortion (whether pro or con), although not viewpoint discriminatory, is nonetheless content based. Such a regulation discriminates on the basis of subject matter or topic. The line between viewpoint and subject matter discrimination is not always clear. In a 1995 Supreme Court decision, five justices thought a prohibition on funding a student publication because it "primarily promotes or manifests a particular belief in or about a deity or an ultimate reality" constituted viewpoint discrimination; four justices thought that the regulation was merely subject-matter discrimination.[19]

Laws that forbid the use of offensive words or symbols have also been readily classified as content-based regulations. The seminal case in the area of offensive language is *Cohen v. California*, a 1971 decision in which the Court upheld the right of an antiwar protestor to wear in public a jacket bearing the message "Fuck the Draft."[20] Finding that the ordinance used to punish Cohen for use of offensive speech was contrary to "the usual rule that governmental bodies may not prescribe the form or content of individual expression," the Court held that the state could not constitutionally excise "one particular scurrilous epithet from the public discourse." "We cannot indulge the facile assumption," cautioned Justice John Harlan, "that one can forbid particular words without also running a substantial risk of suppressing ideas in the process." Harlan noted in addition that "much linguistic expression serves a dual communicative function: it conveys not only ideas capable of relatively precise, detached explication, but otherwise inexpressible emotions as well." Similarly, in *Texas v. Johnson*, a 1989 decision that found a First Amendment right to burn the American flag as a form of political protest, the Court held that forbidding flag desecration because such activity "would cause serious offense to others" rendered the restriction "content based."[21]

The cases invalidating laws forbidding offensive words and symbols have been particularly controversial; both *Cohen* and *Johnson* sparked heated dissents. To the dissenting justices, flag burning and use of vulgar language are, like fighting words, "no essential part of any exposition of ideas"; any idea can, in their view, be "conveyed . . . just as forcefully in a dozen different ways" without the use of inflammatory language or symbols.[22]

Regulations that expressly discriminate on the basis of viewpoint or subject matter or those that proscribe particular words or symbols will almost always be considered content based. But once we get beyond these exemplars of content discrimination, things get murkier. As with most abstract legal concepts, the distinction between content-based and content-neutral regulations blurs around the edges. For instance, in *Turner Broadcasting System, Inc. v. FCC* the Court struggled to classify a federal law requiring cable television operators to devote a portion of their channels to the transmission of local broadcast television stations.[23] Acknowledging that "[d]eciding whether a particular regulation is content based or content neutral is not always a simple task," a bare majority of the Court concluded after extensive analysis that the provision was content neutral. In contrast, four justices thought the provision was content based.

But the most controversial determination of whether a regulation was content based or content neutral—and one particularly relevant to the subject of pornography—came in *Renton v. Playtime Theatres, Inc.*[24] This 1986 decision involved a zoning ordinance that prohibits movie theaters showing "adult" films from locating within 1,000 feet of any residence, church, park, or school. Although the regulation was expressly cast in terms of the content of the films (those "characterized by an emphasis on matter depicting, describing or relating to 'specified sexual activities' or 'specified anatomical areas'"), a majority of the Court found the ordinance to be content neutral.

Justice William Rehnquist found that the ordinance was "aimed not at the *content* of the films . . . but rather at the *secondary effects* of such the-

aters on the surrounding community."[25] The "secondary effects" targeted
by the ordinance were lower property values and increased crime said to
be caused by the mere presence of such theaters and the clientele they attract. The Court found that these harms were distinct from any effects
caused by the impact of the films on the audience. Dissenting, Justice
Brennan, joined by Justice Thurgood Marshall, thought that the city's
"secondary effects" rationale was merely a pretext for burdening the exhibition of these films due to official disapproval of its message. Not only
was the evidence of harmful "secondary effects" in his view "purely speculative," but some of the city's other stated reasons for enacting the ordinance revealed its true purpose. For instance, the city had justified the
regulation on the grounds that pornography "causes a loss of sensitivity
to the adverse effect of pornography upon children, established family relations, respect for marital relationships and for the sanctity of marriage
relations of others, and the concept of non-aggressive, consensual sexual
relations."

That there may be some regulations that are difficult to classify should
not, however, obscure the fact that most speech regulations are easily
identifiable as either content based or content neutral. For the most part,
the dichotomy has proved to be a workable and useful tool. The problem
with the distinction is not lack of clarity but rather that it is sometimes
mechanically applied in ways that lose sight of its underlying purpose.

The Imperfect Fit Between the Rule Against
Content Discrimination and Its Purpose

The Court has offered the following explanation for its hostility toward
content-based regulations: "Laws of this sort pose the inherent risk that
the Government seeks not to advance a legitimate regulatory goal, but to
suppress unpopular ideas or information or manipulate the public debate
through coercion rather than persuasion. These restrictions raise the
specter that the Government may effectively drive certain ideas or viewpoints from the marketplace."[26]

Although content-based restrictions often "raise the specter" of government hostility to certain ideas, they do not inevitably do so. Thus it is far
from clear how a law that requires authors of books describing crimes
they have committed to turn over to the crime victims the proceeds from
sale of these books threatens to "drive certain ideas or viewpoints from
the marketplace."[27] Similarly, a prohibition against residential picketing
that contains an exception for picketing at residences that are also places
of employment would seem to be a reasonable, viewpoint-neutral accommodation between the right of residential privacy and the interests of
workers to picket their place of employment.[28] Yet both of these regula-

tions were found content based and invalidated. Justice Sandra Day O'Connor has candidly admitted that "it is quite true that regulations are occasionally struck down because of their content-based nature, even though common sense may suggest that they are entirely reasonable."[29]

Conversely, although content-neutral regulations will usually not have a discriminatory purpose or effect, they are not always so benign. As has been observed, content-neutral restrictions "may at times have a differential impact or reflect a latent governmental hostility towards certain ideas."[30] A law regulating protests at abortion clinics will have a decidedly disproportionate impact on antiabortion messages, just as a Mississippi law passed at the height of the civil rights movement limiting protests in front of government buildings had a disparate effect on antisegregation messages.[31] Yet First Amendment challenges to these regulations were to no avail, for free speech doctrine notoriously does not account for the disparate impact that content-neutral laws may have on the marketplace of ideas.[32] And irrespective of disparate impact, some content-neutral regulations, such as a ban on the sale or distribution of literature at airports, arguably adversely affect both the democratic self-governance and the marketplace of ideas through the sheer amount of speech that they restrict.[33]

There is, then, less than a perfect fit between the rule against content discrimination and its stated purpose. Such gaps are inherent in legal rules, but the problem is exacerbated in free speech jurisprudence by the rigidly determined result flowing from the classification of a regulation as content based or content neutral.[34] If deemed content based, a regulation will be subjected to "the most exacting scrutiny" (a test the Court borrowed from equal protection jurisprudence). To survive this strict judicial scrutiny, a law must be "necessary to serve a compelling state interest" and furthermore be "narrowly drawn to achieve that end."[35] As has been aptly remarked, such scrutiny is "strict in theory [but] fatal in fact."[36] There are thus few cases on the books in which a speech regulation has survived this test.[37]

As worded, the test for content-neutral speech regulations is not toothless, demanding that such regulations be "narrowly tailored to serve a significant governmental interest, and . . . leave open ample alternative channels for communication of the information."[38] In practice, though, content-neutral regulations are nearly always upheld.[39] Modern free speech doctrine thus creates a rigid two-track system, with one track leading almost invariably to invalidation and the other nearly as certainly to validation. Consequently, all of the important work is done at the classification stage.

An alternative to placing such importance on the classification would be to focus instead on whether the law truly threatens to impair democratic self-governance, warp the marketplace of ideas, or otherwise impair free speech values. The drawback of such an approach, however, would be less certainty. A bright-line rule against content discrimination provides clear guidance to speakers, law enforcement officials, attorneys, and courts as to what types of laws are unconstitutional. In addition, the rigidity of this rule prevents judges from smuggling (perhaps quite unconsciously) their approval or disapproval of speakers' ideas into the analysis. The possibility of such judicial-viewpoint discrimination increases the more flexible the analysis becomes.[40] Perhaps for these reasons free speech doctrine in general and the dichotomy between content-based and content-neutral regulations in particular remain quite mechanistic.

The stark difference in treatment between content-based and content-neutral regulations is, however, mitigated in several respects. Where a regulation, although formally content-based, plainly does not "raise the specter" of viewpoint discrimination, the Court sometimes escapes the formalistic box in which it has imprisoned itself by simply declaring a content-based regulation content neutral.[41] Conversely, the Court occasionally will take a hard look at certain types of content-neutral laws that might mask viewpoint discrimination, such as laws that turn on the speaker's identity.[42] Similarly, it has sometimes viewed laws that constitute total bans on particular media of expression more skeptically than it has run-of-the-mill content-neutral regulations.[43] But the most significant amelioration of the sharply different ways that content-based and content-neutral regulations are treated is achieved by confining the range over which the rule against content discrimination operates. Despite some loose language by the Court suggesting that all content-based regulations of expression are subject to strict scrutiny, there are numerous situations in which content-based restrictions are constitutionally unobjectionable.

The Limited Scope of the Rule Against Content Discrimination

The Supreme Court is fond of sweeping proclamations about content discrimination: "Regulations which permit the Government to discriminate on the basis of the content of the message," the Court has declared, "cannot be tolerated under the First Amendment."[44] Similar is the Court's pronouncement that "the most exacting scrutiny" is applicable to "regulations that suppress, disadvantage, or impose differential burdens upon speech because of its content."[45] Such a rule would provide tremendous protection to speech, as well as greatly simplify the task of understanding and applying free speech doctrine. Unfortunately for both free speech absolutists and others who seek doctrinal simplicity, these proclamations are much too broad. Speech is far too ubiquitous an activity with too many real-world ramifications to permit any such general proscription of content-based regulations. Speech consists not just of political exhortations or social commentary; it is also a means by which people commit crimes and injure others. Furthermore, speech is an essential mechanism by which government manages its own affairs. It is therefore not surprising that in contrast to the Court's rhetoric, its actual decisions reveal many situations in which government routinely regulates the content of speech.

Public Forum Doctrine.   One important and clearly articulated limit on the rule against content discrimination is the Court's "public forum" jurisprudence. Public property that is "by tradition or designation a forum for public communication" (for example, parks and streets) is known in free speech parlance as a "public forum."[46] In such places the government is indeed generally forbidden to regulate speech because of its content. In contrast, public property that is not a public forum but that has been set aside for some purpose inconsistent with unrestricted communication (for example, a classroom at a public university or a faculty mailbox at a public high school) is deemed a "nonpublic forum." In such places the government may generally regulate the content of speech, including its subject matter, if the regulation is "reasonable" in light of the intended purpose of the forum and is not an attempt to suppress a viewpoint with which the government disagrees.[47] For instance, limitations confining speech in the classrooms of state universities to expression relevant to the subject matter of the class is plainly content based but just as plainly constitutional. Accordingly, if a mathematics instructor insisted that a student called to the blackboard confine himself to solving an equation rather than writing political slogans, no serious First Amendment issue would arise despite the blatant content discrimination.

In recent years the Supreme Court has been reluctant to find government property to be a public forum. Thus the Court has held that neither city utility poles nor a sidewalk in front of a post office was a public forum.[48] And in a significant and controversial decision, a sharply divided Court held a major metropolitan airport terminal to be a nonpublic forum.[49] By allowing government considerable leeway to regulate the content of speech on government property dedicated to purposes other than public communication or even to refuse public access for communicative purposes to such property, the public forum doctrine protects the government's ability to conduct its own affairs.

Government Employee Speech.   This same goal is effected even more directly by doctrine that gives government broad power to regulate the content of the speech of its employees. Unless an employee's speech is on "a matter of public concern" (a category that the Court has defined rather narrowly in this context), a government employer has nearly carte blanche to regulate employee speech so as to promote the smooth and efficient running of the workplace. For instance, so far as the First Amendment is concerned, a government employee may be disciplined or even fired for complaining to other employees about her supervisor, so long as the grievance is not of public interest.[50] And even when the speech is a matter of public concern, the government generally has greater latitude to regulate the content of the speech of its employees than it does to impose content-based restrictions on the general public.

Government Subsidies. The government also routinely engages in content discrimination when it subsidizes expression. For instance, the federal government funds only those projects in the arts that meet a standard of excellence, a clearly content-based criterion.[51] The general rule is that when funding speech, government may take account of content so long as the funding decision is not "aimed at the suppression of dangerous ideas."[52] Indeed, lest the First Amendment outlaw all government propaganda, the government may even engage in viewpoint discrimination when it is expending funds to promote its own message. Thus "[w]hen Congress established the National Endowment for Democracy to encourage other countries to adopt democratic principles, it was not constitutionally required to fund a program to encourage competing lines of political philosophy such as communism and fascism."[53]

The Lack of any General Rule Against Content Discrimination. If it were only the nonpublic forum, government employment, and government subsidy cases that readily allowed content discrimination, it still might be said with some accuracy that the First Amendment establishes a general prohibition against content discrimination. The authors of the leading constitutional law casebook appear to take the position that the government's ability routinely to engage in content discrimination is limited to contexts in which the government is acting not in its "sovereign, coercive" capacity but in a "proprietary" capacity as an educator, employer, or patron.[54] The problem with this position is that there are numerous instances in which government is constitutionally permitted to regulate the content of speech in its "sovereign, coercive" capacity. For instance, the content of speech and the impact it has on its audience routinely form the basis of tort suits (i.e., civil cases seeking compensation for injury caused by the defendants' wrongful conduct). Actions for fraud or misrepresentation always involve the content of speech, as do suits for defamation. The Supreme Court has never suggested that fraud and misrepresentation suits are subject to strict First Amendment scrutiny, and although defamation suits brought by public officials or public figures are, as we have seen, subject to considerable First Amendment obstacles, the Court has held that the Constitution poses no strictures on ordinary defamation suits involving private parties where the speech is purely of private concern.[55] Similarly, although in certain circumstances the First Amendment might bar suits by public officials for infliction of emotional distress caused by speech,[56] no such barriers exist in actions brought by private individuals for speech not of public concern. For example, if as a malicious prank Jones falsely tells Smith that Smith's five-year-old child was just run over by a car, there would be no First Amendment barrier to a suit for intentional infliction of emotional distress.[57]

A myriad other tort actions commonly regulate speech because of its content. For instance, product liability actions or ordinary negligence suits can turn on the content of speech, as when an action is brought to recover damages caused by the publication of erroneous instructions for use of a product.[58] Aside from tort suits, there is an almost endless variety of laws that regulate the content of speech but that the Supreme Court easily would uphold against First Amendment challenge. These include securities regulations that forbid the disclosure of certain information relevant to the value of stock; antitrust laws that prevent competitors from sharing price information; copyright laws that restrict the publication of infringing material; regulations that outlaw sexual harassment in the workplace; or to invoke Holmes's hoary example, a law against falsely shouting, "Fire!" in a theater. Indeed, most of these regulations are not thought of as even implicating the First Amendment.

Of course, *particular applications* of these regulations can present First Amendment problems. For instance, an injunction in a copyright suit that prevents the disclosure of important historical information or a sexual harassment suit based on a single statement by an employer that women are not as capable as men to perform certain jobs would raise difficult free speech issues. But the fact remains that every day copyright and sexual harassment regulations along with many other laws are routinely applied to restrict the content of speech in ways that do not even present free speech concerns. In run-of-the-mill cases, such as a copyright infringement suit involving the pirating of computer software or a sexual harassment suit alleging an employer's repeated unwelcome sexual propositions, no one even thinks to raise a free speech claim.

Reconfiguring the Rule Against Content Discrimination in Light of Basic Free Speech Values

Now that we see that no general rule against content regulation exists, where does that leave our understanding of free speech doctrine? Is it but a series of unconnected rules governing particular types of speech, an incomprehensible muddle forming no intelligible pattern? The situation is not quite so bleak. If we look closely, we find some distinguishing characteristics. We discover that speech on "matters of public concern" is much more likely to be afforded rigorous protection than speech purely of private concern, that speech in settings essential to public discourse tends to be highly protected regardless of its content, and that laws having obvious legitimate regulatory purposes tend to be seen as consistent with the First Amendment despite imposing incidental restraints on expression.

Speech on Matters of Public Concern.   "The First Amendment's primary aim," the Court has declared, "is the full protection of speech upon issues of public concern."[59] Thus "speech on matters of public issues occupies the highest rung of the hierarchy of First Amendment values, and is entitled to special protection."[60] We have already seen, for instance, that workplace speech by government employees is eligible for meaningful protection from content regulation only if "on a matter of public concern." In contrast, "when a public employee speaks not as a citizen upon matters of public concern, but instead as an employee upon matters only of personal interest," the government has wide leeway to regulate or even prohibit this speech because of its content.[61]

The constitutional limitations on defamation actions form a similar pattern. The highest level of protection (the "malice" standard of *New York Times v. Sullivan*) is applicable to statements about the official duties of public officials (or matters of public concern about public figures). The First Amendment also extends considerable protection to defamatory statements about private persons, but only if the statement was on a matter of public concern.[62] In contrast, statements about private individuals that are not of public concern have so far been afforded no First Amendment protection from state defamation laws.[63] Similarly, in extending strong First Amendment protection against suits for intentional infliction of emotional distress, the Court pointedly limited its holding to suits by "public figures and public officials," and then only where the injurious speech occurred in the "area of public debate."[64]

These key phrases—"on a matter of public concern" and in the "area of public debate"—suggest that the strong presumption against content discrimination is primarily in service of two instrumental values underlying free speech discussed in the preceding chapter: democratic self-governance and the search for truth in the marketplace of ideas.[65] The pattern of free speech decisions now begins to make sense: The strong presumption against content discrimination is present when needed to protect the public discourse by which we govern ourselves and through which we build our culture. It is largely absent, however, where the regulation is justified with reference to an interest unrelated to the power of speech to persuade people about how to see the world. This special protection afforded speech on matters of public concern is also consistent with the noninstrumental values underlying free speech. It is this value, deeply rooted in the concept of democracy, that explains why free speech doctrine emphatically views the opportunity to participate in public discourse as an *individual* right of moral dimension, one not easily outweighed by consequentialist concerns. The special solicitude that free speech doctrine shows for speech on matters of pubic concern is thus "no mystery."[66]

The power of the "matter of public concern" criterion to explain when a strong presumption against content regulation operates should not (as it often is) be underestimated. This criterion explains why the First Amendment immunizes an animal rights protestor from most any form of content regulation in her attempt to inform the public about the pain cosmetic testing inflicts on animals while imposing no obstacle to laws forbidding officers of cosmetics firms from sharing price information. By the same token, the explanatory power of this criterion should not be overstated.

Speech in Settings Essential to Public Discourse.   Nearly as important to determining when the rule against content discrimination operates as the type of speech is the setting in which the speech occurs. For example, although issues of race and gender are undoubtedly matters of "public concern," an employer could be prevented from beginning every workday with a speech to his employees asserting that blacks are genetically inferior to whites or that a woman's place is at home and not in the workplace. Conversely, that John Smith has sore feet is plainly not a matter of public concern. Yet he has just as much right to pass out a pamphlet on the street corner complaining of this personal problem as an antiwar activist has to distribute leaflets criticizing a war; indeed, Smith may even have a constitutional right to use the same expletive to complain about his feet that Mr. Cohen used to condemn the Vietnam-era draft.

These examples show that in addition to directly serving the underlying values of free speech by bestowing special protection to speech on matters of public concern, free speech doctrine also promotes these values *structurally* by establishing certain settings for discussion of matters of public concern—or as this discussion is sometimes referred to in the scholarly literature, *public discourse*. This phenomenon can most readily be seen in the Court's public forum jurisprudence, which distinguishes between public property that is "a forum for *public communication*" and public property that is not a public forum.[67] As we have seen, government is generally disabled from regulating the content of expression in a public forum. Such a wholesale, structural approach to speech protection has an interesting consequence: If expression occurs within a medium dedicated to public discourse, even expression not on a matter of public concern will tend to be treated as if it were. This phenomenon is analogous to a passenger's being bumped up to first class because the airline has oversold the coach seats. Although the passenger paid only for a coach seat, she will usually be given the same treatment as those who have paid for a first-class seat.[68]

As is true with much of free speech doctrine, the reason for such overprotection is primarily pragmatic. In contexts manifestly dedicated to activities other than public discourse, such as the government workplace, the doctrine allows ad hoc determination of whether speech is on a matter of public concern.[69] But in settings dedicated to public discourse, there is good reason to avoid such ad hoc determinations. The line between matters of public and private concern cannot always be precisely drawn. Where, by definition, the instances of speech on public concern are numerous, as is the case with speech in a public forum, even a small rate of error in classifying matters of public concern as purely private speech could result in significant stifling of public discourse. In addition, ad hoc determinations could mask antagonism (or favoritism) toward the speakers' points of view. It is therefore safer to give a speaker lamenting an issue of purely private concern in a public forum the same protection as someone speaking on an issue of public concern.

A similar phenomenon can be observed in media essential to public discourse. For instance, there is no First Amendment right either to arrange or attend a cockfight in states that have banned cockfighting. But once the event is captured on videotape, significant First Amendment protection attaches both to its distribution and viewing. Thus the protection afforded particular media because of their connection with public discourse often results in protection of individual instances of expression in that medium, even if these individual instances themselves are not part of public discourse.[70]

This phenomenon has an important bearing on why expression whose primary purpose and effect is sexual arousal rather than contribution to democratic self-governance or the marketplace of ideas remains highly protected, subject only to a narrow obscenity exception. Since the media in which pornography appears—books, magazines, film, and the Internet—are essential to public discourse, pornography tends to partake of the protection afforded these media. This phenomenon also explains why nonideational art is highly protected. Although abstract art and symphonic music have little direct connection with self-governance or the marketplace of ideas, many types of art are highly intellectual or overtly political or both. Because art in general is thus connected to democratic self-governance and the marketplace of ideas, First Amendment protection extends across the board, even to art forms that contribute to neither of these functions.[71]

This pattern of free speech decisions, granting rigorous protection against content discrimination to certain speech in particular settings, suggests that free speech doctrine can be usefully viewed as constructing a realm dedicated to public discourse in service of democratic self-governance and truth seeking in the marketplace of ideas.[72] Within this realm there are no verities—every proposition is open to question. Here even the most minimal civility cannot be enforced, for experience has shown that only in such an unconstrained world can the ultimate decisionmakers in a democratic society freely examine and discuss the rules, norms, and conditions that constitute society; only under these conditions will decisions reflect the uncoerced will of the people rather than the preferences of those in power. And only in an environment in which any idea can be expressed can there be that never ending search for the truth upon which cultural, political, and material progress depends. It is in this realm that Justice Marshall's declaration that "our people are guaranteed the right to express *any* thought, free from government censorship" holds sway.[73]

But precisely because public discourse in the United States is so strongly protected, the realm dedicated to such expression cannot be too broadly conceived. Not every setting can be dedicated to public discourse if anything else is to be accomplished. Government must also be able to effectuate results yielded by the democratic process. Although "uninhibited, robust, and wide-open" expression may be essential to democratic self-governance, such speech can also inhibit government from carrying out the decisions reached through this discourse. If there could be no limits on the vituperations with which government employees could complain to each other about their supervisors or on disagreements about the goals of the organization in which they work, accomplishment of the tasks at hand might be impeded. Similarly, personally insulting exchanges in the classroom at a public university can disrupt the learning process—the primary purpose for which the state has dedicated the premises. Accordingly, in settings not dedicated to public discourse where some specific governmental purpose is both manifest and pervasive, such as courtrooms, government offices, and public classrooms, and when that purpose would be frustrated if government could not control the content of expression, government will generally have considerable leeway to regulate the content of expression.[74] Indeed, in some such settings even viewpoint discrimination may sometimes be permissible. Thus an affirmative action officer at a public university could be fired if she persisted in expressing an anti–affirmative action point of view in her official dealings with the public. Similarly, an FBI agent assigned to conduct background checks on presidential appointees could with no hindrance from the First Amendment be prohibited from wearing while on the job a button calling for the impeachment of the president.

The Suspiciousness of the Regulation.   In our attempt to discover when a strong rule against content discrimination operates, we have so far identified two considerations of paramount importance: the subject matter of the speech (whether it is a topic of public concern) and its context (whether the speech occurs in a setting dedicated or essential to public discourse). There is, however, a third criterion that, albeit important, is harder to quantify and thus often remains unarticulated in the case law. Some regulations by their very nature raise the specter that they are motivated, at least in part, by a purpose contrary to core free speech values. Other regulations are the type that dispel such suspicion. For instance, regulations aimed at speech are usually more likely to be motivated by an impermissible purpose than a law aimed at conduct and that burdens speech only incidentally. The antitrust laws regulate the content of what business competitors can say to each other, but because these laws are aimed at anticompetitive practices rather than expression, this regulation is not seen as presenting First Amendment issues. Conversely, although acknowledging that burning a cross on another's property could constitutionally be prohibited under any number of laws aimed at conduct (for example, trespass, arson, and antiterrorism laws), the Court in *R.A.V. v. City of St. Paul* invalidated a law used to convict a juvenile for burning a cross on a black family's lawn because the law was aimed at expression (albeit unprotected expression).[75]

Even if a particular regulation expressly targets the content of speech, it will not ordinarily be seen as raising serious free speech issues if it is part of a larger regulatory scheme aimed at conduct. Securities laws regulating the communication of insider information that could affect the value of stock is a good example of such a regulation. Similarly, because of their connection to a statutory scheme intended to curb discriminatory conduct, regulations prohibiting sexually harassing speech in the workplace are not usually viewed as content-oriented regulations subject to strict scrutiny.[76] There are in addition laws aimed primarily at speech and not part of some larger regulation of conduct that nonetheless do not raise First Amendment concerns. Although copyright law regulates expression, the obvious and undisputed purpose of the law—protection of intellectual property—dispels any concern that the law was enacted to suppress ideas. And although the application of copyright law ordinarily requires an examination of the content of expression (e.g., determining whether one work infringes another), the usually quite mechanical nature of these inquiries and the nonideological context in which they generally occur tend to negate the possibility that government might use copyright law to suppress ideas it finds dangerous or offensive.

Underlying the emphasis that modern free speech doctrine puts on the nature of the regulation is an abiding concern with *government's purpose* in regulating speech. Indeed, as we have seen, key to determining if a regulation is content neutral or content based is whether the regulation can be justified by some speech-neutral purpose. This concern with purpose is why a lawsuit to enjoin a rap group from performing "Cop Killer" on the grounds that it infringes copyright would not present a free speech issue, whereas a suit to prevent this same performance because it promotes disrespect for the law or even because it might endanger the lives of police officers would. Preventing government from regulating speech for some illegitimate purpose reflects the basic noninstrumental value of free speech that government must treat people as autonomous, rational individuals capable of making up their own minds about which ideas are good and which are evil.

In summary, although I can offer no formula that will unerringly predict the situations in which the rule against content discrimination applies, I have suggested that there are three important criteria for making this determination: (1) whether the speech is on a matter of public concern, (2) whether the speech occurs in a setting dedicated to public discourse or in a medium essential to such discourse, and (3) whether the nature of the regulation raises or dispels suspicion that it has been enacted for some purpose contrary to core free speech values. But more important for our purposes than identifying the exact contexts in which the rule against content discrimination operates is the recognition that despite some loose language in Supreme Court opinions, no blanket rule against content discrimination exists. Rather, a strong presumption against content-based regulations operates only within a relatively narrow band of cases. As we shall see, this realization proves particularly pertinent to evaluating the radicals' charge that in denying an exception for hate speech and pornography but allowing numerous other content-based exceptions from First Amendment protection, modern free speech doctrine discriminates against the interests of minorities and women.

4

Modern Doctrine in Action

Its Application to Hate Speech and Pornography Regulation

Many radical critics acknowledge that any attempt to ban the expression of racist ideology or to prohibit sexually explicit material demeaning to women is unconstitutional under current free speech doctrine. Indeed, the essence of radical attack on this doctrine—that it systematically undervalues the interests of women and people of color—presumes this result. Despite inconsistency with their larger claim, however, some radical critics maintain that there may be room under current doctrine for far-reaching restrictions on hate speech and pornography demeaning to women. Some mainstream commentators as well have argued that current doctrine may permit such speech restrictions. But these arguments are really little more than wishful thinking, for it is about as certain as anything can be in constitutional law that broad hate speech or pornography bans are unconstitutional.

I want to emphasize at the outset that in claiming that broad prohibition of hate speech and pornography would violate the First Amendment as currently interpreted by American courts, I am not claiming that this interpretation is either wise or correct. Whether doctrine should allow such restrictions is a much more contestable question, one that is the focus of Part 3 of this book. My assertion here is purely descriptive, namely, that such laws would be declared unconstitutional. I also want to emphasize that my claim of unconstitutionality is limited to laws that would broadly ban the dissemination of racist ideas or pornography, not to more specific measures limited to particular contexts.

HATE SPEECH

Much of the discussion of the constitutionality of hate speech regulation suffers from a failure to specify the type of regulation under discussion. In debates about the regulation of "hate speech," it is often impossible to tell whether the discussion concerns a broad ban on all public expression of racist ideas or a much narrower regulation, such as campus speech codes or prohibition of racist fighting words. Indeed, sometimes even hate *crime* legislation—penalty enhancement for racially motivated crimes, such as murder, assault, and arson—is indiscriminately thrown into the hate speech pot. The problem with failing to distinguish broad hate speech regulations from narrower ones, and both types of hate speech regulation from hate crime legislation, is that free speech doctrine has a very different bearing on each type of regulation. In this chapter I focus primarily on proposals that would generally ban the expression of racist ideas and demonstrate why such laws are unconstitutional under current doctrine. At the end of the chapter, I discuss the much closer constitutional question presented by more limited regulations of racist expression and explain why hate crime legislation is consistent with free speech norms.

The Unconstitutionality of a General Hate Speech Ban

Since the ultimate question here is the constitutionality of a general ban on hate speech, it would be helpful to get examples of such legislation on the table. Because nothing of this sort is to be found on the U.S. statute books, I use as examples a Canadian hate speech provision, an international convention, and a proposal drafted by an American law professor. Section 319(2) of the Canadian Criminal Code provides that "[e]very one who, by communicating statements, other than in private conversation, willfully promotes hatred against any identifiable group" is guilty of an offense punishable by up to two years' imprisonment. Article 4 of the International Convention on the Elimination of All Forms of Racial Discrimination requires signatories to "declare as an offence punishable by law all dissemination of ideas based on racial superiority or hatred, [and] incitement to racial discrimination." Mari Matsuda, a leading proponent of hate speech prohibition in this country, proposes banning any speech whose "message is of racial inferiority . . . directed at a historically oppressed group [and] is persecutory, hateful, and degrading."[1]

From a doctrinal standpoint, the most important thing to recognize about these provisions is that they are all viewpoint-based restrictions on highly protected speech. Anyone who wants to promote racial equality and ethnic diversity is free to do so; those who want to convey opposing points of view may not. As morally reprehensible as hate speech is, it nonetheless expresses a point of view. Moreover, much of the speech proscribed by these provisions would under American doctrine be considered core political speech. Consider, for example, the following expression at issue in two prosecutions under Canada's hate speech law:

> [T]he allegation that 6 million Jews died during the second world war is utterly unfounded. [It is a] brazen fantasy . . . marking with eternal shame a great European nation, as well as wringing fraudulent monetary compensation from them;[2] America is being swamped by coloureds who do not believe in democracy and harbour a hatred for white people; because Zionists dominate financial life and resources, the nation cannot remain in good health because the alien community's interests are not those of the majority; Hitler was right. Communism is Jewish.[3]

Racist speech such as this, although expressing an ugly, twisted view of the world, does nonetheless express a worldview. As we have seen, speech on matters of public concern "occupies the highest rung of the hierarchy of First Amendment values, and is entitled to special protection."[4] And to the extent that such speech occurs in highly protected media, such as books, pamphlets, cable television, the Internet, or in a public forum, such expression is even more certain to be considered highly protected speech. By the same token, not all racist speech is highly protected. Face-to-face racial slurs, for instance, or even undirected racist remarks in the workplace would not be afforded rigorous First Amendment protection. But any general ban on hate speech, such as the three examples cited above, would encompass a great deal of highly protected speech. For example, all of these provisions would apply to a member of the American Nazi Party who spewed venomous ideas in the speaker's corner of the park or a Klan member distributing pamphlets on the street corner, not to mention the racist tracts sold in bookstores or published on the Internet.

Per Se Invalidity. As discussed in Chapter 3, content-based restrictions of speech on matters of public concern occurring in highly protected settings are subject to "strict scrutiny." And as we have seen, once it has been determined that a speech regulation is subject to "strict scrutiny," it is a virtual certainty that law will be invalidated. But if faced with a general prohibition of hate speech, the Court might find even the statute-killing strict scrutiny test too weak. Rather, it is likely to declare such broad viewpoint-oriented restrictions on public discourse per se uncon-stitutional.[5]

As a viewpoint-based restriction on public discourse, a broad hate speech law would be even more constitutionally suspect than the typical content-oriented regulation. A general hate speech ban commits "the car-dinal First Amendment sin"—viewpoint discrimination.[6] As the Court ex-plained in a 1995 decision, "[when] the government targets not subject matter but particular views taken by the speakers on a subject, the viola-tion of the First Amendment is all the more blatant." The government thus must "abstain from regulating speech when the specific motivating ideology or the opinion or perspective of the speaker is the rationale for the restriction."[7] It may well be, then, that the Court would hold any broad viewpoint-discriminatory restriction on public discourse to be in-consistent with the very essence of U.S. free speech doctrine.[8]

Alternatively, the Court might hold a broad hate speech ban unconsti-tutional per se because it is inconsistent with the incitement test estab-lished in *Brandenburg v. Ohio*.[9] *Brandenburg* holds that advocacy of law vi-olation can be punished only if such advocacy constitutes incitement "to imminent lawless action" and then only if "likely to incite or produce such action." Racist speech can, of course, incite imminent lawless con-duct.[10] Such expression could be punished consistent with *Brandenburg* if it could be shown that the expression was likely actually to cause imme-diate lawless action.[11] But a general hate speech ban covers much more than incitement likely to lead to lawbreaking. It includes *any* racist ex-pression, including speech that does not advocate action, illegal or other-wise, but merely tries to persuade others to see the world from the racist's warped perspective. For instance, each of the three exemplars of hate speech quoted above would outlaw the perennial complaint of American racists, expressed in different ways but with the same central message, that certain minority groups are responsible for the decline of American society. But such ravings do not directly advocate illegal activity, nor can it fairly be said that such expression will lead *immediately* to acts of discrimination.

Significantly, however, a frequently cited justification for hate speech bans is that racist propaganda, whether or not advocating illegal acts, ul-timately leads to illegal discriminatory acts against minorities, including violence. But if *Brandenburg* prevents the state from punishing speech that advocates lawless conduct short of incitement, it follows that the state may not forbid speech that does not even expressly advocate illegal con-duct, at least not under the rationale that such speech causes illegal activ-ity. And to the extent that this ban is justified as preventing discrimina-tory activity that is not illegal, it is all the more inconsistent with *Brandenburg*.[12] More generally, I do not believe that the Court ever meant for the strict scrutiny test to apply in areas governed by a specific rule. For instance, strict scrutiny would not be applicable to a state law allowing public officials to recover for defamatory statements about their official conduct if these statements were negligently made. Rather, because such a statute would conflict with the "malice" requirement established in *New York Times v. Sullivan*, it would be per se unconstitutional. By the same token, any law that sought to ban public discourse on the ground that it leads to illegal activity should be analyzed not under strict scrutiny but under *Brandenburg*.

Strict Scrutiny.   If, however, the Court were to subject a general hate speech ban to strict scrutiny rather than declare it per se invalid, the result would be the same. Under the strict scrutiny test, the government must show that the law is "necessary to serve a compelling state interest, and that it is narrowly drawn to achieve that end."[13] Although some of the justifications that would likely be proffered in support of such a law might well pass the "compelling interest" requirement, the law would founder on the requirement that the restriction be "necessary" to accomplishing the goal and that it be "narrowly drawn."

As we have seen, the most powerful justification for a general ban on hate speech is that racist expression causes racial discrimination, including violence. The Court would surely agree that the government has a compelling interest in preventing acts of racial discrimination and violence.[14] But it might well find that a general hate speech ordinance was not "necessary" to prevent racial discrimination and violence. The Court might question whether the public expression of racist ideas significantly contributes to discriminatory acts and whether hate speech laws would effectively remedy this evil.[15]

But it is the narrow-tailoring requirement that would present the greatest obstacle to a far-reaching hate speech ban. Under this requirement, a speech restriction is unconstitutional "if less restrictive alternatives would be at least as effective in achieving the legitimate purpose that the statute was enacted to serve."[16] And as the Court recently stated in applying strict scrutiny to strike down a restriction on indecent speech on the Internet, the broader the content-based restriction, the heavier is the burden on the government "to explain why a less restrictive provision would not be as effective." The state would thus have "an especially heavy burden" to demonstrate that non-speech-repressive remedies such as increasing the scope and rigor of civil rights laws, not to mention the classic free speech solution of "counterspeech," including massive government propaganda denouncing racism, would not be as effective as a general hate speech ban.[17]

There is, however, another justification for banning racist speech aside from the alleged power of this speech to cause others to engage in discriminatory acts. Proponents of broad hate speech legislation also point to the emotional pain that hate propaganda causes: "To be hated, despised, and alone is the ultimate fear of all human beings. However irrational racist speech may be, it hits right at the emotional place where we feel the most pain."[18] But the Court would most likely hold that prevention of psychic injury does not qualify as a compelling state interest. In *Hustler Magazine v. Falwell*,[19] a jury found that the Reverend Jerry Falwell suffered extreme emotional distress as a result of a parody of a Campari advertisement stating that Falwell's "first time" was with his mother in an outhouse. In unanimously nullifying this award as contrary to the First Amendment, the Court referred to "the longstanding refusal to allow damages to be awarded because the speech in question may have an adverse emotional impact on the audience." In holding that public figures cannot recover for infliction of emotional distress caused by media publication (unless they can meet the *New York Times* malice standard), the Court once again recognized that allowing government the power to filter emotionally traumatic speech from public discourse would unduly interfere with the "robust political debate encouraged by the First Amendment."

Finally, some have argued that a ban on such speech would not be subject to strict scrutiny because, like "fighting words" and obscenity, racist speech is categorically outside the protection of the First Amendment. Several recent Supreme Court opinions show that such is not the case. In ruling that a state may not preserve the flag as a symbol of national unity by prohibiting its desecration as a form of political protest, the Court pointed out that "[t]he First Amendment does not guarantee that other concepts virtually sacred to our Nation as a whole—such as the principle that discrimination on the basis of race is odious and destructive—will go unquestioned in the marketplace of ideas."[20] Even more telling is the Court's decision in the cross-burning case *R.A.V. v. City of St. Paul*.[21] Although deeply divided about the reason for the statute's invalidity, the Court was unanimous that the proscription of racist fighting words at issue in that case violated the First Amendment. Such a result is impossible to square with any categorical exclusion of hate speech from the First Amendment. More generally, *R.A.V.* provides proof that a broad prohibition of hate speech would be unconstitutional. For if the state is not constitutionally permitted to regulate *unprotected* speech because of its racist content, it follows that the state may not prohibit protected speech because of its racist ideology.[22]

The Unconstitutionality of Group Libel Laws.   Although a total ban on the expression of racist ideas would plainly be inconsistent with case law, a 1952 decision, *Beauharnais v. Illinois*, did uphold the prohibition of one particularly pernicious category of hate speech—racial defamation.[23] Joseph Beauharnais, the president of the White Circle League, had circulated a leaflet containing a petition to the mayor and city council of Chicago calling for racial segregation. The leaflet stated that if "persuasion and the need to prevent the white race from becoming mongrelized by the negro will not unite us, then the aggressions . . . rapes, robberies, knives, guns and marijuana of the negro, surely will." Beauharnais was convicted under an Illinois statute prohibiting the publication of any matter that "portrays depravity, criminality, unchastity, or lack of virtue of a class of citizens, of any race, color, creed or religion which . . . exposes [such] citizens . . . to contempt, derision or obloquy."

In a 5–4 decision, the U.S. Supreme Court upheld the conviction. Writing for the majority, Justice Frankfurter held that libelous utterances, whether directed at individuals or "designated collectivities," were not "within the area of constitutionally protected speech" and thus could be prohibited without a particularized showing that the speech was likely to cause an imminent danger of harm. In addition, he rejected the argument that truth was a defense to a charge of group libel, holding that it was not unconstitutional to require a defendant charged with criminal libel to show not only the truth of the statement but also that it was made "with good motives and for justifiable ends."

As an initial matter, it should be emphasized that *Beauharnais* does not support the constitutionality of a general hate speech ban. Much hate speech is not legally defamatory. To be defamatory, a statement must contain a factual assertion damaging to the reputation of an individual, entity, or group. Consider, for instance, the refrain uttered by the Ku Klux Klan leader in *Brandenburg*: "I believe the nigger should be returned to Africa, the Jew returned to Israel." An ugly sentiment, indeed, but one that does not make a factual assertion about any group.

More fundamental, the profound doctrinal changes that have occurred since *Beauharnais* was decided in the 1950s has robbed the decision of its vitality. *Beauharnais* is a product of the now largely discredited categorical exclusion methodology, discussed in detail in Chapter 2. In the 1942 decision of *Chaplinsky v. New Hampshire,* the Supreme Court declared that like "fighting words," libelous statements were completely bereft of constitutional protection. Ten years later, Beauharnais argued that the statements in his petition to city officials could not be punished without proof that they presented a "clear and present danger" of violence or law violation. Invoking *Chaplinsky*'s categorical banishment of libel from the realm of First Amendment protection, the Court brushed this argument aside. By the 1960s, however, libel laws had become a powerful weapon in the hands of southern officials in their attempts to suppress protest against racial segregation. Alert to the repressive potential of the *Chaplinsky* approach, the Court afforded libel substantial First Amendment protection. In *New York Times v. Sullivan*, the Court, imposing stringent constitutional restrictions on libel suits by public officials, held that libel could no longer claim "talismanic immunity from constitutional limitations." *Beauharnais*'s basic doctrinal underpinning has thus been swept away.

The leitmotif of *New York Times v. Sullivan* and its progeny is that libel laws are unconstitutional to the extent that they impede "uninhibited, robust, and wide-open" debate on public issues. Group libel laws would obviously have a considerable chilling effect on public debate about matters of race. There are also more specific ways in which *Beauharnais* is at odds with modern doctrine. For one, even if libel were still considered categorically unprotected speech, a group libel law would run afoul of *R.A.V.*'s principle that even regulation of unprotected speech must be content neutral. The constitutional fault that the Court found with the fighting words prohibition in *R.A.V.* was that it did not criminalize all fighting words but only ones with racist content. Similarly, the law in *Beauharnais* did not criminalize all libelous statements, nor even proscribe libelous references to classes or groups of people generally, but singled out racial and religious libel for prohibition.

More basically, the Court would likely hold that almost all of what proponents of hate speech regulation want to punish as group defamation cannot constitutionally be punished as such. Modern First Amendment doctrine requires that statements on matters of public concern must be provable as false before there can be liability for defamation.[24] Consider Beauharnais's statement about "aggressions . . . rapes, robberies, knives, guns and marijuana of the negro." If it means that *all* African Americans are aggressors, rapists, robbers, and knife- and gun-toting pot smokers, the statement is demonstrably unbelievable to any reasonable person and thus not libelous. If it means that *some* blacks are rapists, robbers, and so on, then this statement is demonstrably true, as it would be about some members of any racial or ethnic group, and is, again, not libelous. Another possible interpretation of Beauharnais's statement is that per capita more blacks in Chicago at that time engaged in these activities than did whites. Under such an interpretation, this statement is arguably falsifiable by reference to empirical data. Unfortunately, statements about any subordinated group ghettoized in large American cities to the effect that they disproportionately engage in crime and drug use may well be true. And even if ultimately proved false, such statements would probably be based on enough data to avoid liability under the constitutional immunity afforded false statements under *New York Times v. Sullivan* and its progeny.[25]

But surely Beauharnais did not intend merely to make a dry, descriptive statement about the condition of inner-city blacks, and just as surely that was not the gravamen of the offense for which he was convicted. If an

African American minister had petitioned the mayor of Chicago for more aid for the black community and cited the high and growing incidence of rapes, robberies, and marijuana use among blacks in support of his plea, it is inconceivable that he would have been punished for these statements, even if they turned out to be false according to the best data available and even if the minister was reckless in not consulting these data.

What Beauharnais most probably meant to say, and what the prosecution plainly assumed he meant, is that blacks are *inherently* prone to violent criminal activity and drug use. Thus disagreement with Beauharnais and his ilk is not so much about the existence or nonexistence of particular data but rather about the meaning to be attached to the data. Bigots believe that certain groups commit crimes because that is their nature; others believe that grinding poverty with no hope of escaping it, together with a long and continuing history of discrimination and injustice, will cause crime in any community. Beauharnais believed the solution was state-decreed segregation; others believed that the remedy was integration. Beauharnais's hate-driven conclusions may not be logical or as empirically supportable as nonbigoted beliefs, but the real evil is not that his conclusions are factually false but that they are a product of hateful, racist ideology.[26] As such, however, these statements are not the type of assertions that the Supreme Court would likely characterize falsifiable statements of fact. Rather, the Court would probably find such statements to be "ideas," and under modern First Amendment jurisprudence "there is no such thing as a false idea."[27]

PORNOGRAPHY

Using a model law drafted by Catharine MacKinnon and Andrea Dworkin, Indianapolis in 1984 enacted an ordinance imposing civil sanctions for the distribution of sexually explicit material demeaning to women. The ordinance prohibited the distribution of "pornography," which was defined as "the graphic sexually explicit subordination of women, whether in pictures or words." [28]

U.S. district judge Sarah Evans Barker invalidated the ordinance on First Amendment grounds, and the city appealed. Writing for a panel of the U.S. Court of Appeals for the Seventh Circuit, Judge Frank Easterbrook affirmed Judge Barker's decision in *American Booksellers Assn. v. Hudnut.*[29] The opinion begins by explaining that the "pornography" proscribed by the ordinance was considerably different from "obscenity," which is not protected by the First Amendment. Unlike the obscenity standard, Easterbrook pointed out, the Indianapolis ordinance does not define the prohibited material based on its appeal to the "prurient interest" or its offensiveness as measured by "community standards" or its lack of "literary, artistic, political, or scientific value." But most significant, he found the ordinance was viewpoint discriminatory:

> Speech treating women in the approved way—in sexual encounters "premised on equality"—is lawful no matter how sexually explicit. Speech treating women in the disapproved way—as submissive in matters sexual or as enjoying humiliation—is unlawful no matter how significant the literary, artistic, or political qualities of the work taken as a whole. The state may not ordain preferred viewpoints in this way. The Constitution forbids the state to declare one perspective right and silence opponents.

The city justified the ordinance on the ground that "pornography affects thoughts" and "[m]en who see women as depicted as subordinate are more likely to treat them so." Easterbrook agreed that "[p]eople often act in accordance with the images and patterns they find around them" and that therefore "[d]epictions of subordination tend to perpetuate subordination [of women, including] lower pay at work, insult and injury at home [and] battery and rape on the streets." Nonetheless, he held that under current First Amendment doctrine the ordinance was unconstitutional:

> All of these unhappy effects depend on mental intermediation. Pornography affects how people see the world, their fellows, and social relations. . . . The Alien and Sedition Acts . . . rested on a sincerely held belief that disrespect for the government leads to social collapse and revolution—a belief with support in the history of many nations. Most governments of the world act on this empirical regularity, suppressing critical speech. In the United States, however, the strength of the support for this belief is irrelevant. Seditious libel is protected speech unless the danger is not only grave but also imminent. [Similarly], [r]acial bigotry, anti-semitism, violence on television, reporters' biases—these and many more influence the culture and shape our socialization. . . . Yet all is protected as speech, however insidious. Any other answer leaves the government in control of all of the institutions of culture, the great censor and director of which thoughts are good for us.

The court did not subject the ordinance to strict scrutiny or any other test but rather found this viewpoint-discriminatory restriction per se unconstitutional. The city then appealed to the U.S. Supreme Court, which summarily affirmed the Court of Appeals decision without hearing oral argument or issuing an opinion.[30] Because the court found the primary fault with the Indianapolis ordinance to be its viewpoint orientation, it could be argued that some other approach to pornography regulation, equally broad based but viewpoint neutral, might pass constitutional muster.[31] The problem with this argument is that it runs headlong into the Court's obscenity jurisprudence. As discussed in Chapter 2, the point of the Supreme Court's obscenity decisions has been to draw a line between expression whose sole purpose and function is sexual arousal (i.e., obscenity) and sexually explicit material that has some redeeming literary, artistic, political, or scientific value. The Court has struggled over the years as to where precisely to draw this line, but there has never been any doubt that what the Court had in mind was "hard-core" pornography. Thus at a minimum, to be constitutionally proscribable, erotic material must be extremely graphic, such as films of people engaging in sexual intercourse that show actual penetration. Any attempt to prohibit "soft-core" pornography, such as photographs of naked men or women in erotic poses, or even "medium-core" fare, such as films of people engaging in sexual intercourse that show neither erect penises nor actual penetration, is doomed to failure.[32]

Any lingering doubt that government might constitutionally enact some far-reaching ban of pornographic material that does not meet the Supreme Court's definition of obscenity was dispelled by *Reno v. ACLU*.[33] Concerned that the vast amount of sexually explicit material on the Internet was readily available to children, Congress passed the Communications Decency Act of 1996. The law prohibited anyone from knowingly transmitting by a telecommunications device obscene or "indecent" material to persons under eighteen years of age or from using an "interactive computer" knowingly to send or display any "patently offensive" material dealing with "sexual or excretory activities or organs." In analyzing the law, the Court emphasized that "sexual expression which is indecent but not obscene is protected by the First Amendment." Because the act regulated not just obscene material but other sexually explicit material as well and did so on the basis of its content, the Court subjected the law to "the most stringent" scrutiny.[34] The Court agreed that there is a compelling interest in protecting minors from exposure to "indecent" and "patently offensive" speech. Nevertheless, the Court found that the government failed to carry its burden of demonstrating why several possibly "less restrictive" alternative means for keeping this material from children, such as requiring indecent material to be "tagged" so parents could filter it, would not be as effective as the act. The Court thus concluded that the law unconstitutionally "suppresses a large amount of speech that adults have a constitutional right to receive."[35]

DISTINGUISHING NARROW REGULATIONS OF HATE SPEECH AND PORNOGRAPHY

Often overlooked in discussions about hate speech and pornography is that although free speech doctrine does not permit broad suppression of such speech, it does allow some narrowly focused regulation. This is particularly true of pornography. Indeed, modern free speech doctrine allows sexually explicit speech to be regulated in ways that would be unthinkable with respect to any other form of expression. To begin with, there is the obscenity exception itself, which allows "hard-core" pornography to be suppressed because of its content and with no specific showing of harm. There are, of course, other types of speech that are categorically excluded from First Amendment protection, such as fighting words, perjury, bribery, threats, and still to some extent defamation. But (with the possible exception of fighting words, whose continued status as unprotected speech is doubtful) the harm caused by these other forms of expression is palpable. More important, unlike other forms of unprotected speech (again with the possible exception of fighting words), the exclusion of obscenity because it is "patently offensive" when measured by "contemporary community standards" smacks of the very viewpoint discrimination inimical to core First Amendment values.

As we have seen, although sexually explicit but nonobscene speech may not be totally banned, it may be regulated in ways that impose substantial burdens on those wishing to furnish or receive this material. For example, theaters showing "adult" movies may be subjected to onerous zoning regulations, and "indecent" material may be banned from radio and over-the-air television at times children may be in the audience.[36] Similarly, states may forbid the sale of even "soft-core" pornography to minors and more generally may regulate the distribution of sexually oriented but nonobscene material so as to keep children from gaining access to it, so long as these regulations do not unduly interfere with the rights of adults to obtain the material.[37] For this reason, such expression has been referred to as "lower-value" speech.

Title VII of the Civil Rights Act of 1964, which prohibits racial and gender discrimination in the workplace, has been interpreted to outlaw racially harassing speech. For instance, a number of cases have held that persistent use of the word "nigger" or similar racial slurs by a supervisor to refer to a black employee violates Title VII.[38] Title VII has also been interpreted to outlaw persistent or severe sexually harassing speech, including, under certain circumstances, the display of pornography in the workplace.[39] As the U.S. Court of Appeals for the Third Circuit has explained, "obscene language and pornography could be regarded as highly offensive to a woman who seeks to deal with her fellow employees and clients with professional dignity and without the barrier of sexual differentiation and abuse."[40]

There are still a number of interesting and unanswered questions raised by the use of Title VII and similar state laws to bar racially or sexually harassing speech in the workplace. A few have suggested that even relatively limited application of these laws to racist speech, pornography, and other forms of sexually harassing expression is unconstitutional.[41] So far, however, courts, including the Supreme Court, have shown little concern that these regulations have been or will be applied in violation of the First Amendment.[42]

In considering the possible conflict between workplace antiharassment regulations and the First Amendment, it is important to distinguish two ways in which such a clash might arise. One way is that the law might be too broadly construed. Suppose, for instance, a Title VII suit against an employer for occasionally expressing his opinion that women should not work full time outside the home until their children are grown or that blacks are genetically not as intelligent as whites. Or suppose that a female employee sued an employer for having a painting of a nude woman in his office. The Supreme Court would probably avoid the First Amendment issues in these cases by finding that such "isolated" incidents are neither pervasive nor severe enough to constitute harassment actionable under Title VII. But if forced to reach the First Amendment issue in such a case (for instance, if a state supreme court construed a state regulation as outlawing such expression), the Court might well find the *application* of the law unconstitutional.

Another way Title VII or similar state provisions might be thought to conflict with the First Amendment is that they are content based and thus *always* presumptively unconstitutional when applied to speech. Title VII, for instance, does not outlaw all harassing speech but only expression that harasses on the basis of race and sex (as well as religion and national origin). This might seem to violate *R.A.V.*'s holding that even when regulating unprotected speech the laws may not single out particular content-based categories for prohibition. Realizing that this antiselectivity principle put the constitutionality of Title VII's application to racially and sexually harassing speech in doubt, Justice Scalia in *R.A.V.* issued the following caveat:

> [S]ince words can in some circumstances violate laws directed not against speech but against conduct (a law against treason, for example, is violated by telling the enemy the Nation's defense secrets), a particular content-based subcategory of a proscribable class of speech can be swept up incidentally within the reach of a statute directed at conduct rather than speech. Thus, for example, sexually derogatory "fighting words," among other words, may produce a violation of Title VII's general prohibition against sexual discrimination in employment practices.[43]

It has been suggested that Justice Scalia wrote the *R.A.V.* opinion as a slap at the campus hate speech codes that many universities were promulgating at the time. If so, it is ironic that in protecting Title VII, Scalia drew a road map for drafting constitutional campus hate speech regulations. Campus codes, it is true, have not fared very well either in the courts or with public opinion.[44] Many were badly drafted, focusing on the content of the speech in precisely the way *R.A.V.* condemns rather than prohibiting discrimination, whether accomplished through expression or conduct. In addition, neither the drafters of these codes nor, for that matter, the courts reviewing them distinguished among the various places on campus to which these codes applied. It makes a huge difference whether the university seeks to regulate speech in a campus free speech area, the classroom, or the dormitory. Precisely because these codes did not engage in such "forum analysis" and, more generally, did not attempt to distinguish between legitimate regulatory goals, such as preventing acts of discrimination that materially interfere with students' ability to obtain an education, from illegitimate ones, such as preventing the expression of hateful ideas, the codes were doomed to failure.

For universities that want to impose restrictions on racist speech, *R.A.V.* suggests a way to do so constitutionally. Instead of aiming at racist speech, drafters should track Title VII's prohibition against discrimination on the basis of race, sex, or other categories. They then should draft guidelines modeled after the Equal Employment Opportunity Commission (EEOC) guidelines explaining what conduct, "verbal or physical," constitutes prohibited discrimination. This approach, of course, would not allow the university to apply the code to all speech it may want to prohibit. Even under this approach, it could not prohibit the expression of offensive ideas in the classroom so long as they were germane to the discussion. For instance, it could still not punish a student for expressing the view in a psychology class that homosexuality is a disease that should be medically treated.[45] No matter how carefully the regulation is drafted, the First Amendment does not allow such viewpoint discrimination in this setting. Yet such a Title VII-based approach might allow, for example, the prohibition of the use of racial epithets in the classroom or threats against gays in living areas. *R.A.V.*, then, leaves room for narrowly crafted prohibitions of hate speech in certain settings, such as the workplace and the classroom, even if they are *in effect* content-based regulations of expression.[46]

Nor does First Amendment doctrine impose any substantial obstacle to hate *crime* legislation—laws that enhance the penalty for bias-motivated crimes. Many states have recently passed such laws. A Wisconsin law, for instance, increases the penalty for committing certain crimes, such as battery, murder, and arson, if the defendant "intentionally selects the person against whom the crime . . . is committed . . . because of the race, religion, color, disability, sexual orientation, national origin or ancestry of that person." In *Wisconsin v. Mitchell,* the United States rebuffed a First

Amendment challenge to the Wisconsin hate crime law brought by a black man who received an enhanced sentence for committing racially motivated battery against a white youth.[47] Writing for a unanimous Court, Chief Justice Rehnquist relied heavily on the basic speech-conduct dichotomy undergirding free speech doctrine. He noted that the law punishes only conduct and that the battery committed by the defendant could not "by any stretch of the imagination [be considered] expressive conduct protected by the First Amendment."[48] Rehnquist summarily disposed of the claim that the statute nonetheless violated the First Amendment because it punished "abstract belief." He found that the state's interest in redressing special harms reasonably thought to be caused by hate crimes, such as their tendency to provoke retaliation, inflict emotional harm, and cause community unrest, "provides an adequate explanation for its penalty-enhancement provision over and above mere disagreement with offenders' beliefs or biases."

In summary, there are two important points to be made with respect to the constitutionality of hate speech and pornography regulations. First, there is no doubt that under current doctrine any broad ban on hate speech or pornography would be held unconstitutional. Just as certainly, however, there remains room for narrowly circumscribed regulation of hate speech and pornography, particularly to supplement regulations of conduct and applicable in settings not dedicated to public discourse.

PART TWO

The Radical Attack

A basic tenet of modern free speech doctrine is that government must be ideologically neutral in regulating speech. This requirement of neutrality extends as well to the judiciary, including its formulation and application of free speech doctrine. Radical critics allege that free speech doctrine is infected with the very disease it is supposed to prevent in that it systematically discriminates against the interests of women and minorities. This is a serious charge that should be carefully examined.

Radicals make two quite different claims of discrimination, both of which I consider in detail here in Part 2. Chapter 5 is devoted to analyzing *specific* claims of discrimination, such as the charge that doctrine recognizes numerous exceptions to the free speech principle to protect the economic interests of the rich and powerful yet refuses to afford similar exceptions to protect the interests of women and minorities. Chapter 6 considers the deeper allegation that free speech doctrine is now and has always been an enemy of social progress and equality because it is an essential part of a structure that maintains the status quo and all its inequities.

5

Does Free Speech Doctrine Discriminate Against Women and Minorities?

Radicals claim that contrary to the mythology propagated by civil libertarians, free speech doctrine is riddled with numerous exceptions that when critically examined are found to protect the interests of powerful forces in society. But when people of color and women want hate speech and pornography exceptions in order to defend their interests, they are told that the First Amendment permits no exceptions. A related claim of discrimination is based on the text of the Constitution: Radicals point out that although the First Amendment is just one part of the Constitution, free speech doctrine acts as if it were the only relevant constitutional norm. In particular, they assert that hate speech and pornography implicate the Equal Protection Clause of the Fourteenth Amendment but that free speech doctrine ignores this countervailing constitutional norm. Careful analysis of these indictments shows that they are, on the whole, unfounded.

HATE SPEECH:
IS THERE A DEVIL IN THE EXCEPTIONS?

According to Richard Delgado and David Yun, an examination of "the current landscape of First Amendment doctrine" reveals that the courts have "carved out" dozens of "exceptions" to the free speech principle, each of which responds to "some interest of a powerful group." But when it is suggested that there should be exceptions to protect minorities from the ill effects of hate speech, doctrine is suddenly seen as "a seamless web" permitting no exceptions.[1] To assess the claim that free speech doctrine systemically discriminates against minorities by denying them exemptions afforded other, more powerful interests, we must first closely examine these exceptions.

Delgado and Yun point to exceptions for "words of threat," conspiracy or libel, official secrets, plagiarism, copyrighted and trademarked material, as well as "disrespectful words uttered to a judge, teacher or other authority figure." Mari Matsuda adds exceptions for "false statements about products, suggestions that prices be fixed, [and] opinions about the value of stock"; Matsuda charges that the desire for "smooth operation of the entities of commerce" and for "a stable setting for the growth of capital" have in these instances "overcome the commitment to civil liberties."[2]

This understanding is premised on a profound but widely shared misconception. In this mistaken view, the First Amendment generally confers strong protection to all human utterances subject to various exceptions. But an accurate snapshot of First Amendment doctrine shows a quite different picture, indeed one that is nearly the photographic negative of the one described by Delgado, Yun, and Matsuda. As discussed in detail in Chapter 4, only a relatively narrow swath of expression is afforded strong First Amendment protection. This nearly absolute immunity from content regulation is primarily limited to speech that qualifies as "public discourse"—speech on matters of public concern occurring in settings dedicated to democratic self-governance or truth discovery in the marketplace of ideas. In contrast, most other types of speech are subject to regulation if the government can point to some legitimate interest that the regulation is reasonably calculated to serve. Thus what the radicals (and others) call "exceptions" are in fact the norm—expression routinely regulated incidental to a larger regulatory scheme such as the control of commerce or ordinary criminal activity.

Even a casual glance at the list of so-called exceptions compiled by Delgado, Yun, and Matsuda reveals that most of these items are by no stretch of the imagination speech that critiques society, advocates changes in political institutions, or contributes to the marketplace of ideas. This is most clearly the case with respect to the regulation of industrial and commercial speech Matsuda notes. Agreements to fix prices or statements calculated to manipulate the stock market are obviously quite distinct from the expression through which public opinion is formed or by which we discover truth. The same is true, for the most part, of commercial advertising in general and the false or misleading statements about commercial products in particular. In addition, these are not the type of regulations that raise suspicion that government is restricting speech for some impermissible purpose. Thus we do not suspect that in forbidding price-fixing or securities fraud that government is attempting to manipulate public opinion. Rather, as Matsuda correctly surmises, the impetus for such regulation is the "smooth operation" of free enterprise and capitalism, not to mention concern for individuals and small businesses who might be unfairly victimized by these practices.

Modern doctrine's response to the regulation of commercial advertising underscores the importance of the distinction between public discourse and other types of expression. So long as the regulation of commercial speech is limited to the prevention of false or misleading advertising, the First Amendment imposes little constraint. But as the regulated speech in question moves closer to the realm of public discourse, First Amendment protection increases. For example, advertising by lawyers "seeking to further political or ideological goals" through public interest litigation is highly protected speech.[3]

Much of Delgado and Yun's list is also far afield from the realm of public discourse. The statements at issue in the routine libel suit are typically scurrilous accusations made in the heat of some private dispute and are of no interest to anyone but the combatants. But when the allegedly libelous speech is about a matter of public concern, particularly when it is about the official conduct of a public official, considerable First Amendment protection arises.[4] Similarly, the typical threat, revelation of a state secret, or conspiracy to commit a crime has nothing to do with the formation of public opinion or competition in the marketplace of ideas. But in rare cases in which such speech does have some connection with public discourse, the First Amendment comes into play. For example, as discussed in Chapter 2, the Supreme Court ruled that a federal prohibition on making threats against the president did not extend to an antiwar protestor's declaration that if he were drafted and given a gun "the first man I want to get in my sights" would be the president of the United States.[5] Similarly, in the landmark *Pentagon Papers* case the Court found unconstitutional attempts to restrain newspapers from publishing a purloined top secret study of the history of the Vietnam conflict.[6] And the First Amendment presents considerable barriers to the use of conspiracy laws against political organizations.[7]

The regulation of trademarks will almost never involve public discourse, let alone inhibit it. In contrast, much copyrighted material is part of public discourse. Copyright law, however, does not prevent the dissemination of *ideas* contained in a copyrighted work but only the duplication of the *form* of the expression. And in a rare case in which copyright protection threatens to impede public discourse, courts have interpreted the law's fair use provision as allowing publication without liability.[8] Thus, far from discouraging public discourse, the ability of authors to claim a property right in the form of their expression fosters the exchange of ideas.

In invoking "disrespectful words uttered to a judge, teacher or other authority figure" as an example of an "exception" formulated to protect the interests of the powerful, Delgado and Yun again miss the crucial distinction between public discourse and other expression. Although both the courtroom and the classroom are instrumental to the democratic character of our society, neither is a forum dedicated to robust, uninhibited public discourse. Rather, both places involve highly structured discourse in service of particular ends (justice and learning) that would be undermined by unconstrained debate or use of vulgar epithets. True, the civility rules that operate in these settings may well unduly emphasize respect for the authority figures in charge as opposed to other participants. Still, the rules requiring that judges and teachers be addressed with respect is not a special rule for judges and teachers but part of the civility norms that free speech doctrine allows to be imposed in contexts not dedicated to public discourse.[9]

Proof that these civility norms are specific to place rather than office is that outside the courtroom and classroom the First Amendment generally requires that judges and teachers be subject to the same vituperative exchanges as anyone else. For instance, although the First Amendment would permit Chief Justice Rehnquist summarily to hold in contempt a lawyer who referred to him as a "horse's ass" during oral argument in the Supreme Court, a citizen who delivered the same message by holding up a sign in the public street in front of a public auditorium where Rehnquist was about to deliver a lecture could not constitutionally be punished for this statement. Indeed, there is some suggestion in the case law that at least one type of "authority figure"—the police officer—is required by the First Amendment to endure a greater degree of disrespectful language than the average citizen standing in a public place.[10]

In summary, all the "exceptions" that Delgado, Yun, and Matsuda list are either (1) not a regulation of public discourse (for instance, the prohibition of speech that fixes prices, manipulates the stock market, or defames a private individual on a matter of purely private concern) or (2) a regulation of a broad class of speech that includes public discourse but is neither intended to inhibit nor has the effect of inhibiting robust public discourse (for example, copyright laws).[11] In contrast, although it would cover speech that is not public discourse (for instance, use of racial epithets in the classroom), a general ban on hate speech like the one Matsuda proposes is aimed at regulating public discourse (for example, the expression of racist ideas in books, films, or speeches on the street corner). Indeed, the very purpose of such laws is to cleanse public discourse of vicious racist propaganda. In addition, hate speech laws are a classic example of viewpoint discrimination—prohibition of speech because the government finds its message abhorrent or dangerous. Although a few of the regulations cited by Delgado, Yun, and Matsuda are content oriented (for example, prohibitions against uncivil speech in classrooms and courtrooms), none is comparable to the suppression of a particular political viewpoint such as would be accomplished by a hate speech ban. Thus in every essential way the "exceptions" these critics point to are unlike a general hate speech ban.

The exception to First Amendment protection that comes closest to a viewpoint-discriminatory ban on public discourse is the obscenity exception. Like the proposed ban on hate speech, it applies to media essential to public discourse, such as print and film. In addition, obscenity is defined in terms of "offense" to "contemporary community standards." Accordingly, it has been argued that the obscenity exception reflects society's antipathy toward the Dionysian worldview depicted in most hardcore pornography. Undercutting this argument is that the obscenity exception does not restrict people's ability to criticize our current sexual mores or to advocate their replacement with licentious lifestyles. The obscenity standard's emphasis on offense to the community is thus perhaps best understood not as an attempt to suppress a particular viewpoint but to forbid a particularly offensive *form* of expression. Furthermore, obscenity doctrine's long-standing emphasis on the sexually arousing quality of the material suggests that the state's interest in regulating hard-core pornography may be more akin to the regulation of sex than ideas.[12] In any event, although the obscenity exception may have an odor of viewpoint discrimination, it is not fairly comparable to the explicit and far-reaching viewpoint discrimination worked by a general ban on racist expression.

Contrary to Delgado and Yun, then, the "seamless web" of near absolute protection of speech is not some sanctimonious story told when the less powerful in a society want to regulate speech that harms their interests. Such a "seamless web" does exist, but it covers only the domain of public discourse. Here it does in fact provide exceedingly strong protection against content discrimination and near absolute protection against viewpoint discrimination.

Before leaving the topic of allegedly discriminatory "exceptions," I want to address a particularly erroneous argument made by Charles Lawrence. "[M]uch of the argument for protecting racist speech," Lawrence claims, "is based on the distinction that many civil libertarians draw between direct, face-to-face *racial* insults, which they think deserve first amendment protection, and all other fighting words, which they find unprotected by the first amendment."[13] Lawrence does not give any references supporting this remarkable charge against "civil libertarians."

What many civil libertarians *do* maintain, and with justification, is that the "fighting words" doctrine can be a dangerous tool in the hands of law enforcement officials. Consequently, some argue that *Chaplinsky*, the 1942 case that held that fighting words are not protected by the First Amendment, should be expressly overruled and that face-to-face insults of *all* types (including racial ones) should be afforded First Amendment protection.[14] But I know of no call for special protection of racial fighting words.

Lawrence, in fact, has got things exactly backward. The only arguments for special treatment of racist fighting words have been made by those who (like Lawrence) support "campus codes" and other restrictions on hate speech that single out racist face-to-face insults for prohibition. In *R.A.V. v. City of St. Paul*, a bare majority of the Supreme Court held that a law that singled out racial fighting words for special prohibition was unconstitutional.[15] The opinion makes clear, however, that to the extent the "fighting words" doctrine survives, government can outlaw face-to-face racial epithets as part of a larger prohibition of fighting words. Indeed, any attempt to exclude racial fighting words from a general regulation of hate speech would run afoul of *R.A.V.*'s holding that regulation of fighting words must generally be "all or nothing." But for completely different reasons, *R.A.V.* may provide at least one example supporting the radical charge that modern doctrine discriminates against the interests of minorities.

THE *R.A.V.* DECISION

Justice Holmes once observed that "hard cases make bad law."[16] Perhaps he should have included bizarre cases in his admonition. *R.A.V.* involved the prosecution of a white juvenile under a hate speech ordinance for placing a burning cross on a black family's lawn in the middle of the night.[17] The ordinance made it a misdemeanor to place on public or private property any "symbol, object, appellation, characterization or graffiti, including, but not limited to, a burning cross or Nazi swastika, which . . . arouses anger, alarm or resentment in others on the basis of race, color, creed, religion or gender." Although the statute makes no reference to "fighting words," the Minnesota Supreme Court, recognizing that as written the sweep of the ordinance made it patently unconstitutional, construed the ordinance as reaching only unprotected fighting words. Thus as the case came to the U.S. Supreme Court the question was whether government could single out for special prohibition fighting words with a racial content.

Despite the reconstructive surgery, the Court unanimously found the ordinance to be unconstitutional. Four justices held that the Minnesota

Supreme Court had not sufficiently narrowed the statute and thus still banned protected speech. A majority of the Court, however, found that the ordinance suffered from a deeper flaw. In an opinion by Justice Scalia, the Court found that because the ordinance applies only to fighting words that insult or provoke violence "on the basis of race, color, creed, religion or gender," it discriminated on the basis of the content of the speech (beyond the content discrimination inherent in casting fighting words beyond the pale of First Amendment protection).

The Court explained that even though certain categories of speech, such as fighting words, were often referred to as unprotected speech, this characterization was not "literally true." Rather, the label "unprotected speech" means only that "these areas of speech can, consistently with the First Amendment, be regulated *because of their constitutionally proscribable content* (obscenity, defamation, etc.)—not that they are categories of speech entirely invisible to the Constitution, so that they may be made the vehicles for content discrimination unrelated to their distinctively proscribable content." "Thus," Justice Scalia continued, "the government may proscribe libel; but it may not make the further content discrimination of proscribing *only* libel critical of the government." The Court held that as a general matter such further content discrimination is subject to "strict scrutiny" (i.e., will be upheld only if it is necessary to accomplishing a compelling state interest).

If Justice Scalia had stopped here and simply announced a rule that even when regulating unprotected speech government cannot engage in further content discrimination, his opinion would not be susceptible to the charge of discrimination against minority interests. Well aware, however, that subjecting every content-discriminatory regulation of unprotected speech to strict scrutiny would unduly interfere with legitimate regulatory objectives, Scalia created a number of exceptions to this newly minted rule. One exception is where "the basis for the content discrimination consists entirely of the very reason the entire class of speech at issue is proscribable." "Such a reason," Scalia reasoned, "having been adjudged neutral enough to support exclusion of the entire class of speech from First Amendment protection, is also neutral enough to form the basis of a distinction within the class." As an illustration, Scalia hypothesized an obscenity regulation that prohibited only material most patently offensive in its prurience. He also noted that there is no constitutional problem with the federal law that criminalized only those threats of violence that are directed against the president, "since the reasons why threats of violence are outside the First Amendment (protecting individuals from the fear of violence, from the disruption that fear engenders, and from the possibility that the threatened violence will occur) have special force when applied to the person of the President."

This exception (as well as the others Scalia created) is perfectly sensible.[18] But the following question immediately arises: Why are not racial fighting words and other forms of bigoted epithets worse than garden-variety fighting words for "the very reason the entire class of speech at issue is proscribable"? As noted in *Chaplinsky*, the case that placed fighting words outside the protection of the First Amendment, the harm caused by fighting words is twofold: Their "very utterance inflicts injury" and they "tend to incite an immediate breach of the peace."[19] Measured by either criterion, use of racial fighting words would seem to be worse than other types of abusive epithets.

If in the heat of an argument a colleague called me a "son of a bitch" or an "asshole" or some similar abusive epithet, I would be upset, but with an apology cordial relations could be restored. But if the same colleague had called me a "dirty kike," the injury would be much more severe and any hopes of restoring good collegial relations unlikely. I think that most people, especially those who are members of groups that have historically been victims of such abuse, would feel the same way about the use of racial or ethnic epithets. Furthermore, out on the street or in a bar or on the playground such epithets are particularly likely to provoke violence.

An additional reason that racial fighting words are arguably worse than ordinary personal insults is that they often partake of the harmful characteristics of another class of unprotected speech—threats of violence. As Justice Robert Jackson eloquently explained: "These terse epithets come down to our generation weighted with hatreds accumulated through centuries of bloodshed. . . . Their historical associations with violence are well understood, both by those who hurl and those who are struck by these missiles."[20] This is particularly true of the fighting words at issue in *R.A.V.*: A burning cross placed in front of an African American's house in the dead of night has long been used by the Ku Klux Klan as a threat of violence.

Justice Byron White, in a concurring opinion joined by Justices Harry Blackmun, John Paul Stevens, and Sandra Day O'Connor, was quick to point out that the majority's exception allowing regulation when the basis for the distinction is "the very reason the entire class of speech . . . is proscribable" would seem to encompass racial fighting words. "A prohibition on fighting words," White explained, "is a ban on a class of speech that conveys an overriding message of personal injury and imminent violence, . . . a message that is at its ugliest when directed against groups that have long been the targets of discrimination." Justice Scalia feebly responded to this point by arguing that "St. Paul has not singled out an especially offensive mode of expression—it has not, for example, selected for prohibition only those fighting words that communicate ideas in a threatening (as opposed to a merely obnoxious) manner." Perhaps to

Justice Scalia racial epithets are not "especially offensive" as compared to other types of personal insults, but to those who have been the victims of such epithets (and worse), personally directed racial insults are not only more injurious and more likely to cause a breach of the peace but also more "threatening (as opposed to . . . merely obnoxious)."

I am not arguing here that the result in *R.A.V.* is wrong or even that the majority was incorrect to hold that the First Amendment prohibits government from singling out racial fighting words for prohibition. Although racial epithets are a particularly injurious and inflammatory species of fighting words, their power to injure is intimately connected with the racist message they convey. As the Minnesota Supreme Court emphasized, the message conveyed by the burning cross was "based on virulent notions of racial supremacy." Thus unlike the typical case in which government identifies a subset of proscribable speech as particularly egregious for the very reason the larger category is proscribable (e.g., extremely prurient obscenity), singling out racist fighting words for special prohibition raises the possibility that the motivating force behind the regulation is antipathy toward a certain viewpoint.

Whether a special ban on racial fighting words should be considered an unconstitutional attempt to suppress racist ideas or rather a response to a particularly harmful type of fighting words should depend on the need for such a narrow regulation as compared to a more general prohibition of fighting words. Because the ordinance involved in *R.A.V.* was not drafted as a selective regulation of fighting words but was judicially transmogrified into such a regulation, there was no legislative history explaining why a broader prohibition of fighting words would not have sufficed. And the City of St. Paul did not help its cause when it asserted in its brief that a general fighting words law would not meet its needs because only a specific prohibition of racial fighting words would communicate to the minority that "group hatred" is "not condoned by the majority." The Court might have been wiser, however, to have waited until it had before it an actual legislative effort to selectively proscribe racist fighting words before deciding such a difficult question.[21]

But whether one agrees or disagrees with the result in *R.A.V.*, it seems that this decision is an example of the Court's (albeit a bare majority) ignoring the perspectives of people of color. There is no need, however, to exaggerate *R.A.V.*'s shortcomings, as Catharine MacKinnon does when she implies that in *R.A.V.* the Court found a First Amendment right of racists to burn crosses on African Americans' lawns. "Like pornography," MacKinnon complains, "cross burning is seen by the Supreme Court to raise crucial expressive issues. Its function as an enforcer of segregation, instigator of lynch mobs, instiller of terror, and emblem of official impunity is transmuted into a discussion of specific 'disfavored subjects.'"[22] The charge is unfair.[23] Scalia begins his opinion by noting that the cross burning at issue "could have been punished under any number of laws," such as the prohibition of terroristic threats, and ends by emphasizing that the cross burning involved in that case was a "reprehensible" act.[24]

PORNOGRAPHY:
CONSTITUTIONAL PROTECTION OF SEX CRIMES?

A major obstacle to banning hate speech consistently with the First Amendment is that much of this expression is political propaganda. Indeed, it is precisely because this propaganda is intended to persuade others to think about minorities in hateful, distorted ways that proponents of hate speech regulation want to ban such material. In contrast, the primary purpose and effect of pornography is not political persuasion but sexual arousal. Accordingly, several commentators, including MacKinnon, have argued that pornography is not *about* sex; it *is* sex.

"[S]ocial life," MacKinnon accurately informs us, "is full of words that are legally treated as the acts they constitute without so much as a whimper from the First Amendment."[25] As examples of such speech acts she cites saying "kill" to a trained attack dog, saying "aye" in a legislative vote in return for a bribe, and verbal agreements to fix prices in violation of the antitrust laws. Similarly, she gives a number of examples of expression that is unproblematically categorized as constituting the practice of racial or sexual discrimination rather than expressing an idea in favor of those practices: a sign on a restaurant saying "White Only"; a professor saying to a student, "Sleep with me and I'll give you an A"; or a boss telling his female employee, "Fuck me or you're fired."[26]

All of these examples, MacKinnon insists, involve "only words"; yet they are thought of not as speech but as the acts they constitute, that is, assault, bribery, price-fixing, race discrimination, and quid pro quo sexual harassment. Similarly, to MacKinnon, "[p]ornography is masturbation material. It is used as sex. It therefore is sex." When men masturbate to sexually demeaning pictures of women, it certainly is not "ideas they are ejaculating over."[27] Moreover, MacKinnon claims, like other speech acts that are routinely regulated, pornography is harmful in that it leads to violent assaults on women by men "who are made, changed and impelled by it."[28] Why is it, she asks, that this harmful speech act is thought of as speech protected by the First Amendment rather than as harmful sexual activity such as "rape or child abuse or sexual harassment or sexual murder?"[29] Why is it, MacKinnon continues, that of all types of harmful sexual activity "only pornography . . . is protected as a constitutional right?"[30] MacKinnon answers that the male-dominated power structure, which includes judges who consume pornography, has constructed free speech doctrine so as to render invisible this harm to women.

I agree that we still live in a patriarchal society in which women's interests are often ignored. MacKinnon has not, however, shown that free speech doctrine's treatment of pornography is an example of such discrimination. As an initial matter, it is not at all clear that even hard-core pornography is the idealess "speech act" that MacKinnon claims it is. Owen Fiss, who is generally sympathetic to radical arguments for suppressing pornography, parts company with MacKinnon on this point. "Pornography," Fiss writes, "is an expression of the creators and producers of the work and is most certainly part of the discourse by which the public understands itself and the world it confronts."[31] In contrast, Frederick Schauer insists that watching hard-core pornography is essentially the same as hiring prostitutes to perform live sex acts to stimulate the viewer.[32] What Schauer's interesting analogy misses, however, is that unlike live sex acts, pornography makes use of media (film, books, magazines, and the Internet) that are an essential element of public discourse, thereby raising the possibility that irrespective of any political intent of the producer, government may be seeking to prohibit this expression because of its power to shape public opinion. In addition, precisely because pornography does make use of these media, it inevitably involves some modicum of artistic expression and arguably even the expression of some social or political perspective as well.[33] But even if we were to assume that the *sole* function of pornography is physical arousal, MacKinnon is unpersuasive in her claim that in not allowing the suppression of pornography free speech doctrine discriminates against women's interests.[34]

For one, contrary to MacKinnon's implication, sexually explicit material that can fairly be viewed as more akin to sexual activity than a discussion about sex is in fact afforded *no* constitutional protection under current doctrine. Free speech doctrine has never protected so-called hard-core pornography or, as it is known in legal terms, obscenity. In reaffirming the historical exclusion of obscene material from First Amendment protection, the Court in *Miller v. California* stressed that "the public portrayal of hard core sexual conduct" cannot be equated with "the free and robust exchange of ideas."[35] And though by no means primarily driven by the feminist perspective, the Court did note that "there is at least an arguable correlation" between obscene material and sex crimes. MacKinnon, then, is quite wrong when she complains that of all speech acts it is only pornography that "is protected as a constitutional right."

Indeed, as discussed in Chapter 4, under current doctrine even pornography that is not sufficiently graphic to be legally obscene under *Miller* ("soft-" and "medium-core" pornography) may be regulated in ways that other expression may not. Cities can restrict movie houses specializing in "adult" movies to certain parts of town (or alternatively can forbid such theaters from locating within a specified distance of each other). And government may forbid the sale of soft-core pornography to minors.[36] Current doctrine recognizes no such exceptions for other types of books, films, or magazines, even ones that are thought to be socially harmful. For instance, there are films, books, and magazines that are to violence as pornography is to sex—extremely graphic material with no purpose other than to appeal to a morbid interest in violence. There is, however, no violence analogue to the obscenity exception to First Amendment protection. Nor under current doctrine can government subject movie houses that show violent material to special zoning requirements. Nor is there as yet any Supreme Court decision allowing the government to prohibit material containing explicit violence from being sold to children. Rather, all of these special exceptions are uniquely applicable to sexually oriented material. So MacKinnon has it backward: In affording government a special dispensation to regulate the distribution of sexually explicit materials, free speech doctrine discriminates *against* sexually explicit material.

More centrally, MacKinnon's argument is flawed because it confounds two very different senses in which pornography is claimed to be a speech act.[37] The first (the one just discussed) considers pornography to be an act because it causes physical arousal. But MacKinnon also makes the claim that pornography "constitute[s]" the subordination of women in the same way that commands to trained attack dogs, voting in favor of a law pursuant to a bribe, agreeing to fix prices, or the placement of exclusionary signs in places of public accommodation constitute acts. MacKinnon's comparison of pornography to these speech acts is inapt.

In MacKinnon's view, pornography constitutes subordination of women because men who view this material are "made, changed and impelled by it" to subjugate women through sexual aggression and violence. But men are "made, changed and impelled" to act in this way through pornography's power to shape the way they see women. In contrast, in forbidding verbal commands to killer dogs or the placement of exclusionary signs in places of public accommodation or agreements to fix prices or votes tainted by bribery, the state seeks to prevent harms that are unrelated to the power of speech to affect the way anyone sees the world or social relations in it. In regulating when one can say "kill" to an attack dog, for instance, the state is not concerned with anyone's thoughts about dogs or killing or any other issue but solely that people not be unjustifiably attacked by dogs. Similarly, the justification for preventing restaurant owners from placing "White Only" signs in their establishments is not that such expression may persuade others that integration is wrong or about any other matter of public concern but that places of public accommodation not exclude people of color.

As we have seen, a central purpose of free speech doctrine is to assure that the opinion by which we govern ourselves and the search for truth in the marketplace of ideas is not distorted by government coercion. A ban on pornography justified by its power to socialize men's view of women implicates these core values in ways that the regulation of commands to attack dogs and signs in places of public accommodation simply do not.

MacKinnon insists, however, that pornography affects the way men perceive and hence treat women not because men are persuaded by its ideas but through a form of "primitive conditioning, with picture and words as sexual stimuli," a process that is "largely unconscious."[38] The argument that expression that changes our perception of the world through such "primitive conditioning" should be afforded less First Amendment protection than speech that persuades through appeal to deliberative faculties is an interesting one. But it does not support her claim that free speech doctrine discriminates against women.

To begin with, regardless whether the process by which one's view is changed is conscious or unconscious or whether it is accomplished through "primitive conditioning" or highly rational discourse, justifying the prohibition of certain images on the grounds that these images affect the way viewers perceive social relationships remains entirely different from the rationale for regulating commands to attack dogs, legislative bribes, agreements to fix prices, or the posting of "White Only" signs. It is still the case that the former justification centers on the power of speech to shape people's worldview, whereas the latter rationales do not. More important, much speech, including political propaganda, poetry, and music, influences perspectives through "primitive conditioning" or some other process that is "largely unconscious." If free speech doctrine were to allow the greater regulation of such expression just because of its ability to affect people's perception through noncognitive mechanisms but did not allow similar regulation of pornography, MacKinnon would have a powerful argument that this doctrine discriminates against the interests of women. But free speech doctrine decidedly does not allow any such broad regulation based on this theory, and thus there is no merit to this variation of her discrimination claim.[39]

THE MACKINNON-DWORKIN MODEL
ANTIPORNOGRAPHY ORDINANCE

MacKinnon's particular gripe with current free speech doctrine stems from its incompatibility with a model antipornography ordinance that she and Andrea Dworkin drafted. The model ordinance defines "pornography" as the

> graphic sexually explicit subordination of women through pictures and/or words that also includes one or more of the following: (a) women are presented dehumanized as sexual objects, things or commodities; or (b) women are presented as sexual objects who enjoy humiliation or pain; or (c) women are presented as sexual objects experiencing sexual pleasure in rape, incest, or other sexual assault; or (d) women are presented as sexual objects tied up or cut or mutilated or bruised or physically hurt; or (e) women are presented in postures or positions of sexual submission, servility, or display; or (f) women's body parts—including but not limited to vaginas, breasts, or buttocks—are exhibited such that women are reduced to those parts; or (g) women are presented being penetrated by objects or animals; or (h) women are presented in scenarios of degradation, humiliation, injury, torture, shown as filthy or inferior, bleeding, bruised, or hurt in a context that makes these conditions sexual.[40]

The model ordinance provides civil sanctions, including injunctive relief preventing further distribution.

As discussed in Chapter 4, the U.S. Supreme Court summarily affirmed a federal appellate court decision invalidating an Indianapolis ordinance based on this model.[41] MacKinnon claims that the failure to uphold this regulation is further proof that free speech doctrine invidiously discriminates against the interests of women. This, claim, too is unwarranted. For one, unlike the Supreme Court's obscenity doctrine, the model ordinance focuses neither on prurience nor lack of artistic value but rather is premised on the belief that sexually explicit, demeaning portrayals of women condition men to subjugate women. As MacKinnon has written in defending the model ordinance, "[I]f a woman is subjected, why should it matter that the work has other value?"[42] But if her theory is that pornography is just a masturbatory tool and therefore should be treated like other "speech acts" (e.g., saying "kill" to a trained attack dog), then it must surely matter whether the material in fact has value aside from its ability to sexually arouse.

Unlike verbal commands to attack dogs or a legislative vote cast pursuant to a bribery scheme or words spoken to effectuate an antitrust violation, exclude blacks from restaurants, or sexually coerce students or employees, sexually explicit material *is* often part of serious artistic efforts, some of which involve political or social commentary. Government has often attempted to outlaw important works of art on the grounds that they contain sexually explicit material—works such as James Joyce's *Ulysses* and Henry Miller's *Tropic of Cancer*.[43] Free speech doctrine has attempted to draw the line between expression with erotic content that nonetheless constitutes serious artistic expression or otherwise has "socially redeeming importance" and material that truly is no more than a masturbatory tool. To this end, the Supreme Court devised the following definition of legally proscribable obscenity: The work must, taken as a whole, appeal to "the prurient interest," depict or describe sexual conduct in a "patently offensive way," and lack "serious literary, artistic, political or scientific value."[44]

There can, of course, be reasonable disagreement about whether the Court drew the line in the right place. Some argue that because obscenity prosecutions are expensive to bring and difficult to win, obscenity doctrine is too protective of worthless yet arguably harmful speech. Others argue that this doctrine does not adequately protect artistic and political expression, pointing to such cases as the obscenity prosecution of a museum for showing the homoerotic photographs of Robert Mapplethorpe and an album by the African American rap group 2 Live Crew containing sexually explicit lyrics.[45] But whatever the right answer to the question of where to draw the line, the model ordinance's incompatibility with current doctrine would seem to stem not from some insensitivity to the interests of women but from a genuine desire to protect artistic expression and social commentary.

Also belying the claim that in finding the Indianapolis ordinance unconstitutional the U.S. Court of Appeals and the Supreme Court discriminated against women's interests is the fact that the model ordinance regulates expression based on its viewpoint. As Judge Easterbrook explained, under the ordinance:

> [s]peech treating women in the approved way—in sexual encounters "premised on equality"—is lawful no matter how sexually explicit. Speech treating women in the disapproved way—as submissive in matters sexual or as enjoying humiliation—is unlawful no matter how significant the literary, artistic, or political qualities of the work taken as a whole. The state may not ordain preferred viewpoints in this way. The Constitution forbids the state to declare one perspective right and silence opponents.[46]

As discussed in Chapter 4, laws that regulate speech according to its viewpoint have long been considered anathema to First Amendment values. For instance, in 1959 the Court held unconstitutional a New York law that banned any film that "expressly or impliedly presents [acts of sexual immorality] as desirable, acceptable, or proper patterns of behavior." Pursuant to this ordinance, the state had denied a license to the film *Lady Chatterley's Lover* because "its subject matter is adultery presented as being right or desirable for certain people under certain circumstances."[47] The prohibition against viewpoint discrimination thus cannot plausibly be seen as some novel concept devised for the occasion of invalidating the Indianapolis ordinance.

Cass Sunstein argues that the Indianapolis antipornography ordinance is no more viewpoint oriented than a host of other speech regulations permitted under current First Amendment doctrine. He claims that "bans on advertising for casino gambling, cigarette smoking, and alcohol; the SEC's regulation of proxy statements; the controls on what employers may say during a union election; [and] the prohibition of advertising for illegal products" are viewpoint discriminatory "in very much the same sense" as the Indianapolis ordinance. As Sunstein correctly points out, these regulations are not seen as viewpoint discriminatory because there is "a firm consensus" that the speech at issue causes "real-world harms." These "obvious legitimate justifications" therefore dispel any thought that government has regulated the speech for some illegitimate purpose.[48] The same is manifestly not the case, however, with the Indianapolis ordinance.

As discussed at length in Chapter 7 and the Appendix, it is far from conclusive that pornography that depicts women in demeaning or subordinate positions actually causes violence or discrimination against women. Accordingly, in sharp contrast to most of the regulations Sunstein cites, the Indianapolis ordinance raises the distinct possibility that it is motivated by some purpose other than the prevention of concrete, "real-world" harms, such as violence against women, but is rather an attempt to squelch pornography's offensive images, such as women portrayed as sex objects or as subservient to men. The possibility of illegitimate government purpose is heightened by the inextricable link between the topic of women's sexuality and a host of broader, hotly contested political issues. As Ronald Dworkin has written: "Pornographic photographs, films, and videos are the starkest possible expression of the idea feminists most loathe: that women exist principally to provide sexual service to men."[49] The Canadian Supreme Court candidly admitted that one reason for upholding a ban on degrading and violent pornography is that it "seriously offends the values fundamental to our society."[50] In the United States, the city of Renton, Ohio, justified a pornography regulation on the grounds that such material had an "adverse effect" on "established family values, respect for marital relations and for the sanctity of marriage relations of others."[51]

In contrast, the harm caused by cigarette smoking and alcohol consumption is both palpable and well documented, and it is entirely reasonable to assume that increased advertising of these products leads to an increase in their use. Furthermore, the "socialization" that government seeks to diminish when it regulates advertising for these products is not entangled in broader political issues. We therefore readily accept the government's justification that it has banned cigarette and alcohol advertising for its stated purpose rather than suspecting that it has done so because of disagreement with some worldview that the speech portrays.

The same is true to varying degrees of most everything else on Sunstein's list.[52] What Sunstein's argument does show, however, is that determining whether a regulation is viewpoint discriminatory is not some purely abstract exercise but necessarily involves judgment and interpretation of real-world facts and events, a process that cannot be entirely divorced from the decisionmaker's own political viewpoint. Nevertheless, although his arguments are thought-provoking, Sunstein, like MacKinnon, fails to make a convincing case that contemporary free speech doctrine discriminates against women.

THE ALLEGED FAILURE OF FREE SPEECH DOCTRINE TO ACCOUNT FOR CONFLICTING CONSTITUTIONAL EQUALITY RIGHTS

Proponents of bans on hate speech and pornography often make the following argument: The First Amendment is but one provision of the Constitution. At least as important is the Equal Protection Clause of the Fourteenth Amendment, which outlaws invidious racial and gender discrimination. The expression of vicious racist ideas leads to acts of racial discrimination, and the consumption of pornography causes the subordination of women. Both are class-based injuries implicating the Equal Protection Clause.[53] Accordingly, application of standard First Amendment doctrine, which all but irrebuttably condemns viewpoint-oriented laws as unconstitutional, should not apply to hate speech or pornography bans because, unlike ordinary speech regulation, these laws protect constitutional rights. Hate speech and pornography prohibitions present a special case in which the speaker's First Amendment rights must be "balance[d] . . . directly" against equality rights.[54] The Court's persistent failure to see that challenges to hate speech and pornography involve not just the right of free speech but competing equality rights is another example of how the interests of minorities and women are ignored by free speech doctrine.[55]

At first glance, this argument may seem persuasive, leaving one to wonder how free speech doctrine could have for so long disregarded these countervailing equality rights. Careful analysis, however, reveals that the argument is fallacious, for laws against hate speech and pornography do not really involve conflicting constitutional rights. Like most provisions of the U.S. Constitution, the Fourteenth Amendment is a limitation on governmental, not private, conduct.[56] The Fourteenth Amendment declares that "[n]o State shall . . . deny to any person within its jurisdiction the equal protection of the laws." So a bigot spewing racist venom in the speakers' corner of the park or a video store owner renting a pornographic film cannot possibly violate the Fourteenth Amendment. In contrast, if the proponents of hate speech regulation have their way, the state will enact the law and arrest, try, and imprison the racist speaker and the purveyor of pornography. This is state action plainly implicating the First Amendment. What is involved in a challenge to a general hate speech or pornography ban, then, is not a conflict between constitutional rights but a clash between the constitutional rights of a speaker and the state interest in protecting individuals from harm caused by the speech.

In response, radical proponents of hate speech laws point out that the objection that there is no true conflict between constitutional rights depends entirely upon the distinction between state and private action, a concept that, in the words of Charles Lawrence, "relies upon the mystifying properties of constitutional ideology."[57] It is true that the state action doctrine is among the least coherent of all Supreme Court doctrine, prompting a commentator to refer to it as "a conceptual disaster area."[58] One reason state action doctrine is badly confused is that before Congress passed laws prohibiting discrimination by private persons in housing and public accommodation, the Supreme Court stretched the state action concept to cover instances of these discriminatory practices. For instance, the Court held that judicial enforcement of private racially discriminatory covenants was unconstitutional state action in violation of the Fourteenth Amendment. Similarly, the Court found that state action inhered in racial discrimination practiced by a privately owned coffee shop located in a building owned by the state.[59] And as discussed in detail in Chapter 6, the Court used an expansive notion of state action to upset trespass convictions of civil rights protestors for staging sit-ins at segregated facilities.

Passage of the civil rights laws in the mid-1960s outlawing racial discrimination in housing, employment, and places of public accommodation relieved the pressure to expand the state action concept to cover these areas, and by the mid-1970s the Court's state action decisions were plainly inconsistent with its earlier pronouncements. For instance, in 1974 the Court held that despite extensive state regulation, including approval of the very practice at issue, a private utility company's procedure for terminating service to delinquent customers was not state action and thus not subject to the strictures of the Due Process Clause of the Fourteenth Amendment.[60]

Despite the Court's inability to produce coherent doctrine, recognition of some basic dichotomy between state and private action remains an indispensable element of U.S. constitutional law. Without such a distinction, the concept of constitutional limitations on *governmental* intrusions on *individual* rights becomes meaningless. As Laurence Tribe has explained, "[B]y exempting private action from the reach of the Constitution's prohibitions, [the state action requirement] stops the Constitution short of preempting individual liberty—of denying to individuals the freedom to make certain choices, such as choices of the persons with whom they will associate. Such freedom is basic under any conception of liberty, but it would be lost if individuals had to conform their conduct to the Constitution's demands."[61]

To give some specific examples confirming this point: The Constitution generally forbids sex discrimination, but forbidding individuals from discriminating on this basis in pursuing amorous interests would, aside from being absurd, violate personal autonomy. Similarly, the Constitution forbids the government from discriminating on the basis of religion or even to take a person's religion into account. There could be no such prohibition on private decisionmaking in the religious sphere without contradicting the essential purpose of the Free Exercise Clause. With regard to free speech, the First Amendment generally forbids the government to make content-based decisions in regulating public discourse, but it also presupposes that private persons, such as editors and publishers of newspapers, will routinely engage in content discrimination in deciding which stories to run. In short, the concept of state action cannot be determined in the abstract but, as Tribe suggests, must be bounded by the various realms of decisionmaking reserved to the individual in our constitutional scheme.

Not only is the distinction between private and state action essential, it is, for the most part, quite workable. Indeed, the distinction is usually so obvious that it does not even rise to consciousness in most cases. Only borderline cases call for analysis.[62] But whatever difficulties may arise in these cases, liberal democracy must retain some basic distinction between the actions of the state and those of the individual. Although there can be legitimate disagreement about where to draw the line, a racist speaking in the park or a video store proprietor renting pornographic films must be put on the "private" side of the line.[63] (This is not to say that outlawing racist speech is contrary to basic principles of liberal democracy. I discuss this different and much harder question in Chapter 9.)

Even if a private person expressing racist ideas cannot *technically* violate the Fourteenth Amendment, racial and gender equality is nonetheless a paramount constitutional value. Should not the centrality of this value be factored into the analysis of the constitutionality of laws promoting such equality? In one sense the answer is plainly yes, and current doctrine already accounts for the importance of the state's interest in eradicating invidious discrimination. For instance, the Supreme Court has held that preventing racial discrimination is a compelling state interest and would surely so hold with respect to eliminating violence against

women and other forms of discrimination said to result from pornography.[64] But radical critics argue for something more radical. They believe
the fundamental equality norm expressed in the Fourteenth Amendment
requires that the usual free speech rules should not apply in hate speech
and pornography cases. In particular, they argue, the strong presumption against content-oriented laws should be suspended in such cases. In
their view whenever hate speech or pornography regulations are challenged under the First Amendment, the free speech and equality interests should be "balanced directly." In Chapter 9 I explain why it is far
from obvious that either free speech or equality would be well served by
such an approach. Here, however, I limit the discussion to showing that
in failing to balance free speech rights against other constitutional
norms, the Court has not discriminated against the interests of women
and minorities.

There are a host of other interests that the Constitution protects against
government infringement but that, consistent with the state action requirement, are not secured from interference by private individuals. For
instance, property is guarded by the same amendment that guarantees
equal protection of the laws, yet theft is not treated as raising a constitutional issue in the absence of some state involvement.[65] More pertinent,
the usual free speech analysis applies when business owners claim that
striking employees are interfering with their property rights. Similarly,
the ordinary free speech rules are not suspended in cases in which it is
alleged that expression interferes with constitutionally protected relationships such as marriage or child rearing, as many books and movies
supposedly do. Nor in cases involving advocacy of burglary, murder, or
kidnapping would the Fourth Amendment's protection of the home or
the Fourteenth Amendment's prohibition against the arbitrary depriva-
tion of life or liberty alter the free speech analysis. By the same token, attacks on equality norms by private speakers are treated precisely like all
other private speech that has an impact on values the Constitution
shields from government intervention.

In recent decisions the Court has continued to resist calls to suspend
ordinary free speech analysis just because the speech invades an interest
constitutionally protected against infringement by the state. Although
urged by both academic commentators and litigants (including, to its
discredit, the American Civil Liberties Union) to afford less protection to
protests at abortion clinics because pro-life demonstrations interfered
with a woman's right to obtain an abortion, the Supreme Court has declined to do so.[66] Indeed, even in those rare cases where state action implicating both free speech and some other constitutional right results in a
true conflict of rights, the Court hews closely to its normal free speech
analysis rather than engaging in ad hoc balancing.[67]

Radical critics argue, however, that racial and gender equality are more fundamental than property, protection of the home and traditional family relationships, and other norms reflected in the Constitution. Racial and gender equality is not just some ordinary constitutional value; rather it is, in Owen Fiss's words, "one of the center beams of the legal order."[68] Radicals therefore insist that free speech doctrine's failure to take into account the overriding importance of the equality norm slights the interests of women and minorities.

This claim of discrimination is difficult to substantiate. Democracy is surely also a "center beam" of the American legal order. Indeed, the concepts of equality and democracy are inextricably linked. I take it, however, that the radical critics would not favor the suspension of the normal free speech rules for Marxist propaganda on the grounds that such speech attacks core constitutional norms. Thus these critics do not charge the Warren Court with any lack of commitment to democratic ideals in refusing to suspend normal analysis and "balance directly" free speech against democracy in the later Smith Act cases or in other cases involving communist speech.[69] By the same token, the Court's refusal to suspend the usual free speech rules for regulation of hate speech and pornography should not be seen as reflecting lack of dedication to equality. Rather, this refusal stems from the recognition that such an approach would lead to uncertain and unprincipled decisions.

As the Supreme Court's substantive due process jurisprudence demonstrates, determining what fundamental rights the Constitution actually protects can be an extremely subjective exercise; identifying the central values underlying this document requires even more subjectivity. If a majority of justices happens to believe that national self-defense or protecting U.S. interests abroad is a "center beam" of our national charter, it will be hard to prove them wrong. If they derive from this value the rule that government has a "compelling" interest in preventing disruption of military recruiting during time of war, this, too, seems fair enough. But it would be quite another matter if the Court were to hold that because this value was central to the constitutional scheme, antiwar speech inimical to the war effort should not be measured by the usual rules governing free speech cases but rather protestors' free speech rights should be "balanced directly" against the core constitutional value of national self-defense. Such a "balancing" approach to free speech would invite judges, perhaps quite unconsciously, to smuggle their own views of the underlying controversies—whether the Vietnam War, abortion, communism, labor disputes, or civil rights—into free speech analysis. Such judicial viewpoint discrimination would likely have serious negative consequences for free speech doctrine.[70]

MacKinnon is surely correct that we live in a country that "is suppos-edly not constitutionally neutral on the subject" of racial and gender equality.[71] But we also live in a country that is committed to public dis-course not bounded by the values enshrined in that document. Whether the Court has been right in refusing to apply special rules to speech that arguably undermines the most basic constitutional norms is a question that I address in Chapter 9. My point here is that in failing to suspend the normal free speech rules for hate speech and pornography, free speech doctrine does not discriminate against Equal Protection Clause values. Rather, free speech doctrine merely fails to give equality special immu-nity from the rough-and-tumble of public discourse. Right or wrong, this refusal to exalt equality above the fray of public debate stems not from any failure to appreciate the prominence of equality as a constitutional norm but from fear that reducing protection to speech that attacks consti-tutional norms will lead to unprincipled decisions as well as a stagnant society.

No Supreme Court justice did more to promote gender and racial equality than William Brennan. Yet in his response to Chief Justice Rehnquist's insistence in the flag-burning case that "one of the high purposes of a democratic society is to legislate against conduct that is regarded as evil and profoundly offensive," Brennan wrote: "The First Amendment does not guarantee that . . . concepts virtually sacred to our Nation as a whole—such as the principle that discrimination on the basis of race is odious and destructive—will go unquestioned in the marketplace of ideas."[72] He warned that "decid[ing] which symbols were sufficiently special to warrant [the] unique status" that the dis-sent urged should be bestowed on the U.S. flag would "force [us] to consult our own political preferences, and impose them on the citi-zenry, in the very way the First Amendment forbids us to do." Exalting one constitutional norm over all others as a grounds for limiting speech would similarly involve an illegitimate imposition of "political prefer-ences."

To Stanley Fish, such talk of maintaining ideological neutrality is at best utter nonsense and at worst a bad joke played by elites on an un-suspecting populace. Fish claims that free speech doctrine is inher-ently "political" or "ideological" because the very construction of the rules (for instance, that fighting words are not protected speech or that only certain public places are to be considered public forums) requires judges to engage in value choice.[73] Consequently,

"Free speech" is just the name we give to verbal behavior that serves the substantive agenda we wish to advance; and we give our preferred verbal behaviors *that* name when we can, when we have the power to do so, because in the rhetoric of American life, the label "free speech" is the one you want your favorites to wear. Free speech, in short, is not an independent value but a political prize.[74]

The fallacy of Fish's argument lies in its failure to recognize that the terms "political" and "ideological" cover a multitude of activities, not all of which are sins. Most judicial decisionmaking involves value choice; the formulation of judicial rules is a particularly value-laden exercise, and the formulation of the rules that form free speech doctrine especially so. For instance, the relative importance one attaches to providing sufficient places for robust and unfettered public discourse as compared to allowing government discretion to manage its own affairs might lead different justices to different results in deciding whether airports are public forums. Such value choices are a legitimate as well as an inevitable part of constitutional interpretation. Suppose, however, that in deciding the same issue a justice reasoned as follows: "Airports are the favorite location of those obnoxious Hare Krishnas, whereas the evangelical Christians whose views I agree with prefer to proselytize in traditional public forums such as parks and sidewalks. Accordingly, I find that airports are not public forums." This decision, too, involves value choice, but of a very different kind and one that does violate the central "neutrality" command of free speech doctrine.

Precisely what type of judicial value choice is legitimately part of constitutional interpretation is a much-debated question. But no one can doubt that sympathy for or antipathy to the "substantive agenda" of a particular speaker is plainly inconsistent with a free speech doctrine in service of democratic self-governance, truth seeking in the marketplace of ideas, or the noninstrumental values thought to underlie the American free speech principle. Thus the concept of ideologically neutral free speech regulation means primarily (although perhaps not exclusively) the avoidance of viewpoint discrimination or other species of content discrimination that might mask viewpoint discrimination. But it emphatically does not mean, nor could it sensibly entail, value-free decisionmaking by those who directly regulate speech through legislation or the judges who formulate and apply the constitutional limits on such regulation.

Fish's mistake, then, is to throw all normative judgments into the same pot. Free speech doctrine claims to be ideologically neutral only in the limited sense that government may not prohibit speech so as to advance or inhibit a particular "substantive agenda" or worldview. This is not to say, of course, that there have not been instances in which judges' sympathy for or antipathy against a speaker's "substantive agenda" played a role in their decisions. As Justice Douglas observed about the early "clear and present danger" case: "[T]he threats were often loud but always puny and made serious only by *judges* so wedded to the status quo that critical analysis made them nervous."[75] And as we shall see, sympathy for the goals of the civil rights movement seemed to have influenced several Supreme Court decisions of the 1960s. But by and large, as is evident from cases in which the Court protected the free speech rights of speakers with whose ideas the justices obviously disagreed (for instance, communists urging the overthrow of the government or Klan members threatening to take "vengeance" if the Supreme Court did not stop "oppressing" white people), free speech cases are usually decided on principles that transcend concern about the speaker's "substantive agenda."

Fish's critique does, however, serve to underscore a point often overlooked by defenders of current free speech doctrine: Because this doctrine, including the rule against viewpoint discrimination, is in service of several underlying values flowing from a particular vision of democracy, American free speech doctrine is plainly not ideologically neutral in some larger sense of the term. This recognition raises the possibility that free speech doctrine disserves the interests of women and minorities, not by discriminating against these interests in some rank, easily identifiable way but at a much deeper level. In this view, the very structure of free speech doctrine is seen to prefer democracy's commitment to liberty over its guaranty of equality. It is to this more fundamental charge that I now turn.

6

THE COMPLEX
RELATIONSHIP BETWEEN
FREE SPEECH AND EQUALITY

Neutrality, at least in the formal sense, is free speech doctrine's strong suit. This doctrine steadfastly refuses to exalt any norm, even the most basic ones, above the fray of public discourse and treats the most pernicious ideas as solicitously as benign ones. It is not surprising, therefore, that the radical claim that modern doctrine discriminates against minorities and women does not withstand analysis. Radical critics are on somewhat stronger ground, however, when they argue that the *effect* of this neutrality is to perpetuate and reinforce racial and gender inequality.

The traditional liberal view is that free speech and equality, far from being conflicting values, are consonant and reinforcing. For instance, liberal philosopher Ronald Dworkin writes that "[t]he most fundamental egalitarian command of the Constitution is for equality throughout the political process," which demands that "everyone, no matter how eccentric or despicable, have a chance to influence policies as well as elections."[1] Similarly, the liberal Warren Court pushed both equality and free speech rights further than they had ever been extended before and rarely had to choose between them. In a seminal free speech decision, Justice Thurgood Marshall declared that "there is an 'equality of status in the field of ideas' and government must afford all points of view an equal opportunity to be heard."[2]

Radical critics, in contrast, tend to see free speech and equality as competitors in a zero-sum game: Free speech's gain is equality's loss, and vice versa. They argue that in light of the great disparities of wealth and power, free speech's formal equality results in massive substantive inequality in the marketplace of ideas. They point out that speech capable of shaping public opinion is expensive and thus not accessible to the poor and powerless. Accordingly, to the radicals the claim that free speech doctrine is neutral because it protects all people equally from government censorship is like saying that a law preventing people from sleeping under bridges is neutral because it applies to rich and poor alike. Moreover, radical critics insist, free speech has never been an effective tool for progressive social change in this country. They point out that free speech co-existed with slavery and apartheid and claim that, contrary to popular belief, it did little to help the civil rights movement.[3]

Radical critics are about half right. Much more than First Amendment romantics care to recognize, speech reinforces the status quo. This is particularly true of the most influential media—television, film, and popular romance novels, which tend to reflect the tastes and predilections of the audience and thus reinforce contemporary cultural norms, including racial and gender stereotypes. In contrast, the radical view that free speech has never contributed to progressive social change is unfounded. As we shall see, the relationship between the First Amendment and the status quo—and consequently the relationship between free speech and equality—is a complicated one, not reducible to any simplistic slogan.

FREE SPEECH AS
A REINFORCER OF THE STATUS QUO

Radical critics correctly point out that we live in a society with a marked disparity between rich and poor, the latter being disproportionately people of color and women. They stress that expression that most shapes public opinion is not readily available to the less affluent. Decisions about what to put on the editorial page of the *New York Times* or what television shows to broadcast are made by rich, predominantly white males and reflect, so radical critics claim, the class, gender, and racial biases of these decisionmakers. But especially when it comes to entertainment such as television shows and movies, it is not obvious that the viewpoints reflected are primarily those of the industry executives rather than those of the audience, or at least what the executives perceive the audience's perspective to be.

Media Perpetuation of Racial and Gender Stereotypes

Whatever the source, there can be little doubt that television and films contain racial and gender stereotypes. Indeed, one Hollywood gender stereotype is so prevalent that the screenwriters and producers have a name for it: the "damsel in distress," a comely but not too competent young woman who constantly needs to be rescued by a confident but emotionally blocked male (as in *Romancing the Stone* and *Crocodile Dundee*).⁴ The most reliable sources of gender stereotypes, however, are television commercials, which almost invariably show Mom doing the laundry, cleaning the toilets, and feeding the kids while Dad is at work earning a living. One of the worst offenders in this regard several years ago was a commercial for Tide laundry detergent featuring a little boy playing in the mud who explained that just as his father went to the office, it was his job to play in the mud. This explanation was followed by a voice-over proclaiming, "But moms don't like dirty clothes." There you have it—the natural order of things according to the most powerful medium in contemporary society: Little boys play in the mud, dads go the office, and moms do the laundry. This image of the "proper" role of women is constantly being reinforced by slogans such as "Kix—Kid Tested, Mother Approved" and the cough medicine commercials featuring "Dr. Mom." And then there are the commercials that show the prescribed path for females to become Mom, such as the MasterCard commercial in which a young woman offered an important job in another city reacts with tears of joy when her boyfriend gives her an engagement ring with a note saying, "Please stay."⁵

Richard Delgado and Jean Stefancic have documented how throughout American history popular works have persistently contained false and demeaning stereotypes of racial minorities. Before the Civil War, blacks were portrayed as "inept urban dandies or happy childlike slaves"; after emancipation the "good slave" image continued in the form of "mammies," "uncles," and "Sambos" but was joined by an "ominous shadow figure"—a hypersexual black male who preyed on chaste white women. Both images are grotesquely displayed in D. W. Griffith's 1915 film *The Birth of a Nation*. Echoing the early stereotype of the happy-go-lucky slave, popular culture in the 1920s began to depict blacks as "musically talented, rhythmical, passionate, and entertaining." Beginning with the civil rights movement, the image of blacks in the media once again changed, at least superficially: "the unreasonable, opportunistic community leader and militant; the safe, comforting, cardigan-wearing ('nice') Black of TV sitcoms; and the Black Bomber of superstud films, all mutations of, and permutations of, old familiar forms." Other minority groups have been persistently stereotyped as well: the savage, grunting Indian or more recently the noble savage, still inarticulate but with his goodness exaggerated; the sly, inscrutable, villainous Asian; the greasy, conniving, treacherous Latino.⁶

At least with respect to images of African Americans, I am not sure that the picture is quite as monochromatic as Delgado and Stefancic paint it. The 1990s saw movies in which black actors not only did not play stereotypical roles but in which race played no part in the story line. Morgan Freeman's cowboy in *The Unforgiven* and Denzel Washington's roles in *Crimson Tide, Much Ado About Nothing*, and *Fallen* are examples of this effort to get beyond race. Similarly, in *Star Trek: The Next Generation*, the skin color of the characters played by Whoopi Goldberg and Lavar Burton is mostly irrelevant, as it is in the case of Captain Sisko played by Avery Brooks in *Deep Space Nine*. (The thought here, I suppose, is that the racial differences among humans that seemed so important in the twentieth century have become trivial compared to the differences between humans and the other life forms we encounter in intergalactic explorations.) And although *The Cosby Show* sometimes confronted racial issues, the series was refreshingly free of stereotypes.

Despite this recent progress, I agree with Delgado and Stefancic that false and demeaning racial stereotypes still pervade popular culture. One need look no further than the mascots of several professional sports teams (is there really still a team called the "Redskins"? Why not the "Darkies" or the "Japs"?) or the names of major food brands that nostalgically recall the good ol' days of slavery (Aunt Jemima and Uncle Ben) to realize that we still have a way to go.

Although there has been definite (albeit not nearly adequate) improvement with regard to the images of racial and ethnic minorities in popular culture since the 1930s, the same is not true with the images of women. Indeed, at least so far as film is concerned, it may well be that images of women have regressed. Compare the strong female characters Katharine Hepburn portrayed in the 1930s to the parts Julia Roberts played in the 1990s. True, women are sometimes depicted as successful professionals and executives. But even in these roles they are often shown as unhappy and longing for true fulfillment as wives and mothers.

And even when films do not stereotype women and minorities, these groups are often marginalized. When in *Mississippi Burning* Hollywood finally gets around to producing a movie about the civil rights movement and the violence civil rights workers faced, the story is told from the perspective of two white FBI agents, with black characters in subordinate roles. Similarly, *Disclosure*, the first major motion picture that deals with a long-standing and long-ignored impediment to women's social equality—sexual harassment in the workplace—involves the anomalous situation of a woman who harasses a man.

Thus it is hard to disagree with those radical critics who maintain that much of the speech protected by the First Amendment reflects and subtly reinforces the racism and sexism still prevalent in our society. But although it is accurate to characterize this *speech* as reinforcing the status quo and to observe that such expression is indeed protected by the First Amendment, it is unfair to blame free speech *doctrine* for this problem. No system of free expression compatible with a democracy could possibly permit the pervasive government regulation needed to extirpate offensive stereotypes depicted in popular culture. On a more fundamental level, any attempt to prevent the media from reflecting majoritarian values and prejudices would, as a practical matter, be doomed to failure even in the absence of constitutional constraints. In a democracy the views and values of those assigned the task of regulating the media will to some significant extent share majoritarian values, and thus even if the content of television programs, films, and books were pervasively controlled, the regulations would promote the status quo. (Even in authoritarian regimes, which can to a much larger extent ignore popular sentiments, the views expressed in state-controlled media will over time tend to become consonant with majoritarian views if government propaganda has been at all effective.) There is little that constitutional law in a democratic state can do, then, to keep popular culture from mirroring popular sentiments.

Neither Delgado, Matsuda, nor MacKinnon (nor to my knowledge any other proponent of hate speech or pornography regulation) recommends that free speech doctrine be revised to permit government to censor racially stereotypical images in films, television, or novels. Rather, like most of those who want to prohibit hate speech, they want to ban only the most vicious forms of racist propaganda, such as the material circulated by the Ku Klux Klan or the American Nazi Party. Indeed, Delgado would not even go this far, apparently content with a doctrine that would permit tort recovery for direct personal insults and the regulation of similar speech on campus.[7] Similarly, MacKinnon does not argue that the First Amendment should allow the extirpation of traditional images of women from popular culture but rather that *sexually explicit* expression that is also demeaning to women should find no First Amendment shelter. But surely Delgado and Matsuda realize that the images of Indians on Saturday morning television and the stereotypes of African Americans in films influence the way white Americans see minorities far more than does vicious hate propaganda distributed by fringe groups. Similarly, MacKinnon must know that gender relations most often portrayed in popular culture—in everything from Disney features such as *The Little Mermaid* and *The Lion King* to the Doris Day and Rock Hudson movies of the 1950s to the current box office fare that updates the Cinderella theme for adults—have at least as profound a socializing effect on gender roles as does pornography.[8]

Why, then, do radical critics limit their arguments for government control to doctrine that would recognize restraints on hate speech and pornography? Perhaps the answer is that they recognize that there is no chance that the First Amendment would ever be interpreted to allow such restrictions, so they may as well work for what is at least possible. But I also suspect that they know that even if the First Amendment were no obstacle, Congress would never pass a law setting up such a system of censorship. If they are correct that racism and sexism is ubiquitous in popular culture, then it is unlikely that the political culture would produce legislation eradicating these stereotypical images from mass media. Thus the failure of the radical critics to propose a truly radical solution to the problem of racist and sexist images in the media is a tacit admission that the problem of perpetuation of traditional stereotypes cannot be laid primarily at the First Amendment's door.

Consequently, the radicals' emphasis on the omnipresence of gender and racial stereotyping in the mass media does not directly support their call for revising free speech doctrine to allow hate speech and pornography regulation. Indeed, the existence of expression that would seem to have a much more powerful influence on gender and race relations undercuts the argument that banning hate speech and pornography would significantly improve these relationships. The power of television, films, and popular novels to reinforce false and demeaning images of minorities and women does, however, stand as a rejoinder to those who blithely assert that free speech is always an ally of traditionally oppressed groups.

Unequal Access to Influential Media

Although the existence of stereotypes in mass media and the resulting perpetuation of gender and racial inequality cannot be blamed primarily on free speech *doctrine*, free speech case law has had some role in making the marketplace of ideas less accessible to those of limited wealth and influence. One area in which doctrine is directly responsible for perpetuating the interests of the rich and powerful is campaign financing. In 1976 the Supreme Court, in *Buckley v. Valeo*, reviewed the constitutionality of the Federal Election Campaign Act of 1974, a law passed in the wake of the Watergate scandal.[9] Although upholding restrictions on direct contributions to political candidates, the Court invalidated on First Amendment grounds provisions of the law that limited expenditures that individuals and organizations, including corporations, could make on behalf of candidates or with regard to political issues. The Court stated that "the concept that government may restrict the speech of some elements of our society in order to enhance the relative voice of others is wholly foreign to the First Amendment."

Buckley has been defended on the grounds that despite the good intentions of the expenditure limitations, giving the government such extensive control over political expression will ultimately disserve rather than enhance democratic values.[10] But whatever the ultimate merits of the decision measured in terms of underlying free speech values, the Court's invalidation of the expenditure provision on First Amendment grounds has meant that money remains crucial in electoral politics and hence well-heeled individuals continue to influence the results of these elections. A particularly ironic example of how recent free speech doctrine can abet wealthy interests is decisions that make it possible for monied corporations to control the initiative and referendum process, devices originally introduced to circumvent the stranglehold that these interests had on state legislatures.[11] As one radical critic has written:

> The first amendment has replaced the due process clause as the primary guarantor of the privileged. . . . [S]ince the demise of substantive due process, [a doctrine by which the Court in the early part of this century invalidated progressive business regulations,] their investments in factories and stocks can be regulated by legislatures. Under *Buckley v. Valeo* and [its progeny], however, their investments in politics—or politicians—cannot be regulated significantly. Needless to say, careful investment in politics may prevent effective regulation of traditional investments.[12]

Notwithstanding the contrary dicta in *Buckley*, there are in fact cases in which the Court has allowed government to regulate speech in order "to enhance the relative voice" of those who do not have the means to buy access to the marketplace of ideas. For instance, *Red Lion Broadcasting v. FCC* upheld the fairness doctrine, which required broadcasters to seek out issues of public concern and present them in a balanced fashion, as well as to offer a right of reply to anyone attacked on the air.[13] More generally, current doctrine provides government wide latitude to subsidize speech that for economic or other reasons has not had a fair opportunity to compete in the marketplace of ideas. There thus is no First Amendment obstacle to government programs that favor minority groups in the award of broadcast licenses. Indeed, in rejecting an Equal Protection Clause challenge to such a minority preference program, the Court found that "the diversity of views and information" promoted by this program serves important First Amendment values.[14] Despite the leeway that current doctrine provides government to remedy inequalities in the marketplace of ideas, however, neither Congress nor state legislators have aggressively subsidized those who wish to compete in the marketplace of ideas but do not have the means to do so. As is the case with the perpetuation of racial and gender stereotypes, then, it is not free speech doctrine that is primarily to blame for this continued inequality.

Some have argued that the problem of inequality of access to the influential media will be solved not so much by government regulation but by new technology. The development of coaxial cable greatly expanded the number of available television channels, including public access channels. More significant, the Internet has made it possible for ordinary people to reach a huge audience at very little cost. Nonetheless, the wealthy continue to have an enormous advantage in the marketplace of ideas. At least for now, commercial television, talk radio, movies, and books are still far more powerful than public access stations and Web sites.

Doctrine's Favoring Recognized Rights over Potentially New and Competing Ones

Other ways in which free speech doctrine privileges the status quo are more subtle. Some of the most bitter political battles in American history have been fought over which of two competing and mutually exclusive rights the law should recognize: the property rights of slave owners or the human rights of the slaves; the right of owners of public accommodations and housing to practice racial discrimination or the civil rights of African Americans; a fetus's right to life or women's right to procreative choice. Like an incumbent in a political campaign, the right recognized at any given time will often have an advantage over the interest that seeks to supplant it. This advantage will often be reflected in free speech doctrine, which is, after all, part of the larger legal order.

For example, courts have uniformly rebuffed First Amendment challenges to the Freedom of Access to Clinic Entrance (FACE), a federal law making it a crime physically to obstruct access to abortion clinics.[15] FACE has a decidedly disproportionate impact on this ideological dispute. An antiabortion activist who blocks the path of a woman seeking an abortion is subject to federal criminal penalties under FACE, but a clinic employee who assaults an antiabortion demonstrator is not. Similarly, acts of nonviolent civil disobedience routinely engaged in by the antiabortion movement—sit-ins and blockades at abortion clinics—are the prime objects of FACE; in contrast, similar civil disobedience likely to be engaged in by abortion rights advocates (e.g., a sit-in at a legislator's office) is not covered by this law. Nonetheless, the courts have not viewed this law as an illegitimate attempt by Congress to favor one side in an ideological battle. Rather, they have accepted at face value (so to speak) the argument that the law's purpose is protection of a legal right—the right to obtain abortion services.

Although not often noted, property rights also play an important role in free speech doctrine.[16] The line between public and private property is often also the line between highly protected public discourse (e.g., speech in a public park) and simple trespass speech (e.g., a protestor leafleting at a large but privately owned shopping mall).[17] As we shall see later in the chapter, had it not been for some enormously creative maneuvering by a Supreme Court sympathetic to the goals of the civil rights movement, property rights would have stripped civil rights sit-ins of any constitutional protection.

Equality as Orthodoxy

There is one particularly significant instance in which free speech doctrine's reflection of the status quo actually serves to promote equality. Radicals like to characterize those who carry the message of equality as outsiders or dissidents and bigoted speech as the "dominant narrative."[18] This is an outdated vision: Today blatantly racist expression is the dissident speech, whereas the idea that racial discrimination is wrong, the belief that no one racial or ethnic group is inherently superior to another, and the commitment to equal opportunity regardless of race or ethnicity is official orthodoxy. For anyone who doubts this, I suggest the following thought experiment: Imagine a candidate for CEO of a large public corporation who during the interview proclaims his belief in the genetic inferiority of black people. It is inconceivable that the candidate would be hired.[19]

Several high-profile incidents in professional sports prove this point. In the 1980s an executive with the Los Angeles Dodgers was fired for stating that blacks might not have the "necessities" to be Major League baseball managers; in the 1990s the owner of the Cincinnati Reds was suspended for using racial epithets and expressing admiration for Adolf Hitler, and a professional golfer lost a lucrative advertising contract for making racist jokes. This orthodoxy is so strong that in 1999 a city official in Washington, D.C., was fired (but then rehired) for using the nonracist word "niggardly."[20] And in a constitutionally dubious decision a panel that evaluates the character of state bar applicants found that an applicant's racist beliefs made him unfit to practice law.[21]

Showing just how socially unacceptable blatant racism has become, Ralph Reed, as leader of the conservative religious group the Christian Coalition, acknowledged that white churches' opposition to integration in the South during the 1960s was morally wrong. Further evidence of the new orthodoxy is that in conducting background checks of potential presidential appointees the FBI now routinely asks whether the person being investigated has ever made degrading statements based on race or ethnicity. And although the military does not generally try to regulate the private political activities of its members, it does forbid active membership in racist organizations.[22]

Admittedly, as R.A.V., recent affirmative action cases, and the blithe quotation of Martin Luther King Jr. by affirmative action opponents reveal, the idea of equality that has become orthodox is both narrow and formal, perhaps even superficial. When it comes to deeper, more subtle issues—such as the solution to the continued racial disparity in wealth and education or the causes of the distrust that often pervades relations among ethnic groups in this country—there is no consensus, let alone orthodoxy. And the racial stereotypes that continue to dominate the mass media, together with the absence of interracial couples on television commercials or game shows like the *Dating Game* or the *Love Connection*, suggest that deep in their hearts many white Americans still do not believe that blacks are really their equals. Nor, of course, do I mean to suggest that virulent racism has completely disappeared from the American landscape. Detective Mark Furhman's shameless account of his racially inspired brutality and the horrendous dragging death of James Byrd Jr. in Jasper, Texas, are examples that show that this scourge persists.

When it comes to gender equality, the new orthodoxy is even narrower. For instance, although there is now an overwhelmingly strong social consensus that it is wrong to bar women from entry into most occupations, many people still publicly proclaim that women are not fit for certain tasks (e.g., as combat pilots), a comment that few would make openly about members of racial or ethnic groups. Moreover, although current orthodoxy holds that women should generally have a *right* to equal opportunity in the workplace, there is no consensus that women should exercise this right rather than dedicate themselves primarily to raising a family. Indeed, there does not even seem to be a consensus that women are as "naturally suited" to be business leaders as men.[23] And the feminist critique that gender relations continue to be marked by patriarchy and oppression of women has not achieved orthodoxy, except, perhaps, on some college campuses.

The current orthodoxy about race and the dominant narrative about gender afford these ideas privileges of the status quo, including those bestowed by free speech doctrine. Eradicating racial discrimination is considered a "compelling state interest." And because racism is now seen as destructive of community order, the Supreme Court views laws enhancing the penalty for bias-motivated crimes as legitimate remedies for the disruption to the community caused by racist acts rather than illegitimate attempts to punish ideology.[24] Constitutional law thus has come a long way from the Court's view in *Plessy v. Ferguson* that attempting to achieve a color-blind society amounts to unconstitutional meddling with the natural order of things.[25] Similarly, the basic antidiscrimination principle embodied in civil rights legislation outlawing racial and gender discrimination has become so ingrained in the fabric of American society that in two recent cases it was taken for granted that Title VII was constitutional despite its selective impact on bigoted speech and ideology.[26] Indeed, in one case the Court goes out of its way to draw a protective circle around Title VII.[27]

That the ideal of racial and gender equality has become official American policy also belies the "market failure" theory for the suppression of hate speech. According to this theory, because the influential media are controlled by white males, the message of racial and gender equality is not adequately represented in public discourse.[28] To level the playing field, some have argued, expression that undermines racial and gender equality, such as hate speech and pornography, should be banned from public discourse. It may well be that the more radical views about race and gender are underrepresented in the marketplace of ideas in part because of white male dominance over the most influential media. But it cannot be seriously argued that the basic idea of racial and gender equality is not well represented in the public discourse. Even with respect to the broader concept of equality that has by no means become orthodoxy, the concept of a market failure is hard to sustain. The idea that the legacy of racism in this country accounts for the continued disparity in wealth and positions of power between whites and blacks and that therefore compensatory remedies are both morally justifiable and pragmatically necessary has been widely expressed. Similarly, radical perspectives have long been part of the discourse on racial issues: The separationist, "black power" views of Eldridge Cleaver and H. "Rap" Brown served as a countervoice to the liberal, integrationist message of Martin Luther King Jr.; since then, Louis Farrakhan and Leonard Jeffries have presented alternatives to the mainstream integrationist view.[29] And the radical feminist perspective, including the ideas of Catharine MacKinnon and Andrea Dworkin extensively discussed in this book, is no stranger to public discourse.

In any event, as discussed in more detail in Chapter 10, a "market failure" in the marketplace of ideas might justify the government's *subsidizing* underrepresented groups or views or even supplying the missing perspective in its own voice. It does not, however, justify *suppressing* speech. For one, speech suppression is not a logical remedy for providing an absent perspective. To the contrary, unlike subsidization or government speech, suppression threatens to drive certain perspectives from the marketplace of ideas, including views that are neither racist nor sexist but might be mistaken as such. Any call for the suppression of racist and sexist ideas as a solution to an alleged "market failure" is therefore difficult to see as a legitimate attempt to expand the scope or depth of public discourse to include an "outsider" perspective. Rather, this argument reflects the age-old propensity of the "dominant narrative" to try to silence heterodox views.

In sum, radicals are right that in some important respects free speech doctrine is a conservative institution. This doctrine is not a regime unto itself but part of a legal system functioning in a capitalistic society in which the wealthy have an enormous advantage in everything from housing to education, from medical care to legal services. Current doctrine thus both reflects and reinforces the status quo, including an economic system and power structure in which women and minorities remain underrepresented. To the extent that free speech doctrine merely mirrors deeper inequalities resulting from capitalism or popular prejudice, there is only a limited amount that free speech doctrine can do to rectify this situation. But where inequality is perpetuated by decisions such as *Buckley* and its progeny, which are arguably in tension with deeper democratic values, doctrine can fairly be blamed.

Free Speech as
an Antagonist of the Status Quo

At the same time that it reflects and sometimes promotes the status quo, free speech doctrine rigorously protects speech that challenges the current social order. Indeed, modern free speech doctrine is forged largely from the dissenting opinions of justices who vainly argued that radicals who harshly denounce capitalistic institutions and urge their overthrow should be allowed to have their say. Radical critics, in their fairer moments, do not deny that this is the origin of modern doctrine. They do, however, deny its efficacy as a remedy to systemic social oppression. For instance, according to Delgado and Stefancic:

> Our much-vaunted system of free expression, with its marketplace of ideas, cannot correct serious systemic ills such as racism and sexism simply because we do not see them as such at the time. No one can formulate an effective contemporaneous message to challenge the vicious depiction; this happens only much later, after consciousness shifts and society adopts a different narrative.[30]

These authors therefore reject the "prime tenet of liberal jurisprudence that by talk, dialogue, exhortation, and so on" we are able to "advance society to greater levels of fairness and humanity."[31]

Delgado and Stefancic's argument is self-contradictory. They recognize that over time "consciousness shifts and society adopts a different narrative." But how do they suppose that "consciousness shifts" if not by "talk, dialogue, exhortation, and so on"?

Free Speech and the Abolition Movement

Delgado and Stefancic give the game away when they note that Harriet Beecher Stowe's antislavery novel *Uncle Tom's Cabin* "sold well only after years of abolitionist sentiment and agitation had sensitized her public to the possibility that slavery was wrong."[32] But another name for this "abolitionist sentiment and agitation," as well as Stowe's literary efforts, is "speech"; and as Delgado and Stefancic concede, it was this speech that ultimately persuaded people that slavery was wrong. It is true that deep-seated social norms are difficult to change because they are often seen as an uncontestable part of the natural order of things. Thus public criticism of oppressive but long-standing practices and institutions is rarely effective overnight; such critique usually only triggers the process by which people begin to see things differently. This was certainly true of abolitionist speech.

In part because of their failure to appreciate the enormity of slavery, certainly because of the lack of empathy for blacks, but perhaps primarily because of fear that this speech would alienate the South and thus threaten the Union, northerners at first widely opposed the abolitionist message.[33] Thus the campaign of the 1830s to mail southerners antislavery literature condemning slaveholders as cruel sinners and urging their redemption was opposed by mass antiabolitionist meetings throughout the North and condemned by the northern press as the work of "fanatics" and "incendiaries."[34] Governor George Wolf of Pennsylvania proclaimed that the "crusade against slavery is the offspring of fanaticism of the most dangerous and alarming character; which if not speedily checked may kindle a fire which it may require the best blood of the country to quench."

Nonetheless, the North, relying on the American tradition of freedom of speech, uniformly rejected the southern call to suppress such speech because of its tendency to incite slave rebellions. Even as ardent an antiabolitionist as Governor Wolf realized that "freedom of speech and of the press . . . is the safeguard to free discussion, and the best expositor of public opinion" and thus must not be "infringed upon or controlled by enactments intended to remedy some temporary mischief," even one that threatened the very existence of the Union. Similarly, the U.S. Congress, out of a combination of First Amendment and federalism concerns, refused to outlaw the mailing of abolitionist literature to the South.

A generation later the abolitionists' message that at first fell upon deaf or hostile ears had become orthodoxy in the North. In part because of speech—and the legal traditions that protected it—consciousness shifted so that a once hated sentiment became the moral justification for the North's position in resisting secession. That it took time for abolitionist ideas to replace the dominant ideology does not belie the "prime tenet of liberal jurisprudence" that legally unrestrained public discourse helps "advance society to greater fairness and humanity." For it has never been a tenet of free speech that unrestrained public discourse will *quickly* lead to social progress or even that it will in every instance lead directly to enlightened social policy. Rather, the claim is that, on the whole and over time, unfettered public discussion will lead to a fairer and more just society than will government control over the content of public discourse.

Delgado and Stefancic recognize that what at first seem to be fanatical and dangerous ideas may in retrospect be considered undeniable claims for simple justice. This awareness supports rather than undercuts modern doctrine's insistence on protecting "the thought that we hate."[35] They are correct that social criticism that clashes with the "dominant narrative" will usually not be immediately influential. Indeed, the odds may be long that any idea that challenges "dominant narrative" will ever be generally accepted. But if these "still small voices" are silenced, the chances that new ideas will eventually shift our consciousness will be even further diminished, if not completely extinguished. It is worth noting that only in countries with no tradition of free speech do practices such as torture, slavery, genocide, ritualistic female genital mutilation, lack of rudimentary criminal due process, and legally sanctioned oppression of women continue to flourish as part of the "dominant narrative."

Free Speech Doctrine and the Civil Rights Movement

As part of the claim that free speech doctrine works against the interests of minorities, radical critics dispute the conventional wisdom that the First Amendment was an ally to blacks in their struggle for civil rights during the 1960s. For instance, Delgado and Stefancic write:

> [F]ar from being stalwart friends, [speech and free expression] can impede the cause of racial reform. . . . [W]hen insurgent groups attempt to use speech as an instrument of reform, *courts almost invariably construe the First Amendment against them*. [Thus] civil rights activists in the sixties made the greatest strides when they acted in defiance of the First Amendment as then understood.[36]

It is true that during the first half of this century courts often ruled against "insurgent groups" (particularly leftist ones) who tried to use speech as "an instrument of reform." But Delgado and Stefancic's claim that the courts also "almost invariably" ruled against the free speech claims of civil rights activists of the 1960s is simply wrong. To the contrary, the Supreme Court "almost invariably" ruled *in favor* of the First Amendment claims made by civil rights activists, even when preexisting doctrine seemed to require finding against them.

The civil rights cases fall into three categories: (1) those involving protests, sit-ins, and mass demonstrations; (2) those involving "pure speech"; and (3) those involving attempts by southern states to impair civil rights organizations such as the NAACP.[37] Some of these cases are landmark decisions in which the Court, consciously correcting defects in prior jurisprudence, announced new principles calculated to protect not just the speakers in the cases at hand but future "insurgent groups" who brashly challenge the status quo. Other cases, however, are ad hoc decisions seemingly driven by sympathy for the civil rights movement and antipathy toward the ugly tactics of the southern states.

Protection of Civil Rights Protestors. Before the civil rights era, free speech doctrine invested law enforcement officials with broad discretion to order speakers to stop or protestors to disperse in order to prevent a breach of the peace. For instance, in 1951 the Court in *Feiner v. New York* upheld the conviction of a young leftist who refused to stop a street-corner tirade when ordered to do so by a policeman.[38] The police officer had been told by an offended listener, "If you don't get that son of a bitch off, I will go over there and get him off there myself." Aside from this comment, the only other evidence that a fight was imminent was "some pushing, shoving and milling around" in a crowd of about seventy-five to eighty persons. Twelve years later, in *Edwards v. South Carolina,* a group of black students assembled near the grounds of the South Carolina statehouse to protest racial discrimination.[39] A crowd of about 300 onlookers gathered nearby. Law enforcement officials claimed that they spotted "potential trouble makers" in this crowd and ordered the demonstrators to disperse within fifteen minutes in order to prevent a fight. The demonstrators disobeyed this order and were arrested and convicted for breach of the peace. This time, however, the Supreme Court did not allow the "heckler's veto" to stand and reversed the convictions. Shortly thereafter, the Supreme Court similarly came to the rescue of civil rights demonstrators who failed to obey an order to disperse.

In *Cox v. Louisiana,* Reverend B. Elton Cox, a field secretary of the Congress of Racial Equality (CORE), led about 2,000 students in a demonstration near a Louisiana courthouse to protest the arrest of students for picketing stores that maintained segregated lunch counters.[40] About 100 to 300 whites gathered on the side of the street opposite from where the protestors stood. Approximately seventy-five police officers were stationed on the street between the two groups. Cox gave a speech in which he condemned the arrest of the jailed students and urged the demonstrators to sit-in at segregated lunch counters. Cox's speech elicited some "muttering" and "grumbling" from the white onlookers. The sheriff found Cox's speech to be inflammatory and ordered the demonstration "broken up immediately." When the demonstrators failed to disperse voluntarily, the police fired tear gas shells to break up the demonstration.

Cox was arrested and convicted for breach of the peace and picketing near a courthouse.

The Supreme Court reversed the convictions. Making an "independent review of the record," which included viewing a film of the protest, the Court found that the evidence did not support Louisiana's conclusion that the assembly had become "riotous": "The students themselves were not violent and threatened no violence. . . . There is no indication that any member of the white group threatened violence. . . . And the policemen . . . could have handled the crowd." As to the conviction for picketing near a courthouse, the Court held that although the Louisiana statute that banned picketing near courthouses was facially valid, it could not constitutionally be applied to the demonstrators in this case. By initially allowing the protestors to demonstrate across the street from the courthouse, law enforcement officials had in the Court's view "[i]n effect" advised Cox that the demonstration was not "near" a courthouse within the terms of the statute, and thus the subsequent conviction was "an indefensible sort of entrapment" in violation of due process of law.

Toward the end of the civil rights era, the movement turned toward desegregating various northern institutions. In a 1969 case, *Gregory v. Chicago,* comedian Dick Gregory led a march from city hall to the mayor's residence to protest segregation in city schools.[41] When the "number of bystanders increased" and the "onlookers became unruly," the police ordered the demonstrators to disperse in order to prevent what they believed was "impending civil disorder." The demonstrators refused to disband and were arrested for disorderly conduct. The Court reversed, but on narrow grounds: As the Court read the record, the protestors had been convicted for the *demonstration,* not for a refusal to obey a police officer's dispersal order under conditions in which violence from an opposing group was imminent.

As in *Cox,* the Court in *Gregory* reversed the conviction on a technicality, thereby avoiding a harder, more general free speech question, which if the Court had to reach might very well have gone against the civil rights activists. Such reliance on technicalities became a familiar practice during the civil rights era. For instance, in *Street v. New York,* the Court reversed the conviction of a black man for burning a U.S. flag in protest of the shooting of civil rights leader James Meredith.[42] *Street* was decided in 1969, twenty years before the Court was prepared to afford First Amendment protection to flag burning as a form of political protest. Indeed, if it had been forced to decide the issue in 1969, it is likely that the Court would have found no First Amendment right to flag burning.[43] Nonetheless, the Court reversed the conviction on the ground that the formal charge contained *words* that the protestor had *spoken* as he burned the flag, creating "the possibility" that these words played some role in his conviction.

It is difficult to tell to what extent the ad hoc holdings in *Cox, Gregory,* and *Street* or *Edward's* inconsistency with *Feiner* were driven by sympathy for the civil rights movement as opposed to principled free speech concerns. There are, however, several decisions reversing the convictions of civil rights activists that are difficult to explain other than as driven primarily by sympathy for the civil rights cause.

The civil rights strategy to end segregation included civil disobedience, in particular sit-ins at segregated lunch counters and other places that excluded or discriminated against blacks. By the late 1950s, a series of Supreme Court decisions had made clear that *state*-imposed racial segregation violated the Equal Protection Clause of the Fourteenth Amendment. But because the Fourteenth Amendment applies only to government action, federal legislation was required to put an end to racial discrimination in privately owned places of public accommodation. Consequently, until the passage of the Civil Rights Act of 1964, blacks in many states could legally be refused service at restaurants, segregated at movie theaters, and otherwise discriminated against in privately owned establishments open to the public. Civil rights activists who continued to sit-in at segregated lunch counters after being told to leave by the proprietors were thus violating state trespass law, or so it would seem. Indeed, by definition civil disobedience involves law violation. It is therefore truly remarkable that in every one of the seventeen sit-in cases that reached the Supreme Court from 1961 to 1964, the Court found some defect with the conviction.

Some of the reversals, though technical, identified real legal flaws. For instance, in the first sit-in case, *Garner v. Louisiana,* the state charged the protestors with breach of the peace instead of criminal trespass.[44] The Supreme Court reversed the convictions, finding no evidence in the record that peaceful sitting-in at the lunch counters carried with it the likelihood of imminent violence or otherwise constituted a breach of the peace as defined by state law. And in *Peterson v. Greenville* the Court found that the exclusion of blacks from the lunch counter was mandated by a city ordinance and thus was a result of unconstitutional state action.[45]

In other cases, however, the Court obviously stretched to reverse the convictions. In *Griffin v. Maryland,* for instance, the Court found impermissible state involvement with the discriminatory conduct because the security guard who enforced a policy of racial segregation at a privately owned amusement park had been deputized by the county sheriff.[46] But as the dissenting justices pointed out, the state's role in this instance "is no different from what it would have been had the arrests [for criminal trespass] been made by a regular policeman dispatched from police headquarters," a situation that plainly would not have been a matter of unconstitutional state involvement with the private discriminatory conduct. Similarly strained is the Court's reasoning in *Bouie v. City of Columbia*.[47] Relying on the wording of the South Carolina trespass statute that prohibits "entry . . . after notice from the owner prohibiting such entry," the Court held that this statute could not be constitutionally applied to protestors who legally entered a department store in which blacks were welcome but then sat down and *refused to leave* a lunch counter from which blacks were excluded. Although the South Carolina Supreme Court had, in affirming the convictions, construed the statute to cover remaining on property after being requested to leave, the U.S. Supreme Court held that at the time of the sit-in the protestors would not have had notice that their acts came within the purview of the trespass statute.

Aligned against the host of cases reversing the convictions of civil rights protestors on constitutional grounds are a few that affirmed convictions. One such case, *Adderley v. Florida*, upheld the conviction of demonstrators for trespassing on the premises of a county jail.[48] Another is *Walker v. Birmingham*, in which the Court held 5–4 that demonstrators who defied an injunction prohibiting them from marching could not subsequently defend against a contempt charge by asserting that the injunction was unconstitutional.[49] The Court explained that the protestors should have challenged the validity of the injunction in a higher court rather than disobeying it. (But in *Shuttlesworth v. Birmingham* the Court reversed a conviction of demonstrators in the same march prosecuted for violation of an unconstitutional *ordinance*.)[50]

Review of the civil rights protest cases thus readily belies the allegation that courts "almost invariably construe[d] the First Amendment" against civil rights protestors. There is, however, a purely technical sense in which the claim that the First Amendment was not particularly helpful to civil rights protestors is correct: In many cases it was not actually the First Amendment but other constitutional norms—such as due process (e.g., *Cox* and *Bouie*) and the prohibition against state involvement in racially discriminatory conduct (e.g., *Peterson* and *Griffin*)—that protected the civil rights activists. The Court seemed particularly unwilling to construe the First Amendment as protecting trespass on private property (even when the trespass took the form of social protest) or as protecting mass demonstrations near courthouses that might interfere with the orderly administration of justice.[51] Instead, the Court frequently used the much more malleable concepts of due process and state action to overturn convictions of civil rights activists. We should not, however, lose sight of the First Amendment's crucial role in many civil rights demonstration cases, such as the limitations on the state's ability to convict demonstrators for breach of the peace.

Protection of the Mass Media.   In dismissing the importance of the First Amendment to civil rights activists, Delgado and Stefancic join other radical critics in maintaining that the "greatest strides" toward racial justice came not from peaceful protests protected by the First Amendment but as the result of unprotected activity. (It is not clear if they mean just nonviolent civil disobedience that was the hallmark of the civil rights movement in the South or whether they include such violent episodes as the Watts riots, which many credit with alerting white America to the plight of urban blacks.) The relative role played by law violation as compared to constitutionally protected speech in accomplishing the goals of the civil rights movement is difficult to assess. Any such assessment is made more problematic by the Court's effectively conferring constitutional protection in many cases on activity such as trespass that ordinarily would not find shelter under the First Amendment. In any event, it is probable that neither protected nor unprotected protests played a large direct role in influencing the popular opinion that resulted in civil rights legislation. Rather, it was the brutal tactics of southern law enforcement officials in response to these demonstrations that caused the shift in consciousness.

More than anything, it was the images of hog-jowled police siccing snarling German shepherds on young civil rights protestors or bowling them down the street with high-powered fire hoses that won the sympathy of the American populace.[52] It was the mass media that conveyed the full story of this brutality to the American people. As the United States entered the civil rights era, First Amendment protection afforded media criticism of official conduct suffered from a crucial weakness. In dicta in a 1942 case and in an actual holding ten years later in a case involving group libel against African Americans, the Supreme Court categorically excluded libel from First Amendment protection.[53] This defect was not lost on southern authorities, who used libel laws to attempt to curb protest against their oppression of blacks.

In 1960 an Alabama jury returned a $500,000 libel judgment against the *New York Times* and several black clergymen for a fund-raising advertisement decrying "an unprecedented wave of terror" against blacks engaged in nonviolent demonstrations in the South. L. B. Sullivan, the Montgomery police commissioner, sued the *Times* and the clergymen for certain minor inaccuracies in the advertisement. As discussed in Chapter 2, the Court used this opportunity to remedy the inadequate protection of public discourse provided by free speech doctrine. In the landmark case of *New York Times v. Sullivan*,[54] the Court held that false statements about the official conduct of a government official could not form the basis of a libel suit unless the public official could prove that the statements were made with knowledge of their falsity or with reckless disregard for the truth.

Like many radical critics, Robin Barnes characterizes as a "myth" the assertion that "public protest rights played a pivotal role in securing civil rights for black America." Unlike Delgado and Stefancic, however, Barnes acknowledges the importance of other aspects of free speech doctrine to the civil rights movement:

> It was, in fact, the protection guaranteed to the press which had a crucial impact upon the efforts toward constructive engagement, that led to significant changes for Blacks and other Americans. News reports, stinging editorial columns, and paid advertisements that doubled as fundraising mechanisms, similar to that featured in *New York Times v. Sullivan,* had a far more discernable impact upon the life of the Civil Rights Movement [than did demonstrations].[55]

Like the protest cases, the impetus for the result in *Sullivan* may have been sympathy for the goals of the civil rights movement, as well as abhorrence of the tactics of southern officials. But unlike many of the protest cases, the Court in *Sullivan* announced a general principle calculated to protect all critics of government.[56] And even if, as some radicals claim, the true impetus for this case was the protection of powerful commercial interests in the form of media giants such as the *New York Times* (a dubious proposition, given the long prior existence of powerful publishing empires with no such protection), there can be no doubt that this decision came at just the right time to aid the civil rights movement in its attempt to influence public opinion.[57]

Protection of the NAACP.   As useful as *New York Times v. Sullivan* was to the civil rights movement, a series of lesser-known cases was even more helpful. Soon after the Supreme Court held segregation in public school unconstitutional in *Brown v. Board of Education,* southern states declared war on the civil rights organization that had brought that case on behalf of the black schoolchildren. Organized in 1909 "to promote equality of rights and eradicate caste or race prejudice," the NAACP quickly followed up on its victory in *Brown* with litigation enforcing that decision and new lawsuits attacking segregation in other public institutions.[58] The southern attack on the NAACP took two main forms: legislation that directly disadvantaged the organization or its members and attempts to injure the NAACP indirectly by requiring the organization to identify its members. As the authors of this repressive legislation were well aware, First Amendment protection of political advocacy groups was at that time wholly inadequate. This sad state of affairs was a result of the extreme deference the Court paid to legislative attempts to cripple the Communist Party. Nevertheless, the courts would totally frustrate the efforts of southern states to hamper the NAACP.

An example of a direct attack on the NAACP was an Arkansas law that barred any member of the NAACP from public employment. The law was justified on the ground that because the NAACP had created racial strife in the state and had stirred up "dissatisfaction and unrest among Negroes," membership in that organization was incompatible with the legitimate goals of the state. To underscore the connection with anticommunist laws that the Supreme Court had previously upheld, the preamble to the Arkansas law contained a finding that the NAACP "is a captive of the international communist conspiracy." In *Shelton v. McKinley*, a federal district court invalidated the law, and the state chose not to appeal.[59] That the state would so easily throw in the towel might at first seem surprising given that the Supreme Court had held only a year earlier that members of the Communist Party could be denied public employment.[60] But previous cases had also shown that the Court would steadfastly protect the NAACP (and indirectly its own decision in *Brown*) from the ire of southern legislatures, even when the attack on the civil rights organization was far less direct than those against the Communist Party that the Court had previously sustained. But before turning to these cases, I should mention one more case involving a direct attack on the NAACP.

Rules governing the legal profession traditionally prohibited solicitation of legal business. Prior to *Brown*, Virginia, like most states, did not apply this rule to legal organizations such as the NAACP, which brought lawsuits not for pecuniary gain but to advance a particular social policy. In 1956, however, Virginia, as part of a package of laws passed during a special legislative session called in response to *Brown*, amended the prohibition on solicitation to include legal action groups such as the NAACP. If allowed to stand, such a restriction would have significantly hindered the NAACP, which actively sought out clients to challenge segregation and other discriminatory practices.

In *NAACP v. Button*, the Supreme Court invalidated the prohibition.[61] In an opinion by Justice Brennan, the Court explained that the First Amendment protects not just speech but "vigorous advocacy" in the courts as well: "In the context of NAACP objectives, litigation is not a technique of resolving differences; it is a means for achieving the lawful objectives of equality . . . for members of the Negro community in this country." Such litigation is thus "a form of political expression." Having identified the important First Amendment value in public interest litigation in general, the Court, in a refreshing burst of legal realism, discussed the particular impact that Alabama's law would likely have on the NAACP:

> We cannot close our eyes to the fact that the militant Negro civil rights movement has engendered the intense resentment and opposition of the politi-

cally dominant white community of Virginia; litigation assisted by the NAACP has been bitterly fought. In such circumstances a statute broadly curtailing group activity leading to litigation may easily become a weapon of oppression, however evenhanded its terms appear. Its mere existence could well freeze out of existence all such activity on behalf of the civil rights of Negro citizens.

Returning to doctrine, the Court held that only a "compelling state interest" would justify such an intrusion on First Amendment activities and concluded that traditional interests in regulating solicitation of legal business did not justify the statute's prohibition on NAACP activities.

In addition to such direct attacks on the NAACP, the southern authorities employed indirect measures in their efforts to cripple the civil rights organization. The primary tactic of this sort was to demand disclosure of the NAACP's membership list. Given the intense hostility of many white southerners toward the NAACP as a result of its successful legal battles for civil rights, and in light of the demonstrated willingness of some of these angry bigots to resort to violence to maintain segregation, release of these lists would have had grave consequences for NAACP members. As southern officials no doubt calculated, such disclosure would deter membership in the organization and decrease the dues and other contributions through which the organization financed its litigation. Indeed, there is evidence that just the demands for the membership lists, even though ultimately resisted, served to reduce both membership and contributions to the NAACP in the South.[62]

As was the case with much of free speech doctrine at the dawn of the civil rights era, the sorry state of First Amendment doctrine seemed to offer little hope for constitutional protection against the state's demand for the NAACP's membership lists. This time, however, it was not just cases lost by the communists that seemed to foreclose protection but, ironically, a 1926 decision involving the Ku Klux Klan as well. In *Bryant v. Zimmerman*, the Court had ruled against a Klan member who had challenged a New York law that called for disclosure of member rosters of any organization requiring an oath as a condition of membership.[63] Despite this precedent, the Supreme Court would rebuff every attempt by southern states to obtain names of NAACP members.

The first membership list case, *NAACP v. Alabama*, was decided in 1958.[64] The case grew out of a controversy between Alabama and the NAACP concerning whether a state law requiring out-of-state corporations to qualify to do business in the state applied to the activities of the NAACP in Alabama. (The parent organization was a New York corporation, but most of the NAACP's activities in the state were conducted by local affiliates.) Ostensibly to determine whether the affiliate's parent corporation was doing business in the state, Alabama requested a vast quantity of documents, including lists of members. In a seminal opinion recognizing a constitutional right to association, the Court held that under these circumstances Alabama's demand for the membership list violated the First Amendment. Writing for a unanimous Court, Justice Harlan recognized that "[e]ffective advocacy of both public and private points of view, particularly controversial ones, is undeniably enhanced by group association" and that therefore state action that has the effect of curtailing the freedom to associate is subject to "the closest scrutiny." The Court made clear, moreover, that this scrutiny was applicable even when the state takes "no direct action" to restrict the right to association. Rather, the key inquiry was whether abridgment of the right would "inevitably follow" from the government action.

The Court had no doubt that in these circumstances disclosure of the list would result in such an abridgment, noting that past revelation of the identity of members had "exposed these members to economic reprisals, loss of employment, threat of physical coercion, and other manifestations of public hostility." Because the requested membership list had no "substantial bearing" on the question of whether the parent corporation was doing business in Alabama, the Court found that the state's need for the list was not nearly "compelling" enough to justify the infringement of the group's First Amendment rights. *Bryant v. Zimmerman* was distinguished on the grounds that the Klan's activities involved "unlawful intimidation and violence" and that unlike the NAACP, which had turned over other information requested by the state, the Klan totally refused the state's request.[65]

The southern authorities did not meekly fold their tents after this initial defeat but continued to try to obtain disclosure of the NAACP's membership list. These attempts sparked four more Supreme Court decisions, all of which rebuffed these efforts. The schemes to force disclosure, however, become successively more sophisticated: Alabama's attempt was aimed specifically at the NAACP, whereas the statutes involved in these later cases were more generally applicable. For instance, an Arkansas law required teachers in a state-supported school or college to annually file "an affidavit listing without limitation every organization to which he has belonged or regularly contributed within the preceding five years." In *Shelton v. Tucker*, this law was challenged by a Little Rock schoolteacher and NAACP member whose contract with the school district was not renewed when he refused to file the required affidavit.[66] The Supreme Court invalidated the law on First Amendment grounds, finding that the "statute's comprehensive interference with associational freedoms goes far beyond what might be justified in the exercise of the State's legitimate inquiry into the fitness and competency of its teachers."

A 1963 decision, *Gibson v. Florida Legislative Investigation Committee,* involved the final effort by southern authorities to force the NAACP to turn over its membership list.[67] As part of a Florida legislative investigation into alleged communist infiltration of the Miami NAACP, a legislative committee ordered Theodore Gibson, the president of the NAACP's Miami branch, to turn over the entire list of members of the branch. The Florida Supreme Court refused to enforce this order but stated that the committee could require Gibson to bring the list with him to the hearing as a reference to determine if any specific person identified as a communist was also a member of the NAACP. When Gibson refused, he was held in contempt, sentenced to six months in prison, and fined $1,200.

In prior cases involving investigation of communist activities, the Court had generally upheld the power of legislative committees to compel disclosure of information. For instance, in *Barenblatt v. United States,* the Court had sustained the contempt conviction of a college instructor who would not answer questions concerning his membership in the Communist Party posed to him by a congressional committee looking into alleged Communist infiltration in higher education.[68] And in *Uphaus v. Wyman* the Supreme Court had upheld a contempt conviction against the executive director of World Fellowship for refusing to turn over to a state attorney general investigating subversion a list of guests who had attended a summer camp hosted by that organization.[69]

In *Gibson,* then, the NAACP line of cases, in which the Court had uniformly rejected the states' attempts to force the NAACP to identify its members, collided with the communist legislative investigation cases, in which the Court had generally upheld the requests for disclosure. Which line would control? The Court chose to view the case primarily as one involving investigation of the NAACP, a "legitimate" organization, rather than investigation of the Communist Party, which is not a "legitimate political party" but an organization whose membership "is *itself* a permissible subject of regulation and legislative scrutiny." The Court accordingly reversed Gibson's contempt citation, thereby maintaining its perfect record of protecting the NAACP from various onslaughts by southern authorities who, quite correctly, viewed this organization as the nemesis of an oppressive social structure.

There is much about free speech cases of the civil rights era that is fairly open to differing interpretations. For instance, it could be argued that the lopsided results in favor of the civil rights activists were driven primarily by the Court's sympathy for the goals of the civil rights movement rather than a principled concern that prior doctrine inadequately protected the rights of those agitating for social change. Similarly, reasonable minds can differ as to just how helpful these Supreme Court decisions were to the ultimate success of the civil rights movement. It certainly can be argued that protection of those convicted of sit-ins and other seemingly illegal activity was not very important. In contrast, the Court's protection of the NAACP's membership lists and the press's ability to inform the nation about the reprehensible conduct of the southern authorities would seem to have played a significant role in ending apartheid in this country. More generally, it is hard to imagine the existence, let alone the success, of something like the civil rights movement in a society that does not to some significant extent protect free and open public discourse.

But if the importance of the Supreme Court's protection of the civil rights movement to the success of the movement is open to argument, the fact that the Court provided protection is not. Thus the claim that the courts "invariably construed the First Amendment" against the civil rights movement is not a creative revisionist theory providing a revealing perspective but rather a gross misstatement of knowable and verifiable fact. As this review of the civil rights protest cases shows, in almost every case the Supreme Court either "construed the First Amendment" in a way that favored the interests of the civil rights movement (e.g., *New York Times v. Sullivan; NAACP v. Button*) or found some other, often ad hoc way to rule on the civil rights side (e.g., many of the protest cases). Indeed, as late as 1982, in *NAACP v. Claiborne Hardware*, a case that took decades to wend through the judicial system, the Supreme Court reversed a large monetary judgment against the NAACP arising from its boycott of white merchants in the mid-1960s.[70]

Critique of Economic Inequity

The potentially important role of free speech in exposing economic inequalities, although not as obvious as its role in remedying racial injustice, should not be overlooked. The failure to protect radical critics who saw American involvement in World War I as a capitalist conspiracy and communist agitators during the McCarthy era created an atmosphere in which inequalities of the American capitalistic system could not be safely criticized. Today, in conscious reaction to these shortcomings, doctrine provides strong protection to speech that vigorously and even obnoxiously attacks the status quo, including the economic system. It remains true that those with a vested interest in the status quo—the rich and powerful—have by virtue of their wealth and power an enormous advantage in the marketplace of ideas. There is thus something of a chicken-or-egg problem in looking to public discourse to effect economic equality. Moreover, significant economic reform is usually brought about by economic crisis. Although the world of ideas and public protest doubtless played some role, it was primarily the Great Depression that was responsible for the New Deal. The role free speech will play in any future economic reform is impossible to predict. It is, however, safe to say that without strong protection of radical critique of the current economic order, the possibility of progressive reform will be diminished.

THE FUTILITY OF "FRONT-LOADED" APPROACHES TO HATE SPEECH AND PORNOGRAPHY REGULATION

The foregoing discussion shows that characterizing free speech as either a consistent ally of equality or its eternal nemesis is simplistic and inaccurate. Rather, the relationship between free speech and equality is complex, and the relationship between free speech *doctrine* and progressive social change even more so. Where, then, does this ambivalent relationship between free speech and equality leave us with respect to calls for broad bans on hate speech and pornography? It means, most fundamentally, that questions about the constitutionality of hate speech and pornography regulations cannot be determined simply by framing the issue as a conflict between equality and free expression and then making some general assessment about which value is more important. Singularly unhelpful is the commonly heard radical claim that in not allowing these prohibitions, free speech doctrine exalts abstract values served by free speech over the prevention of real and immediate harms caused by hate speech and pornography.[71]

For several reasons, this approach does not advance the inquiry. On a theoretical level, American free speech doctrine is radically egalitarian: Each person, regardless of race, religion, gender, or social circumstance, has the same right to try to persuade others about matters of public concern. This right, it is true, is quite narrow. For the most part, it offers protection only against direct content regulation imposed by the government and does little to equalize the enormous advantage that a few people have to influence political decisions and the marketplace of ideas. But although free speech doctrine is not an unalloyed force for equality, American free speech right is nonetheless deeply rooted in equality, and thus this value appears on both sides of the equation in any assessment of the values advanced or impeded by hate speech and pornography regulation.

On a practical level, it is not clear whether broad hate speech and pornography bans will serve or obstruct equality. The potential of speech restrictions to backfire against the interest of those they are meant to serve is well known. As discussed in Part 3, experience in other countries shows that racial minorities and lesbians have often been the first targets of expansive hate speech and pornography laws. In addition, such prohibitions on hate speech and pornography might inadvertently chill expression that is neither hateful nor pornographic, including expression that actually promotes racial and gender equality. Whether the net effect of sweeping hate speech and pornography bans would be the promotion of racial and gender equality is thus uncertain.

Even on the assumption that broad bans on hate speech and pornography would foster racial and gender equality, the modification of doctrine that would be necessary to allow such regulations might nonetheless impede the remedying of other injustices. As radical critique so ably demonstrates, the unfairness of long-standing social arrangements—especially those that oppress the least powerful members of society—are often largely invisible to the contemporary eye. As the histories of the abolitionist, women's suffrage, and civil rights movements suggest, the freer the public discussion, the more likely it is that these inequities will come to public consciousness. Only a generation or so ago, the dominant social image of male homosexuals was that of "perverts" who preyed on young boys, and the notion that women could be sexually attracted to each other was so contrary to the prevailing view that it failed even to register on most people's consciousness. The suggestion in the 1950s that gays and lesbians were an oppressed minority would have been an unintelligible statement to most Americans. But due in large part to frank, uncensored public discussion of homosexuality, including sympathetic portrayals of homosexuals in films, plays, and novels, discrimination against homosexuals is beginning to be thought of as closer to racism than righteous persecution.[72]

Surely there exist similar inequities in society today that are as yet invisible to most of us. The radicals are right that the dominant social narrative is often so loud that it drowns out competing voices. But it is precisely for this reason that we need powerful constitutional protection for those who challenge this narrative. Many of these marginal voices are marginal for good reasons, of course: Most advocate crackpot ideas—not particularly harmful or offensive, but not useful either. Others, like the bigoted views the radicals want to silence, are reactionary calls to reinstitute practices condemned by history as oppressive and unjust. But occasionally to be found among this babble is a truly prophetic voice, at first ridiculed or despised, most often merely ignored, but that slowly gains adherents as it exposes the injustice of some well-entrenched practice.

In the song "Bob Dylan's 115th Dream," the protagonist reminds a man who refuses to help him in a time of need that "they refused Jesus, too." The man replies, "You're not him." Similarly, radical critics could reasonably respond that although it is hard for contemporaries to identify the prophet whose words will some day lead to greater social justice, the racist and the pornographer are surely "not him." But whether hate speech and pornography could conceivably be seen as progressive is not the question. The pertinent and much more difficult question is this: Can free speech doctrine be modified in such a way to permit government to exclude from the realm of public discourse ideas that in its view are so terribly wrong and regressive that they cannot possibly promote equality, without risking the chance that government will also suppress highly offensive critiques of the status quo that might well lead to a more just society? Radical critics think that doctrine can safely be altered; the judges and thinkers responsible for formulating current doctrine think otherwise.

Whether as an empirical matter this distrust of government is warranted or whether radicals are correct that government can be entrusted to pluck certain regressive ideas from the realm of public discourse without endangering potentially progressive ones is a difficult question that I address at length in Part 3. For now, suffice it to say that it is not always easy to tell progressive ideas from oppressive ones. This point was brought home to me in the late 1980s in a conversation with two law students, one of whom was a physician and the other a lesbian activist. The topic was homosexuality. The physician said that he thought homosexuality was biological in origin rather than a result of socialization. At first the lesbian activist was offended by this idea; after further discussion, however, she agreed that this theory, rather than providing additional fodder for discrimination against homosexuals, might actually advance arguments *against* such discrimination.

Some of the arguments that cast the controversy as a conflict between liberty and equality have an ad hominem quality to them. For instance, according to Charles Lawrence, those who have an opinion on campus codes are either "civil libertarians" who are insufficiently sensitive to equality concerns and thus oppose these codes or those, like himself, who properly balance the various competing values. As proof of this lack of concern for equality, Lawrence asserts that "[t]hose who raise their voices in protest against public sanctions against racist speech have not organized private protests against the voices of racism."[73] Such accusations are unfair to those who are dedicated to achieving racial and gender equality yet oppose far-reaching bans on hate speech and pornography. My colleague Charles Calleros ardently opposed a campus code at Arizona State University because he thought it too broadly prohibited constitutionally protected speech in public areas; indeed, Calleros was instrumental in the repeal of this code and its replacement with a more narrowly drafted code that targeted harassment that materially interfered with educational opportunities. Yet Calleros has been second to no one in his public condemnation of racist speech and, equally important, has encouraged students to demonstrate against racist incidents on campus.[74] Similarly,

Gerald Gunther, Lawrence's colleague on the Stanford law faculty, was an outspoken critic of the speech code that Lawrence supported. Gunther is a Jewish refugee from Nazi Germany, where he was subjected to anti-Semitic slurs, even from his teacher. In a written debate with Lawrence, Gunther eloquently summarized his position on the regulation of hate speech: "[T]he lesson I have drawn from my childhood in Nazi Germany and my happier adult life in this country is the need to walk the sometimes difficult path of denouncing the bigots' hateful ideas with all my power yet at the same time challenging any community's attempt to suppress hateful ideas by force of law."[75]

No Supreme Court justice can equal the records of Thurgood Marshall and William Brennan for advancing the cause of constitutional equality for women and minorities. Both were fervent foes of invidious discrimination as well as consistent supporters of the constitutionality of affirmative action. Before being appointed to the Court, moreover, Marshall was a legendary civil rights litigator, having argued *Brown v. Board of Education*. Both justices were also champions of free speech. Brennan, as we have seen, wrote such monumental opinions as *New York Times v. Sullivan* and the flag-burning cases. Marshall wrote the influential *Mosley* decision that formally introduced into free speech jurisprudence the presumption against content discrimination and declared that the First Amendment guarantees the right to "express *any* thought, free from government censorship."[76] In contrast, justices with a much more cramped view of constitutional equality, such as Chief Justice Rehnquist and his predecessor, Chief Justice Burger, tend to take a narrower view of free speech as well.

Shortly before he retired, Brennan seemed to go out of his way to make sure that no one could mistake his position on the constitutionality of hate speech regulation. *Texas v. Johnson* involved flag burning, not hate speech.[77] Nonetheless, perhaps because he knew that he would not be around when a hate speech case finally reached the Court, Brennan declared that "[t]he First Amendment does not guarantee that . . . concepts virtually sacred to our Nation as a whole—such as the principle that discrimination on the basis of race is odious and destructive—will go unquestioned in the marketplace of ideas." And in the flag burning case a year later, he wrote that "[w]e are aware that desecration of the flag is deeply offensive to many. But the same might be said, for example, of virulent ethnic and religious epithets."[78]

Years earlier, Marshall wrote an opinion for the Court striking down a law that banned the posting of real estate "For Sale" or "Sold" signs.[79] Marshall agreed that the objective of the law—to promote racially integrated neighborhoods by preventing panic selling by white homeowners—was laudable. He nonetheless found that the means of achieving this end impermissibly impaired freedom of speech by keeping important information from the public. And despite having been leaders in construing the Equal Protection Clause to outlaw invidious gender discrimination, both Brennan and Marshall have long argued that the obscenity exception to First Amendment protection should be overruled so that even the most explicit and offensive sexually oriented material would be protected by the First Amendment.[80] And both justices joined the summary affirmance of the decision invalidating the Indianapolis ordinance that prohibited pornography demeaning to women.[81]

Of course, Brennan and Marshall might be wrong in their assessment of the relationship between free speech and equality in general and in their seeming opposition to hate speech regulation in particular. But no one, not even Charles Lawrence, could ever accuse these justices of being insensitive to equality concerns. Similarly, many liberal feminists with long records of fighting for women's rights oppose far-reaching restrictions on pornography such as the one proposed by MacKinnon.[82] The same is true of the ACLU, which rivals the National Organization for Women in its support of the feminist agenda.

People equally committed to equality can have good-faith disagreements about the best way to attain it. The charge that those who do not support hate speech and pornography legislation are insensitive to equality concerns—or even, as both Delgado and Lawrence have claimed, benefit by bigoted speech because it keeps minorities "off balance"—is unjustified and unhelpful.[83] Such arguments are reminiscent of the accusation that those who advocate fair criminal procedures or oppose the death penalty are "soft on crime" and have insufficient concern for crime victims or the assertion that those who on First Amendment grounds opposed the persecution of communists during the McCarthy era were unAmerican and themselves sympathetic to communism. Radical critics who make these charges (and not all do) would do well to drop them.[84]

But those who favor hate speech restriction are not the only ones who reduce the hate speech controversy to a clash between equality and free speech and then seek to solve the problem by arguing for the primacy of one value over another. In condemning campus hate speech codes, Colin Diver, as dean of the University of Pennsylvania Law School, recognized that "[d]iversity, civility, harmony, respect, [and] community" are important values. He insisted, however, that these values are "secondary to freedom of expression" and concluded therefore that "[i]f the value of free expression conflicts with the value of harmony or diversity, free expression should prevail. Period."[85]

I am not sure whether Diver means for his formula of free expression *über alles* to apply just on college campuses or to society as a whole, but even if it were limited to universities, it is manifestly wrongheaded and unworkable. I doubt very much that if black students had complained to him that a professor continually used racial epithets to refer to African Americans in the classroom that he would refuse to take action because "free expression should [always] prevail" over community and civility norms. Indeed, I suspect that if in one of Diver's own classes students began hurling vulgar epithets at each other during a heated discussion, Diver might seek to reimpose civility norms despite the dampening of free expression.

In summary, the relationship between free speech and equality is not reducible to simple slogans. Nor can we avoid the work of determining whether hate speech or pornography regulation advances or retards equality by resorting to general presumptions. We must instead carefully analyze the particular regulation at issue, including the consequences that upholding it would have on the entire body of free speech doctrine. Also pertinent is the experience of other countries that have enacted such laws. Even then, given the inherent difficulty in deciding causality in a complex social setting, we cannot with certainty predict the effect of such regulations on racial and gender equality. But at least our conclusion will be an informed judgment rather than an ideological assertion.

PART THREE

Should Doctrine Be Modified to Permit Broad Hate Speech and Pornography Bans?

I have so far made two major points regarding proposals to regulate hate speech and pornography: In Chapter 4 I demonstrated that free speech doctrine permits neither a broad ban on hate speech nor the suppression of sexually explicit but nonobscene material; in Chapters 5 and 6, I examined various claims that the failure of doctrine to recognize hate speech or pornography exceptions to First Amendment protection reveals a systemic bias against minorities and women, and concluded that these claims are grossly overstated. But neither of these conclusions does much to answer the question whether doctrine *should* be modified to permit the suppression of racist ideas and sexually explicit material demeaning to women. It is this difficult issue that I explore in this part of the book. Another way to pose the question is to ask whether American society would be better or worse off with such restrictions. This is obviously a large question, involving empirical, doctrinal, and theoretical inquiries. To assess the merits of hate speech and pornography regulations, we need to identify the harms of hate speech and pornography and then judge how effective the proposed restriction would be in eliminating these harms. We would also need to explore the possibility that these laws would be misapplied to squelch the expression of women and minorities. Relevant to these empirical inquiries is the experience of other democracies that have adopted such measures. But even in this part of the book, we cannot escape doctrine altogether: A key question is whether there is any *principle* that would support bans on hate speech and sexually explicit material demeaning to women that would not be so broad as to permit restrictions that would impair basic free speech values.

7

THE BENEFITS
OF BANNING HATE SPEECH
AND PORNOGRAPHY

Assessing the benefits of hate speech and pornography bans involves two related yet separate inquiries: an evaluation of the harms possibly caused by this speech and a prediction of the effectiveness of the prohibition.

THE HARMS OF
HATE SPEECH AND PORNOGRAPHY

In calculating the possible harms of hate speech, it is once again crucial to distinguish between hate speech that is part of public discourse—such as racist ideology expressed at the speaker's area of a public park, in a pamphlet handed out on the street corner, or in a book sold at a neo-Nazi bookstore—and racist expression that is not part of this discourse—such as the use of racist fighting words or racist remarks in the classroom. It is true that the harm caused by face-to-face racist epithets or racist tirades by a classroom instructor overlap to some extent with the injury caused by racist public discourse, but to a much larger extent the harm is distinct. I have already considered racist fighting words and campus hate speech and have shown that current doctrine may well permit the prohibition of much of this expression through properly drafted regulations. Here, however, as throughout most of this book, I am concerned with proposals to broadly ban hate speech from public discourse; thus I focus on the injury caused by this speech.

The expression of racist ideas as part of public discourse is alleged to cause both direct and indirect injury to minorities. Hate speech is said directly to cause psychic injury to those who encounter this material by viciously attacking their race or ethnicity—features crucial to one's personality but over which one has no control. In addition, hate speech is alleged to cause harm indirectly by affecting the way others perceive minority groups, making it more likely that those exposed to racist propaganda will engage in acts of discrimination and even violence against minorities. Pornography, particularly violent and degrading pornography, is similarly said to lead to discrimination and violence against women through its power to shape the way men view women.

Offense, Insult, and Psychic Injury

The most obvious harm of hate speech is that it is deeply offensive and insulting, particularly to members of the groups attacked by such propaganda. But because contemporary free speech doctrine definitively rejects offense and hurt feelings as a legitimate ground for suppressing public discourse, this rationale is rarely mentioned by proponents of hate speech bans. Instead, they argue that such expression causes not mere offense or insult but psychic injury. For instance, Mari Matsuda claims that "[v]ictims of vicious hate propaganda have experienced physiological symptoms and emotional distress ranging from fear in the gut, rapid pulse rate and difficulty in breathing, nightmares, post-traumatic stress disorder, hypertension, psychosis and suicide."[1] But the studies she cites for this assertion deal with racially motivated violence, other acts of racial discrimination, or harassment of individual victims, not racist propaganda aimed at a wide audience. Thus Matsuda reports that a study by the California Department of Justice found that "'racial *epithets* and *harassment*' often cause deep emotional scarring, and bring feelings of intimidation and fear that pervade every aspect of a victim's life." Also beside the point is a psychiatric study finding that "survivors of extreme persecution" suffer serious, long-lasting psychological distress.[2]

This is not to say, of course, that an African American who in the park hears an orator proclaim the inferiority of blacks or a Jew who on a busy street corner is handed a pamphlet denying the Holocaust will not suffer emotional injury. But it cannot be assumed that the severity of this emotional injury is the same as the emotional trauma caused by racist taunts directed at an individual. As Matsuda herself recognizes, "The unprovoked and unpredictable nature of bigoted attacks adds to the anxiety they create. African Americans have been subjected to racist attacks while engaging in commonplace activities such as changing a tire or attending a church picnic."[3] In terms of emotional injury to the audience, the use of racist epithets directed to people simply going about their business is obviously a very different matter from the publication of a book that employs such epithets or otherwise expresses a racist viewpoint. Particularly when racist verbal attacks on an individual are so persistent as to constitute harassment, the harm is likely to be far greater than exposure to a racist tract or speech. Thus Matsuda's reference to a case documenting a nervous breakdown suffered by a woman subjected "to repeated racial harassment, including nooses hanging over her desk,"[4] is certainly relevant to an argument for prohibiting racial harassment in the workplace (which federal law already does). But this and similar reports of injury caused by racial harassment do not tell us much about the harms of racist ideas expressed as part of public discourse.[5]

Instilling Self-Hatred

Matsuda and others have argued that one of the most damaging effects of hate speech is that members of the groups defamed by this expression "internalize" the message and come to believe in their own inferiority.[6] Self-hate, or at least self-derogation, is a well-known phenomenon that afflicts many if not all members of ethnic groups that have suffered centuries of oppression. This is particularly true if they live in a society that prizes cultures other than theirs. K. B. Clark's heartrending account, made famous in *Brown v. Board of Education,* of little black girls' preferring white dolls over brown dolls is one example.[7] And in my own experience most Jews born and raised in the diaspora have to some degree internalized the dominant culture's not always positive view of the Jewish people. A crucial question that proponents of hate speech bans do not address, however, is to what extent hard-core racist expression—as opposed to the more subtle images of minorities in the mainstream media—is responsible for this problem.[8]

Promoting Racist and Sexist Beliefs

According to Matsuda, hate speech is pernicious because "at some level, no matter how much both victims and well-meaning dominant-group members resist it, racial inferiority is planted in our minds as an idea that may hold some truth. The idea is improbable and abhorrent, but it is there before us, because it is presented repeatedly."[9] Although the social science data Matsuda offers in support of this claim are skimpy, it cannot be seriously doubted that to some extent the public expression of racist ideas has perpetuated racist beliefs in this country.[10] Again, however, a key question that Matsuda and other proponents of hate speech laws do not address is to what extent the public expression of explicit racist ideas, as opposed to private racist sentiments passed from parent to child or subtle racist images prevalent in the popular media, contributes to the perpetuation of racist beliefs. My own hunch is that in contemporary American society the public racist statements that proponents of hate speech laws want repressed only marginally contribute to instilling racist beliefs in others. I suspect that a far more significant contribution is made by private conversations and subtly racist public expression, both of which for practical reasons are beyond the law's reach.

I have this impression for two reasons. First, I find it doubtful that most Americans would be influenced by gruesome characters such as the neo-Nazis, skinheads, and Klansmen who make these pronouncements; anyone swayed by such speakers was likely racist before encountering this propaganda, which serves mostly to reinforce their prejudice. Second, until quite recently, hard-core racist propaganda has not been widely available. Indeed, in doing research for this book I had to make an extended effort to find contemporary racist publications. That hard-core racist publications are not part of the regular reading material of a significant number of Americans reduces the possibility that it greatly contributes to formation of racist beliefs in this country. With the advent of the Internet, however, racist materials have become more widely available.[11] It remains to be seen, though, if there is much demand for this noxious fare beyond mere curiosity.

Several recent studies have shown that exposure to sexually violent pornography tends to have at least a short-term negative effect on the way men view women, including increasing beliefs that women secretly want to be raped and that victims of rape are less worthy and less injured.[12] And unlike racist propaganda, pornography is prevalent and easily accessible in this society. Yet the prevalence of *violent* pornography found in laboratory experiments to cause this "sexual callousness" has not been documented. In the Appendix I review in detail the various conflicting claims about the amount and nature of violent pornography and its possible effect on men's attitudes toward women. I conclude that although the evidence is far from conclusive, the possibility that pornography may play a significant role in shaping the way American men view women is cause for concern.

Let us assume, for the sake of discussion, that racist propaganda is a major cause of racist beliefs and that pornography causes men to have sexist beliefs about women. Not everyone would agree, however, that beliefs alone, even the most pernicious ones, count as a harm that government may legitimately redress through coercive means. There is one more step to establishing an effect most would acknowledge as a legally redressible harm, namely, that these beliefs lead to *acts* of racial and sexual discrimination or violence.

Causing Illegal Acts of Discrimination
and Violence Against Minorities and Women

A long-standing argument for banning hate speech and pornography invokes a more familiar rationale for suppressing speech—that the speech will lead those exposed to it to act in harmful ways. That there is a strong connection between racist beliefs and racist acts cannot be doubted. Indeed, it would be unusual for a person engaging in a racially discriminatory act not to have racist beliefs. (A blackmailer who preys on immigrants of certain ethnic groups because he knows that for cultural reasons they are less likely to go to the police might be a rare example of racial discrimination not motivated by racism.) But the converse—that racist beliefs inevitably lead to racist acts—is a much more doubtful proposition. If discrimination is conceived broadly enough to include such private choices as deciding not to marry or to have close friendships with people of certain racial or ethnic groups, then it may well be true that racist beliefs, at least deeply held ones, will virtually always lead to racist acts. But if the racist acts in question are legally cognizable ones, such as discrimination in the workplace or racially motivated violence, then it is simply not the case that all people with racist beliefs engage in racist acts.

Similarly, it is undeniable that catastrophic injuries to racial or ethnic groups such as slavery and segregation in the United States or the Holocaust in Europe could not have occurred in the absence of widespread racist beliefs; it does not follow, however, that the increase in racist beliefs caused by the speech that proponents of hate speech legislation would suppress will lead to the reinstitution of slavery, legally imposed racial segregation, or genocide. Such high-stakes arguments for suppressing hate speech are particularly unpersuasive. There would have to be far-reaching changes in American society and institutions before racist beliefs could lead to such enormous injuries. Thus even if we accept the proposition that public expression of explicitly racist ideas significantly increases racist beliefs and that these beliefs in turn lead to discriminatory acts, the question remains as to the type of discrimination caused by these beliefs. The proponents of hate speech bans present no data showing that racist propaganda is a significant cause of *unlawful* discriminatory acts.

In contrast, those who advocate banning pornography point to studies they claim establish "a causal connection between pornography and violence against women."[13] The studies include experiments showing that exposure to violent (and perhaps nonviolent but demeaning) pornography increases aggression against women in laboratory settings, as well as studies showing a correlation between consumption of pornography and violence against women. I discuss these studies in detail in the Appendix, where I document the obstacles preventing extrapolation from the laboratory to the real world, as well as the limitations on what can be inferred from the quite contradictory correlational data. Although it can fairly be said that these studies supply *some* evidence that certain types of pornography contribute to the complex host of factors causing violence against women, this evidence is not nearly conclusive enough to warrant unqualified statements about causality. A much more accurate assessment of these studies is found in the *Report of the Surgeon General's Workshop on Pornography and Public Health:* "Pornography does have its effects; it is just not yet known how widespread or powerful they really are. There is a clear lack of extensive knowledge or unifying theory, *and global statements about the effect of exposure to pornography have not yet been substantiated.*"[14]

In conclusion, then, those who assert that racist ideas expressed as part of public discourse lead to illegal racist acts (as well as those who deny such a connection) offer little empirical evidence for their position. The causes of human behavior are always complex; the extent to which any particular behavior is caused by the public dissemination of ideas may be unknowable. Given this state of uncertainty, the most that fairly can be said about the relationship between public expression of racist ideas and the occurrence of illegal racist acts is that it is possible that the former significantly contributes to the latter. Any more definite claim is likely to reflect little more than one's deep disdain for the ideas expressed by such speech. With respect to pornography, there are at least some data suggesting a connection between pornography and violence toward women. On the current state of knowledge, however, no confident conclusions can be drawn about whether pornography is a significant cause of this harm.

Group Defamation

Racist propaganda is often defamatory in that it contains scurrilous lies about members of racial or ethnic groups. To the extent that this expression causes offense, insult, psychic injury, self-hate, or acts of discrimination against members of the defamed group, these harms overlap with those just described. But as Matsuda emphasizes, group defamation produces other injuries as well. Irrespective of any illegal discrimination it might cause or hurt feeling it may engender, racist propaganda "distances right-thinking dominant-group members from the victims, making it harder to achieve a sense of humanity." It forces the dominant-group members to use "kid gloves" when dealing with defamed minorities, and it causes minorities to view all "dominant-group members with suspicion."[15] Pornography, according to MacKinnon, similarly defames women.[16]

It may well be that the defamatory images of women and certain racial and ethnic groups interfere with harmonious social relations in this country. More doubtful is whether pornography and blatant racist propaganda are significant causes of this harm or whether, as I have said before, more subtle imaging in the popular media as well as upbringing and other forms of socialization are the primary culprits.

Silencing Women and Minorities

Another harm that hate speech and pornography is alleged to share is the power to silence. In recent years this argument has become a mainstay of those who advocate hate speech and pornography restrictions and is therefore worth examining in some detail.[17] Owen Fiss writes:

> It is asserted that hate speech tends to diminish the victims' sense of worth, thus impeding their full participation in many of the activities of civil society, including public debate. Even when these victims speak, their words lack authority; it is as though they said nothing. This silencing dynamic has also been attributed to pornography. In this view, pornography reduces women to sexual objects, subordinating and silencing them. It impairs their credibility and makes them feel as though they have nothing to contribute to public discussion.[18]

As with many of their arguments in support of banning hate speech and pornography, the proponents of the silencing argument offer no supporting evidence.[19] Despite the lack of any empirical data, however, it may still be possible to engage in some reasonable conjecture about the muzzling effect of hate speech and pornography. First, the potential of speech to quell other expression would seem to depend enormously on the type of speech involved. Although hate speech that is part of public discourse (e.g., racist propaganda published in books or made available on a racist Internet site) might well undercut the "authority" or "credibility" of minorities when they do speak, it is doubtful that such expression is responsible for much literal silencing. In contrast, because of its power to intimidate, a face-to-face racist epithet or other personally directed racist expression might well lead to actual silencing.[20] As to pornography, given its prevalence in this society, it is possible that this material is an important part of the social matrix by which women are sexualized and their intellectual capabilities denied or obscured. It is unlikely, however, that pornography results in literal silencing in the way a threat from the Ku Klux Klan directed to a civil rights activist might.

Let us assume for the sake of argument that hate speech and pornography are significant causes of the devaluing and in some cases actual stifling of the voices of women and minorities. Mirroring the values underlying free speech doctrine, this consequence presents both an individualistic and societal harm. As to the individual, such silencing impairs personal self-expression. But justifying hate speech and pornography bans based on any individualistic interests in speech presents the following daunting problem: What principle justifies shutting up A so that B may speak? Fiss recognizes that there are no legitimate grounds for preferring the self-expressive interests of women and minorities over those of pornographers and racists.[21] He seeks to avoid this problem by focusing entirely on the instrumental value of free speech and arguing that such silencing may well deprive public discourse of worthy perspectives. But this move merely trades a theoretical problem for an empirical one.

Fiss proffers neither evidence nor even a sustained argument that public discourse has been deprived of some idea or perspective because of the stifling effect of hate speech and pornography. Nor can it be assumed that the public debate has been so impoverished, for it is entirely possible that whatever the silenced person would have said will be or already has been expressed by others. Proof that certain perspectives are missing from public discourse is admittedly hard to come by. Still, to investigate this possibility one could conduct a survey of women and minorities hoping they would reveal some suppressed views to a sympathetic interviewer. Or despite the perils of cross-cultural comparisons, one could examine public discourse in countries that have outlawed racist speech and pornography for views missing in American discourse.

Since neither Fiss nor any other proponent of the silencing argument has undertaken any such investigation, we are left to speculate about what ideas or viewpoints hate speech and pornography might be suppressing. One possibility is messages of gender and racial equality—the antithesis of the perspective conveyed by hate speech and pornography. But this seems unlikely. As explained in the analysis of the "market failure" justification in Chapter 6, whether or not the idea of racial and gender equality has become widely implemented or even accepted, it can hardly be maintained that the idea is absent from public discourse. Nor is public discourse bereft of radical perspectives from women and minorities, as is demonstrated by the widespread dissemination of the views of MacKinnon, Andrea Dworkin, Louis Farrakhan, Malcolm X, and other radicals.

Of course, despite the existence of a wide variety of perspectives on racial or gender equality, it is still possible some perspective might be missing from public discourse. But this is pure speculation. Much less speculative is that criminal sanctions against hate speech and pornography will over time deprive the marketplace of ideas of certain racist and sexist perspectives as well as inadvertently suppress ideas that are not in fact racist or sexist. But in disfavoring racist and sexist views in this way, the state is surely not acting "as a fair-minded parliamentarian, devoted to having *all* views presented," as Fiss claims.[22] Fiss's silencing argument therefore cannot be taken seriously.

MacKinnon offers a somewhat more persuasive variation of the silencing argument. She claims that "pornography and its protection have deprived women *of* speech, especially speech against sexual abuse," because women are "seen to love and choose [their] chains because they have been sexualized."[23] In other words, because pornography conditions people to perceive as normal, healthy sexual activity what is in fact sexual abuse, this material effectively silences women (and men) from protesting this abuse or even seeing it as such. Although MacKinnon, like Fiss, offers no concrete evidence for her argument, it seems plausible given pornography's prevalence that this material plays some significant role in defining which sexual behavior is considered acceptable in our society and which is considered abusive and in this sense "silences" protest against sexual abuse.

Harm in the Production of Pornography

The Attorney General's Commission on Pornography reports that "at least some performers have been physically coerced into appearing in sexually-explicit material, while others have been forced to engage in sexual activity during performances that they had not agreed to beforehand."[24] In addition, the commission found that the performers are "normally young, previously abused, and financially strapped; . . . that on the job they find exploitive economic arrangements, . . . strong temptations to drug use, and little chance of career advancement; and . . . that in their personal lives they will often suffer substantial injuries to relationships, reputation, and self-image."[25] No study, however, has attempted to quantify how widespread these various abuses or injuries are. Indeed, the commission acknowledged that "exceptions exist to all these findings, and we concede, as well, that extremely thorough investigation might prove one or more of them untrue."[26]

THE EFFECTIVENESS OF HATE SPEECH AND PORNOGRAPHY BANS

Identifying the harms of hate speech and pornography is only a first step in assessing the probable benefits of far-reaching pornography and hate speech bans. Another key inquiry is evaluating how well such legislation would combat the harms allegedly caused by this expression. But before legislation can be effective, it must be enacted. Thus a question preliminary to any analysis of the likely effectiveness of broad hate speech and pornography bans is whether such laws would in fact be passed even if doctrine were modified to permit such legislation. This inquiry, often overlooked in the debate about hate speech and pornography regulation, is an important one, for it is not at all certain that removal of the constitutional barriers would result in the enactment of laws generally banning hate speech and pornography, either at the federal or state and local levels.

Pornography is big business. Like all powerful interests in this country, the pornography industry has political clout that alone might be sufficient to block bans on its product, especially if such a ban were to include mainstream "soft-core" publications and films. But the political power of the pornography industry is minuscule when compared to the various organizations of publishers and broadcasters who, although not themselves distributors of pornography, could be counted on to oppose a national ban on pornography as interfering with the right of the press. And when the conservative distaste for federal laws regulating areas traditionally left to the states is added to the mix, the political reality is that any broad *federal* ban on pornography is not in the offing, at least not in the immediate future. Similarly, the combined power of the pornography industry and the mainstream press are likely to frustrate widespread bans on pornography at the state and local levels.

In addition, even if the Supreme Court were to modify free speech doctrine to permit broad pornography bans, state court judges interpreting the free speech provisions of state constitutions might invalidate the laws; it is even possible that many state legislators would still believe broad pornography bans are inconsistent with basic free speech principles. As MacKinnon observes, the tenets of current American free speech doctrine are inculcated at an early age.[27] Rightly or wrongly, many Americans have become attached to them, viewing them as part of our national heritage. Then again, if the Court were ever to abandon these principles, their normative force would likely wither over time, making broad hate speech and pornography bans more acceptable to future generations.

Assuming that broad hate speech and pornography bans could be enacted either at the federal level or by state and local jurisdictions, how effective would these regulations be? The current unproductive attempts to ban hard-core pornography suggest that any broader pornography ban might also prove ineffective. Although most states have laws banning obscenity, this material remains readily available nationwide to any adult who wants it.[28] There are many reasons for this phenomenon. To begin with, a few states have chosen not to forbid obscenity. But more important, in many jurisdictions where the sale of hard-core pornography is technically illegal the ban is enforced only sporadically, if at all. And given the ease of transportation among states in this country, citizens in states where bans on the sale of obscene material are enforced can obtain this material in states where it is available. Indeed, despite the federal law against mailing obscene material, they can even obtain it through the mail.[29] The Internet, of course, greatly exacerbates the problem.

Theoretically, the spread of pornography from states that choose not to ban such material into states that do could be halted by a federal law imposing a nationwide ban. But even in the unlikely event that national prohibition on pornography could be achieved, there would almost certainly still be a thriving black market for the product similar to that for liquor during Prohibition and for drugs today. Or perhaps a more apt comparison, in light of MacKinnon's observation that pornography appeals to basic carnal desires, is to the persistent but futile attempts to stamp out prostitution. Because pornography is so pervasive, however, even a relatively ineffective ban in a few jurisdictions might arguably result in significant reduction of pornography consumption and hence possibly a significant decrease in violence and other harmful conduct toward women.

Hate speech is not nearly so ubiquitous as pornography, which is currently available at most convenience stores. The relative unavailability of hate speech cuts both ways in assessing the benefits of attempting to suppress it. On the one hand, even on the assumption that racist propaganda can lead to acts of racial violence and other discrimination, the relatively small amount of hate speech that currently exists in this society suggests it is not a significant cause of racial discrimination. On the other hand, although by no means certain, it may be possible virtually to eradicate the public dissemination of hate speech by force of law. For one, there is for hate speech no parallel to the billion-dollar pornography industry. In addition, despite its attraction to those with deep-seated phobias or other character defects, hate speech does not appeal to carnal desires and thus does not have nearly the same allure as pornography.

It is true that many find pornography as disgusting as hate speech, especially pornography that depicts women in demeaning ways. Indeed, to some pornography *is* antiwoman hate speech. To others, however, sexually titillating material is just good fun. There is not even a consensus among feminists about which sexually explicit material is demeaning or harmful to women and which is benign or even female-empowering erotica. In contrast, there is a strong consensus that virulent racist propaganda is both disgusting and of no positive social value. Like many liberal feminists, Nadine Strossen, the president of the ACLU, defends pornography, not only because she believes government should have no power to censor images or ideas but also because she believes some pornography is beneficial.[30] It is inconceivable that she or any other member of a mainstream organization would similarly praise hate speech. Hate speech, then, is a pariah, having neither pornography's allure nor its support. This accounts for its lack of prevalence in today's society and suggests that, unlike pornography, it may be possible to suppress this material. The question then becomes: What benefit is there in further reducing a type of expression already extremely marginalized in public discourse?

To a large extent this question merges with the previous inquiry regarding the harm of such speech. If it is the case, as I suspect, that publicly disseminated racist propaganda (as contrasted with racist beliefs passed from parent to child) is not a significant cause of racial discrimination or violence, then suppressing hate speech cannot do much to alleviate these problems. Conversely, if this speech does cause these injuries, its already marginalized status suggests that legal suppression might effectively reduce these injuries. But even if its relative scarcity means hate speech is not *now* a significant cause of racial discrimination or violence, it could well become one if such expression were to proliferate, as it is threatening to do on the Internet.[31] A broad hate speech ban could thus be seen as a preemptive strike against such proliferation. Indeed, it has been argued that even the relatively small and uninfluential amount of hate speech that now exists should be extirpated because in times of social unrest it could lead to catastrophic harm such as racial genocide of the type that occurred in Nazi Germany.[32] As discussed above, however, it would require a far more fundamental change in the basic character of our society than social unrest before racist ideology could have such a disastrous consequence.

The introduction to a recent collection of papers examining hate speech regulations in fifteen countries reports that "[m]ost papers share the view that laws which restrict free expression do not reduce hatred or violence."[33] Rather, the effect ascribed to such regulations is the protection of dignity and the maintenance of a civil tone in society. Similarly, many studies in this collection stress the symbolic role of such laws and their important teaching function in reinforcing and instilling proper values.

Because each country's legal system is intimately connected with the nation's unique culture, it is a mistake to place too much emphasis on other countries' experience with hate speech legislation. Still, these examples do suggest that the primary benefit to be expected from a hate speech ban in the United States would not be prevention of illegal acts of discrimination or violence but the protection of individual dignity and the shaping and maintenance of proper societal values. Bans on hate speech and pornography would in addition demonstrate to women and minorities that those in power at long last have begun to take their concerns seriously and reassure them that our lawmakers do not share the degrading view of them portrayed in such material.[34] By showing women and minorities that those in power are on their side in their struggle for dignity and equality, bans on racist and pornographic expression might help women and minorities become less alienated and marginalized. The question with respect to these benefits, however, is whether they can be accomplished just as effectively by other means, thus avoiding the costs of speech suppression. This is a question I return to in Chapter 10, in which I weigh the benefits and costs of broad hate speech and pornography bans.

8

THE COSTS OF REGULATION

Some of the asserted costs of broad hate speech and pornography bans stem directly from the regulations themselves. Such costs include the potential misapplication of these laws to speech not intended to be prohibited and the selective use of these laws against minorities. Other costs are indirect. One potential indirect cost often overlooked, particularly by those who advocate adoption of these laws, is the general weakening of free speech doctrine that might result from modifying it to permit broad hate speech and pornography bans. In this chapter I consider only the direct costs, postponing the question of the effect on free speech in general to the next chapter.

THE SLIDE TOWARD TOTALITARIANISM?

As with the asserted benefits of hate speech and pornography regulation, many of the asserted costs are quite speculative, a few even fanciful. Perhaps the singularly most unpersuasive argument against banning hate speech and pornography is the alarmist claim that modifying free speech doctrine to permit the suppression of hate speech and pornography will lead us down the path to totalitarianism. Like the argument that *not* suppressing hate speech in this country invites another Holocaust, the argument that allowing the suppression of hate speech and pornography will lead to American Buchenwalds and Auschwitzes cannot be taken seriously. To begin with, it was not until 1957 that the Supreme Court suggested that the First Amendment limits governmental power to ban sexually oriented material, and it was well into the 1960s before the Court began to define and enforce these limits with any rigor. Before that, government pretty much had carte blanche to define and ban pornography, at least so far as the federal Constitution was concerned. Similarly, until the landmark Warren Court decisions discussed in Chapters 2 and 3, free speech doctrine presented few obstacles to hate speech bans. Indeed, as discussed in Chapter 4, in 1951 the Supreme Court actually upheld a broad ban on racial defamation. Whatever the shortcomings of the U.S. political order prior to the 1960s, it was not totalitarian.

Most democracies in the world today have some sort of ban on racist speech, including the United Kingdom, Denmark, France, Germany, the Netherlands, Canada, Israel, Italy, and Sweden. And nearly all democracies have long imposed legal limits on the explicitness of sexual depictions, some quite broad. The Canadian Supreme Court has in fact adopted the MacKinnon-Dworkin rationale for the suppression of pornography.[1] Yet none of these countries is sliding down the slope to totalitarianism. Democracy's survival depends not on some detail of free speech doctrine or indeed even on the existence of a charter of judicially enforceable rights but rather on deeply ingrained traditions of liberty, fair play, self-restraint, and respect for the rule of law. The United Kingdom has long been a thriving democracy despite the lack of *any* judicially enforceable limitations on Parliament's power to regulate speech or other basic civil liberties.

The U.S. approach to free speech, with its prohibition of viewpoint discrimination and protection of highly inflammatory words and symbols, is unique. Perhaps other democracies would be even stronger if they were to adopt this approach to free speech. Lacking the necessary familiarity with these societies, I am not qualified to make such an assessment. But that relatively broad hate speech and pornography restrictions did not spell the end of vigorous public debate or otherwise undermine the essential democratic character of these societies is evidence that such restrictions would not have any such catastrophic effect here. Reasoned debate about the wisdom of hate speech and pornography restrictions is not helped by hysterical rhetoric or hyperbole—on either side of the issue.

MISAPPLICATION, CHILLING OF NONTARGETED SPEECH, AND DISCRIMINATORY ENFORCEMENT

This is not to say, however, that broad restrictions on hate speech and pornography would not risk some serious negative consequences. A more realistic fear is that law enforcement officials will misapply these laws to punish expression that is unpopular or offensive but neither racist nor pornographic. Before the Supreme Court narrowly confined the category of obscenity, as I have mentioned, government often tried to suppress what are now seen as important works of art, such as James Joyce's *Ulysses* and Henry Miller's *Tropic of Cancer* and *Tropic of Capricorn*.[2] More recently, hate speech laws have been misapplied in other countries. In

1985 Danish National Television broadcast an interview in which several members of a racist group expressed their views. Although it was undisputed that the purpose of the program was to inform the public of the existence of racism in Denmark, the interviewer and the editor of the program were charged and convicted of violating Denmark's hate speech law.[3] In India, in what an Indian legal expert describes as flagrant abuse of the law, New Delhi banned Salman Rushdie's *Satanic Verses*.[4]

The costs of such misapplication extend beyond the actual punishment of innocent expression. Such misuse will also likely cause would-be speakers to censor themselves for fear that what they want to express, though neither racist nor pornographic, might be mistaken for such. This chilling effect could occur even if law enforcement officials would not in fact misapply the statute to innocent speech. But the degree of self-censorship obviously increases with each misapplication of the law.

Proponents of broad pornography bans argue that this chilling effect can be mitigated by enforcement through civil lawsuits rather than the criminal law. Thus several recent proposals to curb pornography, including the one by Dworkin and MacKinnon, are limited to civil remedies. It is true that as a general matter civil liability is less chilling to protected speech than criminal punishment. A book dealer is more likely to sell a sexually explicit book that is not in fact pornographic if selling pornography invokes a civil sanction rather than a criminal penalty. This is true even if the civil and criminal penalties involve exactly the same monetary assessment, for the civil fine does not carry the stigma associated with a criminal conviction. And where the criminal penalty includes the possibility of imprisonment, the book dealer would ordinarily be much less likely to sell the questionable book than if he faced only the possibility of a fine.

Still, civil remedies are capable of having a considerable inhibiting effect, sometimes even greater than criminal sanctions. For instance, a $10,000 civil fine is likely to be more of a deterrent than a criminal sanction of only $1,000. Even when a criminal penalty carries the possibility of a short prison sentence, this sanction might well be less chilling than a hefty civil penalty, particularly when imprisonment is only rarely imposed. It should also be borne in mind that in criminal proceedings the state must prove each essential element of the crime beyond a reasonable doubt, whereas the burden is usually far lighter in civil proceedings. More telling than the often quite formal distinction between criminal and civil sanctions are the specifics of the remedial scheme in question.

It is not at all certain for instance, that the scheme provided by the Indianapolis ordinance discussed in Chapter 4 would have a significantly less chilling effect than criminal sanctions. Under the traditional criminal approach to regulating obscenity, the decision to prosecute is made by a professionally trained law enforcement official who will ordinarily file charges only after determining that under the applicable law, including constitutional limitation, a conviction is likely. Under the Indianapolis ordinance, in contrast, *any* woman aggrieved by the sale of pornography may file a complaint "as a woman acting against the subordination of women." An administrative agency is then empowered to issue "cease and desist" orders against the sale of pornography and to render monetary awards to compensate for "losses" occasioned by pornography. The determination is subject to judicial review, and courts are empowered to issue injunctions against the sale or distribution of pornography.[5]

Apparently as a safeguard against frivolous suits, the Indianapolis ordinance provides that the administrative process cannot go forward unless a panel of the "equal opportunity advisory board" finds that there is probable cause to proceed. Serious review at this stage could significantly mitigate any overenforcement problems. Conversely, if review at this stage is toothless or otherwise ineffective, producers and sellers of sexually oriented but nonpornographic materials will likely be subject to costly and protracted proceedings and thus may decide that it is easier not to deal in the material in the first place.

Perhaps the greatest danger of broad hate speech and pornography laws is that they will be selectively applied against the very groups that they were designed to protect. The history of speech regulation in this country and recent experience in other countries show the potential for hate speech and pornography laws to be used against unpopular minorities, be they ethnic, religious, or political. As discussed in Chapter 2, the prohibition against content discrimination peculiar to U.S. free speech doctrine is a conscious reaction to persistent misuse of various speech regulations against radical dissidents prosecuted not because their expression realistically posed any danger to interests that the laws legitimately sought to protect but because their ideas offensively challenged the status quo. In this regard, it is noteworthy that the only case in which a musical recording was declared obscene involved attempts to suppress the sexually vulgar music of a black rap group under Florida's obscenity laws.[6] Radical critic Kimberlè Crenshaw, though disturbed by the misogyny expressed in the lyrics, nevertheless notes that the prosecution raises "serious questions of racism," both because of its "apparent selectivity" as well as the court's "apparent disregard for the culturally rooted aspects" of the music.[7]

Experience in other countries shows how hate speech laws can backfire. The first use of Israel's hate speech law, enacted in response to the activities of the Jewish extremists, was against Palestinians.[8] Although "the chief object" of Britain's 1965 hate speech legislation, which outlaws "incitement to racial hatred," was to "curb hostility to immigrants from the

Caribbean and the Indian sub-continent," there were "few prosecutions," and of the few that were brought the jury often acquitted. But "some of the successful prosecutions were of black people accused of inciting hatred of white people."[9] In 1991, under an amended version of this law, a notorious bigot who for years had distributed highly inflammatory anti-Semitic literature was given a suspended sentence; that same year a Jewish manager of a shop selling Nazi memorabilia was sentenced to two months' imprisonment.[10]

In 1986 Britain passed a law that made it a crime to use "threatening, abusive or insulting words" or displays or behavior likely to cause "harassment, alarm or distress" to another.[11] Despite the "aim of [this law] to take action against those who intimidate the vulnerable," it has been used to "prosecute students who tried to put up a satirical poster of then Prime Minister Margaret Thatcher, demonstrators who ran onto a cricket pitch to protest against cricketers playing in South Africa, and a demonstrator outside Downing Street."[12]

Two provisions of Canada's penal code expressly prohibit hate speech: Section 318, which forbids the advocacy of genocide, and Section 319, which outlaws inciting or promoting "hatred against any identifiable group." In addition, Section 181, which bars the spreading of false news, has been used to punish racist lies such as Holocaust denial. Although in recent years these provisions have been applied mainly to hard-core racist expression by whites,[13] in the past they were often brought to bear on nonracist speech by minorities. At the beginning of the century, Section 181 was used against an American who posted a sign on his store saying that he was leaving because Americans were not welcome in Canada; in the 1950s it was used against civil rights activists for publishing a pamphlet critical of the government's treatment of Jehovah's Witnesses; in 1970 it was applied to publishers of an underground newspaper for running a parody of a mainstream newspaper.[14] Later in the 1970s, Section 319 was used to convict francophone rights activists who, in order to garner support for a French-language school, circulated a pamphlet purporting to be from an anti-French group.[15] In the 1980s, Canadian customs officials detained at the border for more than a month a film about Nelson Mandela on the grounds that it might promote hatred against white South Africans.[16]

The cases in other countries thus suggest that there might well be *some* misuse, particularly the selective prosecution of minorities, if a broad hate speech ban were enacted in the United States. Just how much misuse would occur is impossible to say, although the experience elsewhere provides some evidence that it might not be extensive.[17] We should not, however, take too much comfort in this. In other democracies with hate speech laws, the decision to prosecute hate speech is usually made at the highest levels of the national government (often by the attorney general). As a result, prosecutions are relatively few and carefully chosen, usually reserved for the most blatant forms of hate speech. In contrast to most other nations, where the criminal law is primarily the responsibility of the national government, in the United States state and local governments have primary authority to make and administer criminal law. Our federal system would probably not allow for the centralized control that is largely responsible for the restraint in enforcement of hate speech laws in other democracies. And it is worth emphasizing that it would not only be states that might enact hate speech restrictions but local authorities as well. Indeed, almost all the recent hate speech cases in this country involve local ordinances.[18] With so many jurisdictions potentially enacting and enforcing hate speech laws, the possibility of widespread prosecutions by ambitious, publicity-hungry district attorneys cannot be ruled out.

Experience in other countries similarly reveals the potential for broadly worded pornography laws to be selectively used against gays and lesbians. As Catherine Itzin, a British advocate of MacKinnon-Dworkin-style antipornography legislation, has written:

> The deliberate vagueness of the definition of obscenity and indecency [in Britain] has left the legislation open to abuse. It has consequently been used as an instrument to censor art and literature, to oppress gays and lesbians and to control women's fertility. . . . As recently as the 1970s, obscenity legislation was being used against the radical, counter-culture "underground" press. . . . *Last Exit to Brooklyn* was prosecuted in 1967 as obscenity because of its portrayal of homosexuality and drug-taking.
>
> Homosexuality, whether gay or lesbian, has historically been regarded as inherently obscene. In 1936, Radclyffe Hall's *The Well of Loneliness* was declared obscene because it dealt with lesbianism, and as recently as 1984 Gay's the Word Bookshop was prosecuted [and prosecutors seized] 142 titles (800 items) on the grounds that they were "indecent and obscene." . . . The material was prosecuted because it was homosexual not because it was obscene: it included literature which would merit no legal action if it were heterosexual, books already available in the UK, on syllabuses of respectable higher education institutions by writers such as Oscar Wilde, Kate Millett and Jean Genet. Silver Moon, the women's book shop, reported that . . . their imported feminist and lesbian books were regularly opened by custom officers under the guise of a search for obscenity—a form of informal unauthorized harassment.[19]

Itzin advocates replacing the current, vaguely worded British obscenity law with "civil rights" legislation that defines pornography as the "sexually explicit subordination of women." She argues that this change will "greatly reduce if not actually eliminate the censorship" of lesbian and gay material.[20] Recent events in Canada suggest that Itzen's hope is misplaced. In a 1992 decision, *Regina v. Butler,* the Canadian Supreme Court, at the urging of feminist lawyers inspired by MacKinnon and Dworkin's approach to pornography regulation, interpreted Canadian obscenity laws as outlawing not only sexually graphic violent material but also nonviolent material that is "degrading" or "dehumanizing" to women.[21] MacKinnon and Dworkin both enthusiastically praised this decision as a triumph for women. Within a year of the ruling, however, a feminist lawyer who worked on the brief urging adoption of the MacKinnon-Dworkin approach condemned prosecutors for using this decision to target lesbian bookstores. Since then, other feminists have made the same complaint, and there is indeed considerable evidence that *Butler* has led to discriminatory prosecution of lesbian publications.[22]

LEARNING FROM EXPERIENCE:
THE POSSIBILITY OF DRAFTING
HATE SPEECH AND PORNOGRAPHY BANS
SO AS TO AVOID MISUSE

Just because broad hate speech and pornography laws have a tendency to be misused does not mean that such abuse is inevitable. At the same time it underscores the potential for misuse, experience in other democracies also provides guidance on how to avoid misuse. If those who draft hate speech regulations were to carefully heed these lessons, it might be possible to draft a hate speech prohibition that would minimize the potential for misuse. I am less sanguine, however, about the possibility of doing so with respect to bans on sexually graphic material demeaning to women.

A statute describing a class of hard-core racist propaganda with sufficient specificity would minimize its misapplication to nonracist (or arguably nonracist) expression. Such specificity and narrowness of scope would also, I believe, eliminate any significant chilling effect. Just as there have for the past twenty-five years been bans on highly explicit sexually oriented speech (obscenity) without *widespread* misapplication or significant chilling effect, it may be possible to target extremely explicit and highly inflammatory racist propaganda. Of course, the price for such specificity is that analogous to the constitutional protection now afforded medium-core pornography such as *Hustler* and *Penthouse* magazines, material with racist ideas would be immune if the author made an effort either to disguise its racist intent or soften its message. In addition, pseudoscientific claims of racial inferiority and pseudohistorical claims such as Holocaust denial might have to be given safe harbor if presented without racist invective. It is probably not possible to draft a law that could ade-

quately distinguish between crackpot racist theories dressed up as scholarship and genuinely academic but arguably racist works such as *The Bell Curve*.[23]

This need to provide breathing space for nonracist discourse raises the
question whether such a narrow statute would effectively serve the goals
that proponents of hate speech laws wish to accomplish. In recent years
some countries with hate speech bans have minimized misapplication
and the chilling effect by reserving prosecutions for the most egregious
examples of racist speech. This restraint, however, has drawn criticism
from those who believe that a cautious approach has robbed the laws of
their effectiveness.[24]

Even if application to nonracist speech can be avoided or minimized by
careful drafting, there remains the problem of disproportionate impact on
minority groups. The difficulty is not simply one of selective prosecution.
The disparate impact that the British hate speech law had on black-power
advocates in the 1960s was apparently not just a result of selectivity on the
part of prosecutors but stemmed also from the tendency of juries to acquit
white defendants while convicting black ones.[25] The application of the
death penalty in the United States, which was traditionally imposed more
often on blacks than whites and still depends to a large extent on the race
of the victim, suggests that hate speech laws might be used disproportionately against black racists, such as Louis Farrakhan and his followers.[26]
Whether there would be significant disparate impact on minorities is impossible to determine in the absence of actual experience with hate speech
laws in the contemporary United States. My guess is that under current
conditions there would be some but not widespread discriminatory application. If, however, black activism such as that which occurred in the 1960s
were ever again to scare or enrage the white majority, the possibility of
widespread discriminatory application would be more likely.

The potential of hate speech laws to be discriminatorily applied against
minorities reveals a contradiction in the radical theorists' position. If their
premise is that society is so profoundly racist that even apparently neutral free speech rules are deeply biased against minorities, is there not at
least as much reason to believe that the legislatures that draft the hate
speech laws and the prosecutors, judges, and juries that apply them will
similarly discriminate against minorities?[27]

Although careful drafting and sensible administration might minimize
misapplication, chilling effect, and discriminatory application of hate
speech laws, these problems will be much harder to contain with regard
to laws banning sexually graphic expression demeaning to women. There
is little agreement, even among feminists, as to which sexually oriented
depictions are demeaning to women.[28] A recent book by Nadine Strossen
includes illustrations of a number of works of art that some feminists

have praised as depicting women in a positive light or for making a pro-feminist political point. Other feminists, however, have condemned these same images as demeaning pornography.[29] Strossen also notes the following passages from a 1987 novel:

> She is lean and tough. She fucks like a gang of boys. . . . She fucks everyone eventually, with perfect simplicity and grace. She is a rough fuck. She grinds her hips in. She tears around inside. . . . The first time she tore me apart. I bled and bled.

>   *   *   *

> He tears into me. He bites my clitoris and bites it and bites it until I wish I was dead. He fucks. He bites my clitoris more, over and over for hours. . . . He leaves. I hurt so bad I can't even crawl.

>   *   *   *

> I scratch, I bite, I tie him up, I hit him with my hand open, with my fist, with belts: he gets hard. He does each thing back to me. . . . I ended up cowering, caged, catatonic.[30]

Do these depictions constitute, in the words of MacKinnon and Dworkin's model legislation, "the graphic sexually explicit subordination of women," in which women are "presented as sexual objects who enjoy pain or humiliation" or are "presented as sexual objects tied up or cut or mutilated or bruised or physically hurt"? Does it matter that the author is Andrea Dworkin and that the overall theme of her works protests the subordination of women? It obviously did not matter to Canadian custom officials, who after the *Butler* decision adopting MacKinnon and Dworkin's approach to pornography regulation seized two of Dworkin's books, claiming that they violated Canada's pornography laws.[31]

Especially when dealing with human sexuality, terms such as "subordination" or "demeaning" will not sufficiently confine the prosecutorial discretion of law enforcement officials. As the Dworkin example shows, even if there is agreement that certain material depicts the subordination of women, the question remains whether this depiction is an endorsement or a protest against such behavior. Because of this inherent subjectivity, antipornography laws based on the MacKinnon-Dworkin model are likely to be used to punish a significant amount of artistic and political expression not intended to be prohibited by these laws and consequently to chill even more such expression. This deep subjectivity also increases the potential of these laws to be used disproportionately against sexual minorities.

Any vague legal standard for regulating sexual conduct enforced primarily by heterosexuals would tend to have a negative disparate impact on homosexuals. But terms such as "degrading," "dehumanizing," "demeaning," and "subordinating" positively invite such abuse. Because many heterosexuals (even some who support homosexual rights) find homosexual sex acts disgusting, it would not be surprising if heterosexual prosecutors, judges, and jurors more readily found graphic depictions of homosexual acts to be more "degrading," "dehumanizing," "demeaning," and perhaps even more "subordinating" than depictions of similar heterosexual acts. The restriction on public funding of art sponsored by Jesse Helms applied not to erotic art but to *homo*erotic art. Similarly, it can be seriously questioned whether the museum that exhibited Mapplethorpe's photographs would have been criminally prosecuted if the display showed heterosexual activities instead of homosexual ones.[32]

A possible solution to the potential misuse of laws banning pornography demeaning to women is to adopt a page from the Supreme Court's book and specify that it applies only to hard-core pornography. This would minimize any chilling effect on serious artistic expression, and although it would not necessarily reduce disproportionate impact on homosexual material, it would at least cut down on the range of homosexual material that is eligible for prosecution. So far, however, most advocates of bans on pornography demeaning to women have refused to limit the regulation to hard-core material, insisting instead that they include all "graphic sexually explicit" material. Perhaps they have been right not to make this concession if the harm inheres not in the degree of sexual explicitness but in the degree of subordination depicted in an erotic context. But the trade-off for the breadth of coverage is abandoning the anchor that has prevented current pornography regulation from being extensively misused. Alternatively, since violence is easier to define than subordination, it might be possible to design a ban on sexually violent material that would not result in widespread misapplication and abuse.

PUBLICIZING RACIST
ORGANIZATIONS AND IDEAS

The risk of prosecutorial misuse is a potential cost that hate speech and pornography bans share. A possible cost unique to hate speech bans is that prosecutions will publicize racists and the virulent ideas they espouse. Whether prosecution of racist expression in the United States would serve to spread this propaganda in such a way as to exacerbate its alleged harm is a complex question, but experience in other countries as well as here suggests that it might. For instance, in a recent French prosecution for Holocaust denial the defendant stated that he intended to repeat his views in court. Associations representing Holocaust survivors requested that the court forbid him from doing so and that the proceedings be closed to the public. The court denied this request, and at trial the defendant maintained that the Holocaust had not occurred. He was convicted and ordered to pay a fine, which was suspended so long as he did not commit this crime again within five years.[33] In the UK "Attorneys-General became increasingly reluctant to authorize prosecutions because they feared that trials would provide platforms for racists who, if convicted, would claim martyrdom and, if acquitted, would claim vindication."[34]

In the United States, the Skokie controversy of the late 1970s underscores how attempts to suppress racist expression can result in giving publicity to racist organizations and ideas. Frank Collin and his small band of neo-Nazis originally wanted to demonstrate in a Chicago park but were prevented from doing so by a prohibitively costly insurance requirement. Collin then announced plans to march in Skokie, a Chicago suburb with a large Jewish population, including many Holocaust survivors. Skokie responded by passing an ordinance forbidding the dissemination of material that "promotes and incites hatred against persons by reason of their race, national origin, or religion," as well as a law requiring applicants for parade permits to obtain $350,000 in insurance. There followed several rounds of highly publicized litigation; in the end the ordinances (as well as an injunction against the march) were declared unconstitutional.[35] Having won the right to march in Skokie, Collin then canceled plans to do so. Instead, he held a small rally in a Chicago park, relying on the Skokie litigation to invalidate the insurance requirement that had previously blocked this demonstration. Collin explained that the threatened Skokie march was "pure agitation to restore our right to free speech."[36] In retrospect, some members of the Jewish community in Chicago thought it would have been far better if Collin had simply been allowed to demonstrate in the Chicago park as planned rather than for his organization and ideas to have been given extensive publicity.

The Skokie incident suggests that if the Supreme Court were ever to clear the way for hate speech prosecutions in this country, these prosecutions would attract extensive public interest and media coverage. Moreover, in some jurisdictions the trials would likely be broadcast on television. (It is possible, however, that over time the public's interest and thus the media attention would wane, especially as these prosecutions became commonplace.) As in the recent French case, the prosecutors in the United States would likely try to limit defendants' opportunity to repeat their calumnies in court. But given extensive rights of criminal defendants in this country, including the right to testify on their own behalf, to cross-examine witnesses, and even to represent themselves, such containment may often prove difficult.

In prosecutions for use of racial epithets or advocating that certain groups be stripped of basic civil rights, deported, or subjected to violence, it may be possible to keep the defendant from repeating this expression in court or defending its propriety. But in prosecutions for group defamation based upon pseudoscientific claims about the genetic inferiority of certain ethnic or racial groups or for pseudohistorical claims such as Holocaust denial, disallowing the defendant from attempting to prove a factual basis for these beliefs would be problematic. Under current First Amendment doctrine, truth must be recognized as a defense in all defamation actions based on statements on matters of public concern. Indeed, the burden is on the plaintiff (or prosecution in criminal cases) to prove that the defamatory statement is false.[37]

Of course, if doctrine were changed to permit hate speech prosecutions, this rule could be altered as well. Perhaps the elimination of truth as a defense in pseudoscience and pseudohistory prosecutions could be justified by conceiving of the essence of the offense not as spreading false facts but as making hateful statements about a group of people. Constitutional limitations aside, however, there is still something troubling about charging people with a crime of spreading malicious falsehoods and then forbidding them to prove that the statements were true. For one, it gives the appearance that the government is afraid of examining the truth. At a minimum, it will gave racist organizations ammunition to make just this charge. And even if defendants can be kept from using the courtroom as a platform for reiterating their racist views, they can still publicize these views in media interviews outside the courtroom.

Law does, however, have an important teaching function. It is possible, therefore, that racist ideas expressed in the context of a criminal prosecution will not be nearly as persuasive or damaging as racist speech in the speaker's corner of the park or in a book or pamphlet, especially if defendants are convicted and led away in handcuffs. But what if they are acquitted? Even if acquittals were for purely technical reasons, some are likely to see this outcome as a vindication of the defendants' views. Certainly racists will urge the public to view every acquittal in such a light. And even convictions carry certain dangers. Racists convicted of hate speech are likely to paint themselves and to be viewed by others (not all of whom are racists) as free speech martyrs.[38] In this regard there has been a tendency to romanticize the high-ranking members of the American Communist Party convicted in the 1950s Smith Act prosecutions as free speech champions rather than as the hard-line Stalinists they actually were.

In the final analysis, hate speech prosecutions run the very real risk of creating some of the dangers that hate speech laws are meant to prevent by giving publicity to racist organizations they could not purchase at any price. If I am correct that at present hate speech is neither particularly prevalent nor influential, it would be a sad irony if hate speech laws generated large-scale interest in material that would be largely ignored if simply left alone. As is the case with so many of the possible effects of hate speech legislation, there is no way to predict with certainty the likelihood and the magnitude of this potential cost. But unwittingly giving hard-core racists a far greater audience than they could ever hope to reach in the absence of such prosecutions is a potential cost that anyone favoring broad hate speech restrictions should seriously consider.

THE POSSIBLE BENEFITS
OF HATE SPEECH AND PORNOGRAPHY

Even on the assumption that hate speech and pornography cause harm, it is possible that this expression has certain beneficial aspects as well that would be negated by its suppression. Strossen claims that pornography can convey a message of sexual egalitarianism (women like sex, too, and should initiate it); is used to treat sexual dysfunction and paraphilias; provides a way for couples to spice up their sex lives; and offers an important source of information about sex, including "information about women's bodies and techniques for facilitating female sexual pleasure, which is otherwise sadly lacking in our society."[39] Similarly, Kathleen Sullivan argues that pornography can promote women's sexual liberation: "[I]f social convention, backed by religion and law, confines sexuality to the heterosexual, monogamous, marital, familial, and reproductive, then the ambisexual, promiscuous, adulterous, selfish, and gratification-centered world of pornography is a charter of sexual revolution that is potentially liberating rather than confining for women."[40] It is also relevant that many people seem to derive pleasure from this commodity, as is shown by the billions of dollars a year that Americans spend on pornography.

Supporters of pornography bans such as the civil rights model drafted by MacKinnon and Dworkin might argue that most if not all of pornography's benefits could be produced by sexually graphic material that is not demeaning to women and does not show women in subordinate positions. But "demeaning" and "subordinate" are extremely uncertain and subjective terms. As Nan Hunter, a feminist lawyer who opposed the Indianapolis ordinance, has observed: "[I]f a woman [in a pornographic work] says to a man, 'fuck me,' is that begging, or is it demanding? Is she submitting, or is she in control?"[41] Any law that defines pornography in terms of whether it is demeaning to women or depicts women in subordinate positions is certain to cast a pall on the production and distribution of all sexually explicit material and thus interfere with any benefit this material may produce.

Another claim sometimes made by opponents of hate speech restrictions is that racist speech and pornography provide a safety valve by which potentially violent racists blow off steam rather than commit violent acts. Removing this outlet through suppression of hate speech and pornography, they say, might actually increase violence against minorities and women. Similarly, it has been argued that pornography can be a catharsis for men who would otherwise engage in sexual violence. As it relates to hate speech, I find the "safety valve" theory particularly unpersuasive. It strikes me as implausible that racists would turn to violence just because they are denied the right publicly to proclaim their ideas. It is possible, of course, that any given racist might be driven to violence because he may no longer legally publish his propaganda. What is unlikely is that this would be a common reaction. The causes of violence are many and to a large extent unfathomable; hate speech restrictions, however, would not seem to be among them.[42] With respect to pornography, some have claimed that use of pornography may be an outlet for people who would otherwise engage in sex crimes.[43] But recent studies suggest that if anything, pornography demeaning to women causes rather than prevents sexual violence.[44]

A related claim is that preventing racists from publicly expressing their views will give us all a false sense of security that virulent racism no longer exists. At first this objection may seem far-fetched. But what makes it plausible is the remarkable tendency of some Americans to deny the existence of racism in this country. Such denial is a result of ignorance or sometimes even the denier's own racist tendencies. Whatever the reason, racist expression as part of public discourse serves as a reminder that virulent racism has not yet gone the way of smallpox. But since hate speech laws are unlikely entirely to eradicate hate speech in this country and since any attempt to do so would generate a lot of publicity about (and for) racist organizations, there is little reason to fear that racist expression would as a result of these laws become unavailable as proof that racism still exists.

Finally, the following possible benefits of hate speech should be considered: Although racist propaganda mostly contains scurrilous lies, it may, in Mill's words, "contain a portion of the truth." And even if we are certain that this is not the case, the presence of highly inflammatory racist speech in public discourse may prevent the ideals of equality that it attacks from becoming dead dogma.

SENDING THE WRONG MESSAGE

In canvassing the possible benefits of laws banning hate speech and pornography, I considered the symbolic value of such legislation, both in terms of the psychological boost it gives minorities and women and the normative statement such bans would make to society as a whole. Here I want to note the possibility that such legislation might also send the wrong message. It has been argued that hate speech restrictions imply that minorities are emotionally weak and in need of special protection by the state, thus adding to the "victim mentality" that keeps minorities down, when what is really needed is mental and emotional toughness.[45] Similarly, some feminists have condemned proposals to ban pornography demeaning to women as paternalistic interference that is itself demeaning to women's status in society.[46] I am dubious that hate speech laws will have this kind of deleterious effect, at least to any substantial degree. There is no evidence of any such outcome in countries that have hate speech laws. In addition, this possible result can be minimized by laws that ban all hate speech—as most proposals to ban hate speech in fact do—not just speech aimed at minorities.[47] And if the argument for banning pornography is to protect women from palpable harm, such as rape and other forms of violence and job discrimination, it is hard to see why such legislation should be demeaning to them.

A more powerful argument that suppressing hate speech sends the wrong message is that forbidding the expression of *any* idea undercuts the commitment to critical inquiry. By expressly holding that within the realm of public discourse no idea is off limits, no thought unthinkable, and no orthodoxy immune from challenge, current doctrine reinforces the commitment to critical thinking that has been a strength of our society, contributing to both our material and moral progress. One cost of modifying doctrine to allow for the suppression of hate speech would be the dilution, if not outright repudiation, of this message.

DISTRACTION FROM REMEDYING
ROOT CAUSES OF DISCRIMINATION

Another argument against the symbolism of hate speech legislation is that using such laws for symbolic purposes detracts from the much more important work that needs to be done in the area of racial and gender equality. Like the death penalty for drug "kingpins," hate speech and pornography legislation can be seen as just another quick fix that Americans are so fond of—splashy, superficial remedies that do nothing to address the complex issues underlying large societal problems but may well detract from finding real solutions. A review of hate speech laws in Britain and Israel concludes that

> the experience of both countries is that the existence of incitement laws has
> distracted attention away from the need to enact legislation which addresses

root causes of discrimination. In Israel, a bill to extend the law which prohibits discrimination in employment and public services on the basis of sex to discrimination on national, ethnic, and religious grounds has languished in the Knesset for years. In Britain, members of minority groups remain woefully underrepresented in government, the judiciary, the professions, and in crucial government departments such as the police. This situation prompted one of the four minority members of the 650-member House of Commons in 1988 to comment that racist behavior is more socially acceptable in the UK than in the US.[48]

Whether or not we have made greater strides than has Britain in eradicating racism, there is still obviously a lot of work to be done in the United States. A disproportionate number of women and minorities in this country live in poverty, and the highest jobs in industry and government are still primarily held by white males. Racial violence still plagues us, and violence against women, in the form of both domestic violence and rape, is epidemic. Even if hate speech and pornography contribute to these ills, few believe that they are the root causes. Thus it is rare to find veteran civil rights litigators or women who have spent their lives battling for gender equality in this country calling for broad bans on hate speech and pornography. They know that this is not the real battleground.

But if distraction from more important work is possible, it is not inevitable. For one, hate speech and pornography legislation and civil rights legislation addressing root problems are not mutually exclusive remedies. Indeed, on the surface at least they appear mutually reinforcing in that enactment of one will spur interest in the other. Moreover, the civil rights community in this country is wise enough to keep its eyes on the prize and not stray from working for solutions that will address core issues. The danger, however, is that the white male establishment might prefer to enact some cosmetic remedy rather than address root problems.

IMPAIRING THE EXPRESSIVE RIGHTS
OF RACISTS AND PORNOGRAPHERS

The possible costs of hate speech and pornography regulation I have listed so far have been primarily detriments to society as a whole rather than to the would-be racist speaker or pornographer. But if we accept the view that free speech is valued not just for instrumental reasons but as a fundamental personal right grounded in a moral conception of the relationship between the state and the individual, then these restrictions implicate fundamental rights of those wishing to express racist views and arguably of those wishing to produce or view pornographic images demeaning to women. This cost is most salient with respect to hate speech.

Although some racist speakers may intend merely to inflict emotional in-jury on minorities, others, perhaps most, sincerely want to convey a worldview, as twisted and malignant as that perspective may be. The heart of the noninstrumental view of free speech, however, is that all indi-viduals are entitled to try to persuade others to see the world the way they do. Racists' right to do so will obviously be impaired by hate speech bans.

It is not as obvious that those who make or distribute pornography are attempting to persuade others to view the world in a certain way or that those who consume pornography are seeking new perspectives on social issues. Nor is it obvious that pornographers are engaged in serious artis-tic efforts. Still, there may well be some modicum of political, social, or artistic expression to be found in the sexually explicit material that those opposed to pornography wish to outlaw.

9

IN SEARCH OF
A CONFINABLE PRINCIPLE

So far I have considered the possible direct costs of hate speech and pornography bans. I now turn to a potentially significant indirect cost of modifying current doctrine to permit such bans—a general weakening of the constitutional protection afforded debate on matters of public issues. Even radical critics do not favor totally abandoning judicially enforceable First Amendment limitations on governmental regulation of expression. Rather, they urge that free speech doctrine be modified to accommodate hate speech and pornography bans. But such proposed modification presents the difficulty of finding a principle that permits the suppression of hate speech and pornography but at the same time protects expression that must be allowed in a democracy—or, to personalize the inquiry somewhat, still protects speech that radicals like.

Of course, there is always the possibility of adopting an ad hoc, unprincipled rationale for suppressing hate speech and pornography, some much-hedged "exception" that has the appearance of principle but that does not bear up to analysis. An example of such an unprincipled approach is Chief Justice Rehnquist's dissent in the flag-burning case calling for an exception to the principle that government may not forbid offensive words or symbols used in public discourse.[1] To be sure, unprincipled decisions by the Supreme Court are not unheard of. But each unprincipled decision undermines respect for the Court and hence the popular acceptance of judicially enforceable constitutional limitations. It is especially important that free speech decisions be principled, lest free speech doctrine degenerate, as some radical critics wrongly allege it already has, into a crudely political exercise in which free speech protection is bestowed only on those speakers whose views advance the "substantive agendas" the justices favor.[2]

Finding a principle for suppressing hate speech that would not also gut core free speech protection would appear to be a particularly difficult task because, unlike pornography, racist propaganda often takes the form of core political speech. Racist tracts commonly denounce the morality, intelligence, or culture of minorities as part of an attack on existing government policies such as affirmative action or integration or, in more extreme cases, in support of some horrific policy such as the deportation or even extermination of members of certain racial or ethnic groups.[3] What principle can be proffered for stripping such speech of the strong protection usually afforded criticism of social policy?

The "Harmful Tendency" Rationale

Let us begin with a rationale based squarely on the harm that such expression is alleged to cause. As we have seen, a long-standing argument for suppressing racist speech is that hateful statements about minorities will tend to lead others to view them as inferior or loathsome, which in turn might cause those so persuaded to commit illegal discriminatory acts. This rationale does not require that the speech in question expressly advocate such conduct nor proof that this expression will in fact lead to law violation or other manifest injury. It is sufficient that the "natural tendency and reasonably probable effect" is to cause such harm.[4] This is the "harmful tendency" approach to speech regulation that was in effect in the early years of the twentieth century.[5] Under this approach, rousing denunciations of U.S. involvement in World War I were punished for their likely interference with the war effort. The verdict of history, however, is that such a principle for speech suppression disserved democracy in general and progressive causes in particular.

Conscious of the defects of the harmful-tendency approach to speech protection, the Warren Court, the most progressive Court in this nation's history, discarded it. Reviving this discredited approach might well impose a significant cost on all speech that challenged the status quo, including expression that progressives hold dear. A principled application of this rationale would allow the suppression of any speech that might persuade people to break the law or to inflict some palpable injury on another. For instance, under this principle a movie depicting loving homosexual relationships could be suppressed on the grounds that it might lead people to commit illegal acts of sodomy. Or if abortion were ever to lose its constitutional protection and again be prohibited in some states, a book celebrating women's reproductive choice could similarly be banned.[6]

Unlike racist propaganda, sexually graphic material designed primarily to arouse is not so centrally connected to public discourse. Later in this chapter, I discuss in detail the argument that because pornography does not appeal to our "deliberative capacities," it should be excluded from the highly protected realm of public discourse and suppressed merely on the possibility that it may lead to violence or other discriminatory harms to women. Suffice it here to say that although pornography may not be core political speech, it nonetheless has been argued, even by some who support the suppression of pornography, that pornography is "part of the discourse by which the public understands itself and the world it confronts."[7] And whether or not pornography should be considered public discourse, reserving rigorous constitutional protection only for speech that expressly appeals to our "deliberative capacities" and allowing all other expression to be forbidden merely on a showing of a "harmful tendency" would leave most art vulnerable to suppression.

Radical critics often belittle as "slippery slope" arguments those such as I have just made against the harmful-tendency rationale.[8] I agree that "slippery slope" arguments are not particularly persuasive, if what is meant by that term are arguments claiming that if government is permitted to regulate in a certain area, it will continue to do so until that area is pervaded with oppressive regulations. A classic example of this sort of argument is the National Rifle Association's position that any prohibition of weapon ownership (including automatic weapons and armor-piercing bullets) will lead to the banning of all guns, including hunting rifles. And "slippery slope" arguments do abound in the First Amendment arena, such as the commonly voiced objection that regulations such as the V chip, which allows parents to block out violent and sexually graphic television programs, will lead to government censorship of core political speech.[9]

But my objection to the harmful-tendency rationale is in fact quite different from such a "slippery slope" argument. The objection is not that hate speech restrictions will inevitably lead to restrictions on prohomosexual speech (although this would be a real danger, particularly in certain communities) but that the *breadth* of the harmful-tendency rationale is such that if courts were to apply it in a principled manner they would have to uphold suppression of prohomosexual speech, as well as any other expression that has a tendency to lead to law violation. Although legislation often is a product of compromise and expediency, constitutional adjudication should be based on principle. As the Supreme Court recently emphasized, "[L]egislatures may draw lines which appear arbitrary without the necessity of offering a justification. But courts may not. We must justify the lines we draw."[10]

A major challenge to those who support bans on hate speech and pornography demeaning to women is finding a rationale for the suppression of this speech that can be applied in a principled fashion in future cases that will not dilute the strong protection currently afforded speech that denounces the status quo. Of course, many radical critics claim that this protection is not particularly useful to advancing the interests of women, minorities, and other less powerful groups. In their view, even an across-the-board weakening of this protection would be no great loss. But if I am right that these critics sorely underestimate the protection modern doctrine provides to those agitating for progressive social reform, then weakening this protection might impose significant costs.

Preventing Psychic Injury

Another commonly proffered rationale for suppressing hate speech is that it inflicts psychic injury on minorities who encounter it. But is there some principle to distinguish the emotional injury caused by racist propaganda distributed to the general public (as opposed to expression targeted at specific individuals) from the emotional injury caused by other types of inflammatory public discourse? What grounds are there for concluding, for instance, that the psychic injury racist public discourse causes minorities is any greater than the emotional injury those who had sons killed in Vietnam suffered on seeing "Support the Vietcong" signs carried by antiwar protestors? Or more damaging than the emotional injury inflicted on Jerry Falwell as a result of the *Hustler* magazine parody claiming that his first sexual experience was with his mother in an outhouse? Or more severe than the emotional harm antiabortion pamphlets that display aborted fetuses in gory detail cause to women who have had abortions? Like the "harmful tendency" rationale, the psychic-injury rationale applies to more than just hate speech and thus could have a considerable dampening effect on the robustness of public discourse.

Combating the Silencing Effect

A recently minted rationale for suppressing hate speech and pornography posits that hate speech silences minorities and pornography silences women. According to Fiss, a distinct advantage of the silencing argument over other justification for prohibiting hate speech and pornography is that the state is not "us[ing] its power to skew debate in order to advance particular outcomes" but is merely making sure that "all sides are heard."[11] Thus rather than compromising core free speech values "by trying to control the people's choice among competing viewpoints by favoring or disfavoring one side in a debate," the state is instead promoting these values by "acting as a fair-minded parliamentarian, devoted to having all views presented."[12]

At first blush it may seem as if Fiss has found a rationale for suppressing hate speech and pornography that will actually promote, not compromise, core free speech values. Careful analysis, however, shows that the promise is not fulfilled. First, it is important to note that Fiss is not arguing that hate speech or pornography *literally* silences minorities and women through its power to intimidate, as might well be the case with personally directed hate speech (e.g., a burning cross placed on a black family's lawn) or perhaps even with personally directed pornography. Rather, he argues that hate speech deprives the victims' words of "authority," making it "*as though* they said nothing," and that pornography "impairs [women's] credibility." But pornography and hate speech can have such ill effects only through their power to persuade others to see women and minorities in some demeaned status, such as sex objects or second-class citizens.[13] As Fiss recognizes elsewhere, regulations that are justified in terms of their power to influence people on how to see the world are contrary to core First Amendment values.[14] The silencing rationale, therefore, does not avoid implicating basic free speech values.

Nor is the rationale a narrow one. Although it is conceivable that hate speech and pornography discourage minorities and women from participating in public debate, it is just as likely that strong condemnations of racism and sexism discourage people from airing views that are in fact neither racist nor sexist but might be misunderstood as such, or that the widespread condemnation of drug use silences people from pronouncing dissenting opinions on this subject, or that harsh professional criticisms may stifle scientists or physicians from expressing novel ideas (a few of which may even be useful).[15] I do not mean to suggest that it is always a bad thing for strong negative reaction to inhibit speech. That the expression of racist and sexist views is no longer socially acceptable is decidedly to the good. More generally, that some perspectives drive others from the marketplace of ideas is part of the inevitable winnowing process by which public opinion is formed.[16] My point here is that allowing the suppression of speech just because it tends to "silence" other expression is a rationale that if applied in a principled way has the potential to dilute the robust nature of public discourse.

But it is not just that the harmful-tendency, psychic-injury, and silencing rationales are extremely broad; their application necessarily calls for extremely subjective judgments. As a result, use of these rationales will invite prosecutors, judges, and juries selectively to punish those who advocate unpopular viewpoints. On an even more pragmatic level, because these rationales are so broad and subjective, there is no chance the Supreme Court will adopt them or even that many who would like to see hate speech banned will support them.

THE COUNTERVAILING
CONSTITUTIONAL RIGHTS RATIONALE

Another currently popular rationale for the suppression of hate speech and pornography is the "conflict of constitutional rights" rationale. If this rationale allowed only for the suppression of speech that actually implicates other constitutional rights, it would be both fairly narrow and objective. It would not, however, cover most instances of hate speech. As explained in Chapter 5, the typical examples of hate speech that radicals want to ban—a bigot's oratory in the park, a neo-Nazi parade, or the distribution of Klan literature on the street corner—do not implicate the Fourteenth Amendment or any other part the Constitution. The same is true of the pornography sold by the local "adult" bookstore or rented at the corner video outlet. Rather, such speech implicates constitutional *values*. But unlike a theory that allows the suppression of speech that actually violates other constitutional rights (as the case would be, for instance, if government sponsored religious speech in violation of the Establishment Clause of the First Amendment), a rationale permitting suppression of speech because it undermines constitutional values is extremely broad and subjective.

Constitutional values are numerous—ranging from respect for private property to protection of states' rights, from the commitment to robust public discourse to ensuring a strong national defense. In addition, they change over time, sometimes dramatically. A century ago the Court thought that racial segregation was consistent with the Fourteenth Amendment and that confining women to the domestic sphere was part of the natural order of things. Today these practices are thought to be contrary to basic constitutional norms. A free speech system that disfavored speech that attacked societal norms so basic that they find expression in the Constitution as interpreted at any given time would particularly imperil speech that challenges the status quo. Justice Holmes long ago explained that the essence of free speech is "not free thought for those who agree with us but freedom for the thought that we hate."[17] Radicals often sneer at this aphorism, calling it a cliché.[18] Less well known, however, are the circumstances that prompted Holmes to write these words.

Rosika Schwimmer, a Hungarian immigrant, was denied American citizenship because, as a pacifist, she could not commit to take up arms in defense of the country. The District Court upheld the denial of citizenship on the grounds that she had not satisfied a requirement of the naturalization act of "attachment to the principles of the Constitution." The U.S. Supreme Court affirmed the denial of citizenship. Although Schwimmer, a forty-nine-year-old woman, was in any event not eligible for military service, the Court noted the "power" of her counterconstitutional ideas to "influence others."

Some proponents of hate speech bans attempt to cabin the "contrary to constitutional values" rationale by seeking to privilege equality (or more precisely, today's conception of equality) over other constitutional values. Fiss, for example, argues that equality has a preferred place in the constitutional order because "it is one of the center beams of the legal order. It is architectonic."[19] But a free speech principle that allows the suppression of speech because it challenges "one of the center beams of the legal order," albeit narrower than a rationale that allows suppression of speech that offends any constitutional norm, is nonetheless a formula for a conservative society. As Fiss notes in arguing for constitutional protection of homoerotic art from discriminatory funding decisions, speech regulations that reinforce "an orthodoxy" betray "one of the fundamental purposes of the First Amendment."[20] But "architectonic" in this context is just another word for "orthodox."

Still, since only a limited number of values can qualify as "center beams of the legal order," Fiss's rationale is fairly narrow. But is it principled? By what criteria is today's vision of equality privileged over property, democracy, national security, or other potential core constitutional values, including, by the way, free speech? Perhaps there is a principled way to make this determination, but those who advocate the privileging of the modern view of racial and gender equality over all other constitutional norms suggest none. Without such an explanation, however, elevating the contemporary vision of equality over all other constitutional norms seems little more than an attempt artificially to constrain a rationale for the suppression of hate speech and pornography.

HARM IN THE PRODUCTION OF PORNOGRAPHY

Citing both the coercion of young women into the pornography industry and abuse and mistreatment of these performers on the job, Sunstein argues that this harm justifies the suppression of the distribution of pornographic materials.[21] Justifying suppression on this ground, however, would have serious negative consequences for free speech doctrine. Under this rationale, action films could be banned because of the danger to stuntpeople, westerns suppressed because of the danger to animals, and any movie with child actors censored because of the documented exploitation of juveniles in the film industry. A more direct solution to such harm is, of course, regulation of production rather than distribution. Just as there are safety rules for stuntpeople, restrictions on the use of animals, and limits on the hours children may work and laws safeguarding their wages, special protection governing pornography production might be warranted.

Sunstein, however, argues that because of the "peculiar setting" in which pornography is produced and because of "special enforcement" problems, directly trying to eliminate the harms in production would not be effective and thus banning pornographic material may be the only realistic remedy.[22] There are several problems with this argument. Since there has never been an attempt directly to regulate practices alleged to cause harm in production, it is not at all certain that direct regulation would in fact be ineffective. Moreover, there is no reason to believe that insurmountable enforcement problems exist in all parts of the pornography industry, including mainstream, high-budget productions. Thus even if for some types of pornography direct regulation of the production would not be sufficient to do away with the harm to models and actors, this would be no justification for banning all sexually graphic material. Indeed, such a broad pornography ban might have a perverse effect of driving production underground, where abuse would likely increase.[23] More significant, permitting suppression of an entire category of speech just because there is often harm associated with its production is a rationale that few would embrace. For instance, we would not think it a sufficient reason to ban investigative reports on the grounds that their production often involves deceit, fraud, trespass, or other illegal practices.[24]

REDUCED PROTECTION FOR SPEECH THAT ATTACKS IMMUTABLE CHARACTERISTICS

Borrowing an idea from equal protection jurisprudence, some proponents of hate speech legislation have tried to confine the rationale for punishing hate speech by emphasizing that such expression attacks people because of an immutable characteristic. It is not at all clear, however, why this fact justifies suppressing speech. The reason that immutability is important in equal protection jurisprudence is that penalizing someone for an accident of birth is exceedingly unfair if it bears no reasonable relationship to any legitimate government purpose. But just because speech is grossly unfair would not seem to be a sufficient reason for suppressing it. Perhaps, though, immutability is invoked not as a rationale for suppressing speech but merely as a vehicle for *limiting* the breadth of other rationales. For instance, it could be argued that because discrimination on the basis of race is particularly unfair and because racially motivated violence is worse than other types of violence, it is principled to suppress speech that has a tendency to cause racially based harm. Similarly, it could be argued that speech that viciously attacks groups of people because of an immutable characteristic is likely to inflict greater psychic injury than other types of speech causing emotional harm.

But the concept of immutability fails to provide a principled way of confining the harmful-tendency and psychic-injury rationales. With respect to the harmful-tendency rationale, it is not at all clear that the discriminatory harms that racist propaganda tends to cause are more grievous than the harms of many other types of speech. It certainly could be argued that the tendency of antiwar speech to impede the war effort or the antipolice rap music to lead to the death of police officers is as grave a harm as racial violence and a far greater harm than nonviolent forms of racial discrimination, such as discrimination in the workplace. And as noted in Chapter 7, it is hard to make the case that racist tracts inflict greater emotional injury than other forms of caustic and insulting public discourse.

Another problem with an immutable-characteristic limitation of the psychic-injury and harmful-tendency rationales is that race is by no means the only immutable characteristic. Indeed, the list of immutable traits is virtually endless, including (at least arguably) sexual orientation, intelligence, mental illness, various physical characteristics (including obesity and ugliness), alcoholism, and antisocial or criminal inclinations. The large number of immutable characteristics suggests that this limitation may not be very confining. It also reveals that immutability may not be a very good criterion for identifying particularly harmful speech. Is a publication that makes fun of the physically handicapped really more emotionally injuring or more likely to cause greater discriminatory harm than an essay that ridicules a particular religion? The lack of any obvious correspondence between speech that attacks immutable characteristics and increased harm undercuts the claim that this rationale is a principled limitation rather than just another result-driven justification.

REDUCED PROTECTION FOR DEFAMATORY ATTACKS ON PEOPLE

A related argument often made by proponents of broad hate speech bans is that unlike the expression involved in the World War I Espionage Act cases, the Smith Act prosecutions of communists, and the other classic free speech cases, hate speech involves vicious attacks on *people*, not criticism of government or its policies.[25] The point here seems to be that hate speech, though it takes the *form* of public discourse, is really an attack on people rather than a legitimate part of the debate on matters of public concern. Like the immutable-characteristic argument, however, this rationale is probably not offered as a sufficient reason for suppressing hate speech (few believe that speech that does not qualify as public discourse should be completely bereft of First Amendment protection) but as grounds for denying hate speech the rigorous protection afforded speech on matters of public concern.

The problem with this argument is that the group defamation that often pervades hate speech is inextricably linked to social and political commentary. We can certainly question the morality and character of those who engage in such expression, perhaps even their mental health. There is no reason, however, to doubt the sincerity of their political and social views. It is untenable to maintain that all those who write racist propaganda have no broader social or political agenda beyond defaming minorities. Rather, any fair assessment of hate propaganda as a social phenomenon must acknowledge that it commonly encompasses arguments for social and political change. In any event, allowing the suppression of speech just because it involves attacks on groups of people is an extremely broad principle. It would include, for instance, the vicious critiques of the male character found in some feminist literature, including that of Dworkin and MacKinnon, as well the disparaging remarks about the capitalist classes that pervade much leftist literature.[26]

But even if racist speech cannot be safely excluded from public discourse just because it involves attacks on groups of people as part of a critique of social policy, there may be other grounds for excluding at least some types of racist speech from public discourse that would not unduly compromise core free speech values.

EXCLUDING HATE SPEECH
FROM PUBLIC DISCOURSE

As we have seen, modern doctrine generally reserves its most rigorous protection for public discourse. Although doctrine generally confines this protection to speech on matters of public concern in certain settings, such as the "public forum" and media essential to public communication, it is extremely reluctant to exclude any speech from public discourse because of its content. Rather, the virtually irrebuttable assumption of current doctrine seems to be that any speech on matters of public concern occurring within these settings will be highly protected no matter how horrific the ideas or how uncivil the expression. Thus the major obstacle to broad hate speech legislation under current doctrine is that much hate speech is considered to be part of public discourse. Some hate speech—for instance, racial epithets directed to a black person waiting for a bus—is of course not public discourse. But included in the speech that proponents of hate speech legislation wish to ban are racist ideas expressed as an integral part of an argument for social or political change. Although racist propaganda often advocates abhorrent policies, such as stripping minorities of basic human rights, racist tracts sometimes also advocate mainstream political reforms as well, such as ending affirmative action or curtailing welfare. But is current doctrine correct in concluding that hate speech is legitimately part of public discourse just because it espouses political or social change? A useful line of inquiry in the search for a principled rationale for banning hate speech that would not gut the protection afforded other public discourse might be to reexamine this conclusion.

Advocacy of Law Violation

Not all hate speech advocates *legal* social change. The worst of it urges law violation, violence against minorities, and even genocide. As discussed in Chapter 2, current doctrine protects advocacy of law violation unless the expression amounts to incitement to imminent lawless action that is likely to produce such conduct. But if the primary instrumental values served by free speech are democratic self-governance and truth discovery, why should advocacy of law violation be protected? The very concept of democratic self-governance presumes a *process* for making and changing laws, and so long as this process is itself democratic and subject to critique and change through collective self-determination, then there would seem to be nothing undemocratic about insisting that this process be followed. As Judge Learned Hand wrote long ago: "Words . . . which have no purport but to counsel the violation of law cannot by any latitude of interpretation be a part of that public opinion which is the final source of government in a democratic state."[27] As a theoretical matter, then, forbidding express advocacy of breach of the democratic process would not seem inconsistent with the democratic self-governance value of free speech. Similarly, as long as individuals are free to advocate any political or social change through lawful process, it would seem that prohibiting express advocacy of law violation would not impair the search for truth in the marketplace of ideas.

Suppressing express advocacy of law violation is also arguably consistent with the noninstrumental values of free speech deriving from the postulate that government must treat individuals as equal, rational, and autonomous agents.[28] So long as one may advocate and work to achieve the repeal of any law, it is far from obvious that this equality precept yields a right to try to persuade others to break the law as it stands. There is a stronger argument that forbidding such speech denies the rational capacities of listeners to decide for themselves whether to violate the law. But if such speech is likely to lead some people to commit crimes, it may be that government is justified in suppressing this speech even if it does not amount to incitement likely to cause an imminent danger of law violation, as is required under current doctrine. In other words, perhaps suppression of express advocacy of criminal activity on a harmful-tendency rationale is consistent with the theoretical underpinnings of free speech.

As we have seen, however, the substantial protection now afforded advocacy of law violation is a product not so much of theory but of experience. The most important lesson learned from a half century of trying to formulate doctrine that would adequately protect both free speech values and legitimate governmental interests is that drawing the line between legitimate and illegitimate public discourse where theory suggested resulted in the punishment of legitimate social criticism. Arguably, however, the Court may have overreacted to this history. Thus it could be argued that these pragmatic concerns could be addressed by means that better strike the balance between protecting dissident speech and preventing lawless activity than does current doctrine. For instance, robust public debate might, as Hand suggested, be sufficiently safeguarded so long as only clear and unequivocal calls to violate the law were punishable, with ambiguous statements and innuendo retaining protection. Furthermore, it could be argued that since only advocacy of illegal racist conduct would be excepted from the general prophylactic rule afforded advocacy of illegal activity, any cost to free speech would be minimal.

Again, however, the following question arises: What principled basis is there for limiting to racist speech the rationale concerning advocacy of illegal conduct? It is not at all certain that advocacy of racial lawlessness is demonstrably more harmful than advocating draft resistance in time of war or advocating the blowing up of government buildings as revenge for alleged government misconduct. To be principled, the rationale may well have to include all express advocacy of criminal activity. Although adoption of this rationale may result in some diminution of the robustness of public discourse, it will at the same time allow the suppression of what is arguably the most pernicious type of hate speech. Such a rationale, however, would not permit the suppression of all racist speech, including the use of highly inflammatory epithets or symbols used in pubic discourse. Banning this expression involves quite a different line of reasoning.

Breach of Civility Norms

It has been argued that even if the expression of racist *ideas* must generally be considered part of the debate on public issues, there is no reason to protect the use of vulgar racial epithets or horrific racist symbols such as burning crosses and swastikas, even when not directed at any particular individual. Those who wish to express racist ideas, the argument continues, can express their views without use of such inflammatory words and symbols.

As discussed in Chapter 2, under current doctrine speakers involved in public discourse have a First Amendment right to express not only any idea they want but to choose the words or symbols for expressing these ideas, even if these words or symbols breach widely accepted civility norms. Like the protection of advocacy of lawless conduct, the protection afforded offensive words and symbols as part of public discourse may be primarily the product of pragmatic, prophylactic consideration rather than some deep theoretical concern. If this is true, then the rule suspending the enforcement of civility norms might be modified to permit the punishment of the use of highly insulting racist language or symbols without compromising core free speech values. And because the modification would be limited to use of *racist* epithets and symbols, any negative practical consequences would be limited.

Again, however, the problem is finding a principle for stripping only offensive racial epithets and symbols of constitutional protection. Although a strong argument can be made that use of racial epithets in *face-to-face* confrontations is demonstrably in a class by itself so far as its tendency to provoke violence and inflict emotional injury is concerned, it is not at all certain that use of racist language and symbols as part of public discourse breaches civility norms more severely than does use of other inflammatory language. Is a sign held up by a protestor in a town square that reads "Down with Niggers" really more offensive than one that says "Fuck Blacks"? And by what criteria are we to conclude, other than through our own political preferences, that the Klan's burning a cross at a political rally is more offensive than protestors' burning an American flag at an antiwar rally? What these examples show is that it is often difficult to separate the offense caused by the way an idea is expressed from the offense caused by the idea itself.

A more principled and workable approach would be to modify free speech doctrine to allow for a *general* imposition of civility norms on public discourse. Conservative justices have urged precisely this approach for decades. Dissenting in *Cohen v. California*, which protected the right of an antiwar protestor to wear a jacket bearing the slogan "Fuck the Draft," and in *Texas v. Johnson*, which upheld the right to burn the American flag as a form of political protest, these justices argued that ideas can adequately be expressed without resort to vulgar words or inflammatory symbols.[29]

On the one hand, modifying free speech doctrine to allow the banning of vulgar words and inflammatory symbols within public discourse, including racist slurs and symbols, although principled, would involve significant costs. Civility norms are purely creatures of social convention and will vary from culture to culture. In a pluralistic society such as ours, it is not clear that there is sufficient consensus about such norms to make their enforcement practical. More likely, only the dominant culture's norms will be enforced. And as Mill long ago recognized and U.S. case law documents, uncivil language used to express ideas challenging the status quo will likely be seen as much more egregious than the same coarse expression used to refute these dissidents.[30]

On the other hand, this near total suspension of civility norms in public discourse may have come at its own cost. Conservatives have long argued that the protection of highly offensive speech has had a negative effect on the tone of society. More recently, people across the political spectrum have suggested that brutal attacks on government and on the character of public officials that have become commonplace on talk radio contributed to violence such as the Oklahoma City bombing. And even if the consequences of the breakdown of civility norms have not been that severe, it has been argued that the lack of civility norms detracts from rational public debate. Particularly if reviewing courts are watchful of selective prosecution, it is arguable that society in general, and public discourse in particular, would be better off if free speech doctrine were modified to allow the suppression of flagrant breaches of widely shared civility norms. Protestors could still criticize American involvement in wars, radicals could still decry the unfairness of capitalistic institutions, and racists could still contend that certain groups are genetically inferior. They would, however, have to make these arguments without using vulgar words or inflammatory symbols.

Those who support the suppression of inflammatory racist words and symbols seldom urge that doctrine be modified to permit *general* enforcement of civility norms, and the radical critics among them never do so. Aside from fearing selective prosecution of minorities and those expressing radical ideas, radical critics do not support modifying doctrine to allow a general imposition of civility norms because they want antiwar protestors to be able to burn American flags or wear jackets that say "Fuck the Draft."

Modifying doctrine to permit the banning of advocacy of lawless conduct as well as the breach of civility norms would be a principled basis for suppressing a significant amount of hate speech from public discourse without gutting the protection that current doctrine provides public discourse. Even in combination, however, these rationales do not cover all racist speech. Still protected would be advocacy calling for the implementation of racist policies through legal means, including advocacy of such appalling measures as stripping certain groups of basic civil rights or legally expelling them from the country. Is there any theory under which this expression, too, could be considered no legitimate part of the debate on matters of public concern?

Speech Advocating Antidemocratic Policies

We have already considered the theory that speech contrary to basic constitutional norms should be less protected than other public discourse. I pointed out that reserving rigorous protection for speech that conforms with contemporary understanding of constitutional norms will likely impair the ability of the democratic process to effectuate change, particularly progressive reform. This conclusion was based on the premise, more empirical than theoretical, that for there to be progress, all norms, including constitutional norms, must be contestable in the public debate.

But is it really true that *all* norms must be contestable for this progress to occur? We have already considered the argument that the contemporary understanding of race and gender equality should be exempt from the rough-and-tumble of public discourse because such understanding is "one of the center beams of the legal order," a position I rejected as both unprincipled and contrary to basic free speech values. There is, however, a more defensible variation on this theme. If, as suggested in Chapter 2, the strong protection afforded public discourse is seen as promoting certain basic values, why should this protection extend to advocacy of political change fundamentally inconsistent with these values? In particular, why should a free speech principle in service of democracy protect expression that advocates antidemocratic measures? Of course, not all racist speech advocates policies deeply inconsistent with democracy. But the worst of it surely does—tracts calling for the reinstitution of slavery or the deportation of certain groups or herding them into concentration camps. If democracy is to mean something more than mere majoritarianism, there must be some respect for the rights of minorities, be they political, ethnic, or religious. Political theorists may differ on just how much protection of minority rights is inherent in the concept of democracy, but most would agree with Abraham Lincoln that a society that permits slavery is to that extent "no democracy."[31] Thus the suppression of speech advocating that minorities be stripped of their basic human rights would seem to advance, not compromise, democracy.

There are, of course, a number of objections that can be raised against this argument. The most basic is that a policy that prevents the abandonment of democracy by democratic means is itself inconsistent with democracy. If after full discussion the people in their collective wisdom choose to abandon democracy, it may be that basic democratic principles must allow this choice. If this criticism is valid, then it follows that a policy that not only prevented this substantive outcome but also forbad its advocacy would also be inconsistent with democracy. As Justice Holmes long ago observed: "If in the long run the beliefs expressed in proletarian dictatorship are destined to be accepted by the dominant forces of the community, the only meaning of free speech is that they should be given their chance and have their way."[32]

It is not, however, at all clear that forbidding the abandonment of democracy is itself inconsistent with democracy. To explore this question, let us imagine a country that has historically had an authoritarian form of government, a communist state, say, or a theocracy. During the past few decades, this country has finally succeeded in establishing a democracy with a constitution that provides for near universal suffrage, governance by a popularly elected legislature and executive, and protection of basic civil rights, including free speech, religion, and equal treatment on the basis of race, ethnicity, and gender. Recently, however, many have been calling for return to "the old ways." Indeed, a recent poll shows that if elections are held as scheduled, the antidemocratic forces will be elected in such numbers that they will be able to amend the constitution so as to reinstate dictatorial rule by the communist party or imams, as the case may be. Would canceling the election so as to save democracy be consistent or inconsistent with democracy?

The answer depends on one's theory of democracy. If one is committed to a *liberal* democracy in which government must respect basic individual rights, then it may well be consistent for a democracy to insist that it remain so, even if a large majority of the people have decided otherwise. In this view, majority rule is not an end in itself but a means of achieving the deeper purposes of democracy, such as ensuring that government respect basic human rights and treat everyone with equal concern and respect. Ordinarily, the basic commitment to equality requires that governance decisions be made by the majority, lest one person's preferences be privileged over another's. But there are occasions in which this commitment to equality requires that majority rule be suspended, such as when a majority attempts to deprive minority groups of basic civil rights or when a party that has gained majority support seeks to lock itself in by restricting free speech or other basic political rights. In such instances any violation of equality resulting from the suspension of majority rule is superficial in comparison to the profound blow to equality that will occur if the majority is allowed to have its way. It is for this reason that many of the fundamental rights ensured by the constitutions of most liberal democracies, though antimajoritarian, are not considered antidemocratic. But if such specific antimajoritarian provisions are consistent with democracy, then it is also consistent with democracy to deny the majority (or even a supermajority) the power to obliterate democracy in its entirety, including the majority rule that ordinarily promotes democracy.[33]

If it *is* consistent with democracy to prevent the majority from abandoning that enterprise, then it may be consistent for a free speech principle in service of democracy to rule out of bounds advocacy of any measure deeply inconsistent with democracy, regardless of the legality of the means proposed for bringing it about. Specifically, it may be that certain racist policies are so anathema to the deepest values of democracy that their advocacy can be excluded from the realm of highly protected public discourse. If democratic self-governance were, as some have argued, the only reason for protecting speech, this might be a persuasive argument, at least on the theoretical level. But as we have seen, another important purpose of free speech is truth discovery in the marketplace of ideas. Under this rationale, a reason for protecting speech inconsistent with democracy is that there may be better forms of government than democracy, and thus taking advocacy of such systems off the table diminishes the possibility of discovering better forms of government. And even if it were to be assumed that democracy is universally and for all time the best possible form of government, allowing democracy to be openly challenged by advocacy of other types of political ordering might, as Mill suggests, reveal partial truths, such as defects in the present forms of democracy.[34] In addition, such rigorous challenges might lead to richer understanding of and a more secure allegiance to democracy. With respect to hate speech in particular, it might be argued that racist challenges to the orthodox, liberal notions of equality might trigger rebuttals that will keep our commitment to racial equality from becoming dead dogma.

But although it may be true that as a general matter we gain a better understanding of issues and a more secure grasp on the truth if all competing ideas are heard, it is not at all certain that much would be lost if *express advocacy* of policies antithetical to the core of democracy were excluded from the marketplace of ideas. As long as any idea, including current understandings of racial and gender equality, could still be vigorously critiqued, it may well be that most of the truth-finding function of speech could be secured without allowing direct advocacy of grossly undemocratic political change. With regard to hate speech in particular, I seriously doubt that the idea of racial equality will become stultified if people are not allowed to advocate amending the Constitution to reinstitute slavery or permitting the expulsion of certain ethnic or religious groups. And even if forbidding such expression resulted in some stultification, it may be that this cost is more than offset by the harms avoided by suppressing this speech.[35]

In addition, there are noninstrumental reasons for not suppressing advocacy of antidemocratic political changes. As discussed in Chapter 2, a primary value underlying free speech is assuring that government treat people as rational agents capable of choosing between good and evil counsel. Even though government consistent with this value may step in at the last moment to keep the majority from irreversibly choosing a regime that would disrespect not only equality but individuals' rationality as well, it would arguably violate respect for individual rational capacity to stop discussion until society has actually reached the edge of the abyss. Thus even if a democracy consistent with its own ideals can put certain political *results* off limits, I am not sure that *advocacy* of these results can similarly be excluded consistent with the values underlying free speech in a liberal democracy.

Aside from these various theoretical objections, there would likely be serious practical problems in declaring antidemocratic speech no part of legitimate public discourse. It would be very difficult to distinguish between critiques of current democratic institutions that might lead to a more just, although radically different democracy and ideas that are truly antithetical to that form of government. Once again I fear that it would be progressive ideas, or those expressed by marginalized groups, that would be most easily condemned as contrary to democracy.[36] One of the justifications offered for suppressing communist speech during the McCarthy era was that speech that advocated the end of democratic institutions had no place in democratic discourse.[37] Radical critics are well aware that such a rationale could easily apply to certain types of leftist speech, including, ironically, calls to radically modify free speech doctrine. It is not surprising, therefore, that they have not embraced a democracy-based rationale for suppressing hate speech.

My purpose here is not to resolve the merits of allowing the prohibition of expression because it advocates political change antithetical to democracy. Rather, I want to suggest that this is a principled rationale that is arguably consistent with at least some of the basic values underlying the rigorous protection afforded robust public discourse. Together with the advocacy-of-criminal-conduct and breach-of-civility-norms rationales, this theory might well support a fairly broad ban on hate speech. And unlike some other rationales favored by radical critics, principled and sensible application of these theories arguably would not gut the protection provided core political speech. Still, their adoption would weaken the strong constitutional protection currently afforded public discourse.

EXCLUDING PORNOGRAPHY
FROM PUBLIC DISCOURSE

It would seem that finding a principled rationale for suppressing pornography without jeopardizing public discourse would not be so formidable a task as finding such a rationale for banning hate speech. If hate speech can be suppressed because it is not *legitimate* public discourse, then pornography could, it would seem, be suppressed because it is not public discourse at all. It has been argued that pornography is essentially a means of sexual arousal, not social or political commentary. If one accepts the premise that the most rigorous protection should be reserved for public discourse, then there would seem to be a principle for suppressing pornography that would not jeopardize democratic self-governance or impair the proper functioning of the marketplace of ideas.

The argument that pornography may be suppressed because it is far afield from the speech by which we govern ourselves and makes no contribution to the marketplace of ideas is a view held not just by radical critics such as MacKinnon but by some mainstream thinkers as well. Sunstein, for instance, argues that "[m]any forms of pornography are not an appeal to the exchange of ideas, political or otherwise; they operate as masturbatory aids and [thus] do not qualify for top-tier First Amendment protection." Because pornography "does not appeal to deliberative capacities about public matters, or about matters at all," this material should, in Sunstein's view, be considered "low-value" speech. As such, pornography, like "misleading commercial speech, libel of private persons, conspiracies, unlicensed medical or legal advice, bribes, perjury [and] threats," should be suppressible on a lesser showing of harm than is required to ban high-value speech.[38] To Sunstein, the scientific evidence of the harm caused by violent pornography described in Chapter 7, though not definitive enough to justify restricting high-value speech, is sufficient to ban low-value speech. Since these studies suggest that the combination of sexually explicit material and violent images leads to violence and other discriminatory harms to women, this is sufficient grounds for banning violent pornography.[39]

Sunstein is to be credited for attempting to find a principled rationale for banning certain forms of sexually explicit speech. Indeed, he is virtually alone among those who favor broader bans on pornography than is permitted under current doctrine in considering the impact that this principle would have on protection of other types of speech. Sunstein's argument for the suppression of pornography is part of a larger critique of current doctrine, which he views as already incorporating a two-tiered approach to speech, but in a selective and unprincipled form. Noting that existing doctrine recognizes several categories of low-value speech (e.g., commercial speech and private libel not on matters of public concern), Sunstein complains that "the Court has yet to offer anything like a clear principle to unify the categories of speech that it treats as 'low value'" and that its current practice of "selective exclusions" from "first tier" protection cannot "be justified as a matter of principle."[40] Sunstein insists that his approach—denominating all speech that does not "appeal to deliberative capacities on public matters" as low-value or "second-tier" speech— is more principled. This approach, however, would relegate to second-class status an enormous amount of speech, including much art and literature. Sunstein contends, however, that "there is little reason to fear a large increase in official censorship" if his approach were adopted.[41] I am not so sanguine.

Sunstein acknowledges that the principle that high-value speech is only that expression that "appeals to deliberative capacities about public matters" fairly calls into question whether art and literature should be classified as "high" or "low" expression.[42] But he argues that under his approach much art and literature would continue to be afforded top-tier constitutional protection. In Sunstein's view high-level speech includes not just "political tracts," but all works of art and literature "that have characteristics of social commentary." He thus finds that James Joyce's *Ulysses* and Charles Dickens's *Bleak House* "political for First Amendment purposes" because *Bleak House* contains "a great deal of comment on the fate of poor people under conditions of industrial profit-seeking" and *Ulysses* "deals with the role of religion in society." Similarly, according to Sunstein, the homoerotic art of Robert Mapplethorpe should be considered high-value speech entitled to rigorous First Amendment protection because it "attempts to draw into question current sexual norms and practices."[43]

As the Mapplethorpe example shows, a major problem with Sunstein's approach is that it requires ad hoc, subjective judgments about whether a given piece of art or literature has sufficient "appeal to the deliberative capacities about public matters" to qualify for rigorous First Amendment protection. To Sunstein, a photograph of a man with a bullwhip inserted in his anus or a picture of a man with a finger inserted in the head of his penis is an attempt "to draw into question current sexual norms and practices." Others, I would wager, view these photographs not as political commentary but as "masturbatory material" for sadomasochistic homosexuals. By what standards are we to determine whether these photographs are sufficiently political to deserve "top-tier" First Amendment protection? Where such subjectivity abounds, the determination is likely to be made not on some detached view about "appeal to the deliberative capacities" but on some judge's view of rough homosexual practices or, worse yet, on the morality of homosexuality.

Moreover, if Mapplethorpe's sexually explicit photographs are entitled to full First Amendment protection because they question "current sexual norms and practices," why is the same not true of pornography in general? Certainly *Playboy* challenged norms when it first came on the market in the 1950s, and some say hard-core pornography does so today. It could be argued that *Hustler* and other magazines that routinely show women as objects for sexual conquest and subordination attempt to question the current view of sexual equality.

My point is not that pornography makes much of an "appeal to the deliberative capacities about public matters." Rather, I am concerned that this construct is far too abstract and slippery to be entrusted with the important task of determining whether a work of art or literature should be relegated to second-class status. In addition to inviting judicial bias, the uncertainty of the "appeal to the deliberative capacities" standard will mean that except in the case of expressly political art or literature, neither the creator of the work nor law enforcement officials will know whether the art in question is entitled to full First Amendment protection or is punishable on some lesser standard.

The top-tier protection that current doctrine extends to all art and literature stems from the realization that there is no practical way to separate art and literature that "appeals to the deliberative capacities" from material that does not make such an appeal without jeopardizing the ability of art and literature to contribute to the deliberative process. Sunstein is well aware of these risks, recognizing the dangers of "[a]d hoc determinations of free speech value," through which the "prejudices and myopia of particular judges, even judges operating in good faith, would produce unacceptable dangers."[44] He thus understands that current doctrine "protect[s] materials that would not, in the best world of perfect judges and costless administration, receive protection—simply because without such protection people in a position of authority will, in our world, draw and implement lines in a way that is too threatening to the system of free expression."[45] Sunstein nonetheless rejects the wisdom of extending rigorous constitutional protection to all art and literature, arguing that such blanket overprotection is unnecessary. In his view the First Amendment protection applicable to lower-value speech is sufficient to prevent governmental abuse. He emphasizes that government is forbidden from regulating even low-level speech for illegitimate reasons and thus must justify the regulation with "reference to genuine harms."[46]

I do not share Sunstein's confidence that the minimal protection afforded the huge category of second-tier speech he would create would adequately prevent government from illegitimately controlling debate on matters of public concern. This is especially true with the protection of art and literature relegated to the second tier because of its irrelevance to public discourse. Sunstein too facilely assimilates "nondeliberative" art and literature in general, and pornography in particular, with "misleading commercial speech, libel of private persons, conspiracies, unlicensed medical or legal advice, bribes, perjury [and] threats," speech that, as Sunstein notes, is treated as low-value speech under current doctrine.[47] When government bans the other forms of expression on Sunstein's list, there is usually no reason to be concerned that it is targeting this speech for some illegitimate reason.[48] In contrast, when government seeks to suppress art and literature—even the "nondeliberative" variety—it is much more likely that it is doing so for some reason that the First Amendment forbids. Totalitarian regimes routinely ban even "nondeliberative" art for reasons that Sunstein would find impermissible.[49]

Suppose that the U.S. government in the 1950s had tried to ban rock 'n' roll from the airwaves on the grounds that it was a particularly ugly and unpleasant form of music. Under Sunstein's approach, the ban would have been upheld because aesthetics, though not an especially compelling justification, is not an impermissible rationale.[50] Under current doctrine, in contrast, such a restriction would be patently invalid. Precisely because all art and literature is considered high-level speech, such a justification would not be nearly compelling enough to pass the "strict scrutiny" that such a ban would elicit. This scrutiny is a product of the suspicion that although aesthetics is the stated rationale, the real reason for the ban is probably something more nefarious.[51]

A similar point can be made about pornography bans. There is reason to believe that the motivation for such bans is "disagreement with the ideas that have been expressed" or "ensur[ing] that people are not offended by the ideas" found in sexually explicit material, rationales that Sunstein lists as illegitimate.[52] Pornography has been condemned for conveying the idea that engaging in sex for recreation rather than as part of a committed relationship is proper behavior, for teaching that there are no negative consequences to such activity, and for leading men to view women as sex objects or even as secretly wishing to be raped.[53] In contrast, bans on false advertising, unlicensed medical or legal advice, bribes, perjury, or threats do not raise the specter that the prohibition is motivated by disagreement with some worldview the expression is assumed to convey.

In addition, the undoubted connection between unlicensed professional advice, bribes, perjury, and threats and harms that government may legitimately address dispels suspicion that government has suppressed this speech because it opposes or is offended by the message this speech delivers. Sunstein suggests that there is a similar connection between pornography and violence against women, citing the scientific studies discussed in Chapter 7. The comparison is inapt. Although not all misleading advertising results in fraud nor all unlicensed medical or legal advice in bodily injury or loss of legal rights, there can be no doubt that as a class this expression would cause significant harm if left unregulated. The clarity and certainty of the harm caused by bribes, perjury, or threats is even more manifest. In contrast, as detailed in the Appendix, the link between violent pornography and violence against women is both murky and contested.

Finally, the suspicion that the true motivation for banning pornography is disagreement with its worldview is magnified by the explanation that pornography causes violence by altering men's attitudes toward women. The various rationales for suppressing misleading advertising, unlicensed professional advice, bribes, perjury, or threats, in contrast, posits no such change in attitudes about how people see the world.[54]

I have spent considerable time critiquing Sunstein's view because it is a sustained and thoughtful effort to find a principled rationale for suppressing pornography. But precisely because it is principled, his approach would strip a vast amount of art and literature of the strong constitutional protection it now enjoys. What Sunstein's argument most clearly demonstrates, then, is that it may not be possible to find a principled basis for banning pornography that would not also imperil core free speech values.

At first it may seem odd that I am more sanguine about finding a principle supporting a broad hate speech ban that would not jeopardize core free speech values than I am about finding such a principle for the suppression of pornography. Hate speech, after all, is much more connected to the debate about public affairs than is pornography. But although free speech doctrine does not permit even the most offensive racist propaganda to be banned, it already allows hard-core pornography to be suppressed. There thus may be no more room for broader pornography bans consistent with adequate protection for public discourse and serious artistic effort. As a theoretical matter, it can certainly be argued that current doctrine affords too much protection to sexually graphic material, just as it overprotects libel and advocacy of lawless conduct. But as we have seen throughout this book, free speech doctrine is more a product of experience than theory. And in the pragmatic judgment of nearly every Supreme Court justice who has wrestled with the problem of pornography regulation since the 1970s, at least this degree of protection is necessary.[55] Thus with respect to the relationship between public discourse and pornography, free speech doctrine has already separated the wheat from the chaff.

10

WEIGHING THE COSTS AND BENEFITS OF HATE SPEECH AND PORNOGRAPHY BANS

The primary purpose of the survey of the costs and benefits of broad hate speech and pornography bans has been to give readers sufficient information to draw their own conclusions about the wisdom of such regulations, including whether doctrine should be modified to permit such speech suppression. Although I have strived to be fair and objective, I of course have my own views on the various arguments for and against banning hate speech and pornography, some of which I have expressed along the way. Here I want to both summarize these views and offer some overall conclusions.

GAUGING THE STAKES

With respect to hate speech bans, my firmest conclusion is that the stakes are not nearly so high as many of the proponents and opponents of such bans claim. If there were strong reasons to believe that racist propaganda is a major cause of violence and discrimination against minorities in this country, and if modifying doctrine to permit the suppression of this speech would likely have a disastrous effect on free speech, we might have to make some hard choices. Fortunately, we are not faced with such a dilemma. There is no evidence that outlawing hate speech will significantly reduce violence and discrimination against minorities. Indeed, it is doubtful that hard-core racist propaganda significantly contributes to the formation or perpetuation of racist beliefs in this country. The primary responsibility for such beliefs lies with much more subtle influences, such as attitudes transmitted from parent to child. Making it even more un-likely that racist propaganda is a primary cause of racial discrimination or racist beliefs is that until relatively recently this material has not been widely available. The Internet, however, has made racist speech more ac-cessible. Although this development is troubling and should be carefully monitored, there is as yet no evidence that it has led to a marked rise in ei-ther racial discrimination or beliefs.

By the same token, there is no reason to believe that the enactment of hate speech laws or the modification of free speech doctrine to allow for such a ban would have a catastrophic effect on free speech in this country. With sensible drafting and proper vigilance by the courts, misapplication and selective enforcement of hate speech bans could be minimized, thereby limiting (though not eliminating) the chilling effect on nonracist speech. Moreover, there are arguably principled rationales for upholding the constitutionality of such laws, such as the exclusion of speech that ad-vocates illegal conduct, breaches civility norms, or advocates changes in-imical to a democracy. Precisely what the cost to free speech would be if any or all of these broad rationales for speech suppression were adopted is difficult to say. My best guess is that there would be considerable dampening of public discourse but that the negative consequences would not be monumental.

Even if the First Amendment were repealed, traditions of free speech are sufficiently strong in this country that legislatures would generally (though not always) respect core free speech values. Still, unlike those in some other democracies, Americans have come to rely on judicial protec-tion of free speech. Any sudden gutting of this protection could have a significant negative effect on public discourse. For this reason, if the Court were ever to uphold a ban on racist propaganda, it might well in-voke a much narrower rationale than the ones suggested above, a ratio-nale with the patina of principle but that could not withstand critical ex-amination. Such an unprincipled decision, though harmful to both free speech doctrine and the Court's authority to some indeterminate extent, would not be disastrous for either.

With respect to pornography, the stakes may be somewhat higher. There is some evidence that violent pornography and perhaps other types of pornography as well cause violence and discrimination against women. And unlike hate speech, pornography is extremely prevalent in this soci-ety. On the present state of the evidence, however, it cannot be confidently concluded that pornography is a significant cause of violence or discrimi-nation against women or that banning pornography will significantly re-duce this harm. In addition, any ban on sexually graphic material notably broader than the one permitted under current obscenity doctrine is likely to inhibit artistic expression as well as political discourse.

A much more certain benefit from banning hate speech and pornography would be preventing insult to minorities and women inflicted by this expression and reassuring them that government does not share the hateful or demeaning views portrayed in this material. Although not nearly as compelling as preventing violence and discrimination, these interests are nonetheless important. They can, however, be achieved by means other than speech suppression.

THE IMPORTANCE OF
CONSIDERING ALTERNATIVE REMEDIES

Government can demonstrate to minorities and women that it does not share the hateful or demeaning views expressed in racist propaganda or pornography by condemning these views in its own speech. Similarly, counterspeech by private individuals can show that most people do not share these views and thus can go a long way to relieving the insult inflicted by racist or pornographic speech. The existence of alternative remedies also undercuts several other rationales for suppressing hate speech and pornography. For instance, if, as Fiss claims, public discourse has been robbed of certain perspectives because of the silencing effect of hate speech and pornography, government can remedy this harm by using its own voice to provide missing perspectives. Similarly, if MacKinnon is correct that pornography obscures the fact that coercing women into unwanted sex acts is sex abuse, government could make this harm visible, either by subsidizing those who will expose this abuse or through its own campaign.

Fiss apparently sees no difference between the state's "allocating public resources—[metaphorically] hand[ing] out megaphones—to those whose voices would not otherwise be heard" and "silencing the voices of some in order to hear the voices of others."[1] Pace Fiss, the distinction is crucial. For one, government suppression involves dangers that subsidization or the government's own speech does not, such as misapplication, selective enforcement, and chilling speech that is neither racist nor pornographic. More important, subsidization and government counterspeech is a more precise response to inadequate representation of certain viewpoints than is the clumsy and indirect solution of speech repression. In addition, unlike subsidization or counterspeech, suppression threatens to eliminate completely a particular point of view from the public debate. Speech suppression thus cannot possibly be justified as promoting the proper functioning of the marketplace of ideas. Finally, suppression infringes upon the basic moral right of each individual to try to persuade others to see the world in a certain way. In contrast, government supplementation and counterspeech do not implicate this core value.

Especially because there is no conclusive evidence that hate speech and pornography are a significant cause of violence or discrimination, it is crucial that alternatives to speech suppression be considered as remedies to these harms as well. Such alternative means for addressing these harms include increased enforcement of civil rights and domestic violence laws, educational campaigns that raise public consciousness about the possible harms of pornography,[2] and vociferous official condemnation of racism in all its manifestations.

THE HIDDEN INFLUENCE OF NONUTILITARIAN POSITIONS

In an interesting way, the arguments for the repression of hate speech and pornography are similar to the arguments for the death penalty. In both debates the arguments are often stated in harm-based, utilitarian terms, with the proponents drawing on dubious or inconclusive statistical analyses or scientific studies. Just as many proponents of the death penalty will latch on to any evidence showing that it is a greater deterrent to murder than life imprisonment, so, too, many proponents of hate speech and pornography bans are convinced on very thin evidence that hate speech and pornography are a significant cause of violence and discrimination against women. Most people who are strongly in favor of the death penalty will admit, however, that even if it could be shown with certainty that capital punishment is not a more effective deterrent than life imprisonment, they would still favor execution of murderers. They will argue that deterrence aside, killers of innocent people should be put to death because they deserve to die.

I suggest that something similar may underlie at least some of the arguments for banning hate speech and pornography. Even if it could be conclusively proved that hate speech and pornography were not a cause of violence and discrimination against minorities and women, I suspect that many proponents of such bans would still favor suppression because they believe that this expression is profoundly offensive to any moral view of humanity. This moral view emerges at the end of Matsuda's argument for the suppression of hate speech when she writes that racist propaganda should be banned "not because it isn't really speech, not because it falls within a hoped-for neutral exception, but because it is wrong."[3]

A nonutilitarian moral vision may similarly lurk in some arguments *against* broad hate speech and pornography bans. Although many who oppose such bans argue that they would have disastrous consequences for the democratic nature of our institutions, these claims are hard to support. I suspect that if it could be shown that hate speech and pornography bans would not in fact lead to any significant impairment of free speech, many opponents of such bans would still oppose their enactment. Many who argue against hate speech and pornography bans may not be conscious of some deeper opposition. Ronald Dworkin, however, captures this view when he argues that government insults us when it suppresses speech out of fear that it may persuade people to see the world in a way that the authorities find dangerous or offensive.[4]

At its deepest level, then, the arguments both for and against suppressing hate speech and pornography may have less to do with preventing harm, either to women and minorities or to free speech and democracy, than with preventing insult to human dignity. At bottom, the hate speech and pornography controversy may pose the question whether it is better for minorities and women to be insulted by demeaning images of them or for all of us to be insulted by the government's deciding the proper way for us to perceive the world. This may explain why those who tend to see political issues in stark moral terms tend to have intractable views on hate speech and pornography bans. Radicals who reflexively support almost any measure that seems to advance racial and gender equality, even if only symbolically, passionately support hate speech and pornography bans. In contrast, libertarians who see any restriction on liberty as anathema are unalterably opposed to such bans. Liberals who have strong commitments to both liberty and equality, however, find the choice more difficult and will tend to rely on instrumental assessments to resolve the issue.

Although deep-seated moral reactions to proposals to ban hate speech and pornography may be in play more than we recognize, the practical consequences of such proposals, for minorities and women as well as for free speech doctrine, remain crucial. Difficult though it may be, it is important to try to make these empirical assessments as free as possible from the distorting influence of deeply held preconceptions.

SUMMARY AND CONCLUSION

On the one hand, it is unlikely that broad hate speech and pornography bans and the modification of free speech doctrine that these bans would entail would have disastrous consequences for free speech. On the other hand, such developments would likely impair the vitality and robustness of public discourse to some considerable extent. The danger is twofold. Any broad ban of hate speech would likely deter nonracist political commentary, just as a broad ban on pornography would inevitably chill the production of serious art and literature dealing with sexual matters. Second, it is difficult to conceive of a principled rationale for such suppression that would not also diminish the constitutional protection that experience has shown is necessary to robust public discourse. There thus would likely be sobering costs involved in suppressing hate speech and pornography.

On the other side of the ledger, the most important benefits that banning hate speech and pornography might produce are extremely speculative. Because proof of the relationship between these forms of speech and violence or illegal discrimination against women and minorities is sparse, there is no guarantee that a ban would alleviate these harms. The more certain benefits, such as reassuring minorities and women that neither the government nor the majority of Americans share the distorted and offensive worldview portrayed in these materials, can be accomplished by means other than speech repression.

On the present state of the evidence, therefore, the better course in my view is to combat the harms that hate speech and pornography might cause through means other than speech repression. If future studies demonstrate with more certainty that certain types of pornography are a significant cause of sexual violence or discrimination, then modifying doctrine to allow for the suppression of this speech might be justified. Similarly, if hate speech were to proliferate, and it could be demonstrated that this expression was contributing to increased violence or discrimination against minorities, I would reevaluate this conclusion.

Although I have confidence in my position that current doctrine's refusal to allow broad bans on hate speech and pornography is on our present state of knowledge correct as a matter of policy, it bears repeating that my ultimate purpose is not to convince the reader of this result. Rather, my primary aim is to provide the background for people to reach their own conclusions about this perennial problem of social policy.

It is true, of course, that whether to modify doctrine to permit broad hate speech and pornography bans is the prerogative of the U.S. Supreme Court. Thus to some extent discussion about these issues is, as they say, academic. But more than might be supposed, Supreme Court decisions tend to reflect the basic beliefs of the American people. It is inconceivable, for instance, that in the climate of the 1950s the Court would have found a constitutional right to abortion or held that the Virginia Military Institute had to admit women. Public attitudes toward free speech in general and its relation to hate speech and pornography in particular could well in the long run have an effect on social policy, including Supreme Court doctrine. In any event, our current system of free speech invites debate on all matters of public concern, among them the controversies about the limits of free speech.

11

CONCLUSION

Public debate on important issues such as abortion, affirmative action, and presidential impeachment increasingly resembles professional wrestling more than rational discourse among citizens. Such no-holds-barred screaming matches, marked by invective, distortions, and even outright lies, are no doubt the product of the mass media's concern for ratings and audience share rather than for intellectual content. Perhaps this unfortunate state of affairs is also partly due to the mistaken belief that the best way to offer a balanced presentation is to encourage two people with views on opposite extremes to fight it out. It is regrettable enough, although perhaps understandable, that popular debate has tended to degenerate in this way. More troubling and less understandable is that academic discussion is often marked by the same defects.

In the early 1990s, I attended a free speech conference at a large midwestern university. On a panel with me was a well-known radical critic who claimed that contrary to popular belief, free speech is useless to oppressed minorities, as is shown by the Supreme Court's invariably construing the First Amendment against civil rights protestors. On another panel a speaker took the position that free speech doctrine did not allow the prevention of racially or sexually harassing speech in the workplace. At about the same time as this conference, I was doing research for an article on hate speech regulation on campus. I was dismayed with how much participants on both sides of the debate distorted facts to support their position. For instance, in a law review article attacking campus codes, Congressman Henry Hyde alleged that "at UCLA, the editor of the student newspaper was suspended" for running a cartoon critical of affirmative action.[1] In fact, the student was not suspended from the university, as Hyde implied, but was suspended from the newspaper by a student-run communications board.[2] Similarly, in an article arguing in favor of campus hate speech codes, Richard Delgado misleadingly re-counts an incident in which he claims a fraternity held a "slave auction" in which the pledges wore "black face-paint and Afro wigs."[3] In fact, the blackface and wigs were part of a skit in which pledges lip-synched Jackson Five songs and imitated Oprah Winfrey; this regalia had nothing to do with the "slave auction" theme of a fund-raiser in which people bid for the services of a pledge.

Over the years, the quality of discourse about hate speech and pornography regulation has continued to deteriorate. The distortions persist, and the discussion has often taken on an ad hominem quality, such as the charge that opposition to hate speech and pornography bans stems from a desire to keep minorities and women "in their place," or the charge made by a colleague of mine that the *purpose* of hate speech codes on college campuses is to stifle criticism of university affirmative action policies. In this book I have tried to contribute a degree of moderation to this polarized debate, in the hope of providing the reader with a more balanced perspective on this difficult issue. To this end, I have shown that many of the extreme charges that radicals have leveled against free speech doctrine cannot be substantiated. Particularly unsupportable, though repeatedly alleged, is the charge that free speech doctrine is discriminatory because it prevents far-reaching hate speech regulation and banning of pornography demeaning to women while permitting speech regulations that serve the interests of the rich and powerful. As we have seen, free speech doctrine does not allow *any* viewpoint-based restriction on public discourse, no matter whose interest it may serve. But the radicals are correct when they emphasize that free speech doctrine is not neutral in any deep sense. Although it supplies an important check on the majority's power, free speech doctrine does not operate outside the legal system but as an integral part of it. As such, this doctrine will to some degree reflect the legal system's basic norms, including capitalism. As a result, the wealthy, which in this society disproportionately include white males, will have more access to the marketplace of ideas. And to an even greater degree, the speech itself (as opposed to the doctrine) will tend to reflect majority sentiment, including lingering racist and sexist views.

The question whether broad hate speech and pornography restrictions are good social policy is a difficult issue about which reasonable people can differ. My own view is that in the United States at this time such restrictions would on balance be inimical to continued social progress, including increased race and gender equality. As I have said, however, my primary purpose here is not to persuade others of this position. It is instead to demonstrate that the right answer to this complex question cannot be derived from slogans or preconceptions but must be determined through careful analysis.

APPENDIX:
EMPIRICAL STUDIES ON THE
EFFECTS OF PORNOGRAPHY

Science Meets Ideology

In contrast to the dearth of scientific research on the harm caused by hate speech, recent studies have focused on the question of whether pornography leads to acts of aggression and violence toward women. There have, however, been a number of conflicting claims about what these studies show. For instance, in the mid-1980s the Attorney General's Commission on Pornography found that "the available evidence strongly supports the hypothesis that substantial exposure to sexually violent materials . . . bears a causal relationship to antisocial acts of sexual violence and, for some subgroups, possibly to unlawful acts of sexual violence."[1] In contrast, the American Civil Liberties Union claims that the commission "wildly overstates" the "tentative results of a limited number" of studies.[2] Academics debating the wisdom and constitutionality of banning pornography make similarly disparate claims. Sociologist Diana Russell refers to the "very strong evidence" that pornography causes harm, whereas philosopher Ronald Dworkin asserts that "no respectable study or evidence has shown any causal link between pornography and actual violence."[3] In Chapter 7 I concluded that like so many of the claims about hate speech and pornography and the regulation of this material, the truth lies somewhere in between: Although there is some evidence that violent pornography (and perhaps "demeaning" pornography as well) causes violence against women, the evidence is far from conclusive. In this Appendix I discuss in detail both the claims made about these studies and what these studies actually show.

THE PRESIDENT'S COMMISSION ON PORNOGRAPHY

In 1970 the President's Commission on Pornography reviewed the pertinent studies on the effects of pornography, including research it had funded, and concluded:

> Research to date . . . provides no substantial basis for the belief that erotic materials constitute a primary or significant cause of the development of character deficits or that they operate as a significant determinative factor in causing crime and delinquency. . . . On the basis of the available data . . . it is not possible to conclude that erotic material is a significant cause of sex crime.[4]

At the time the president's commission reported, however, scientific inquiry into the effects of pornography was at an early stage. Many of the experiments were rudimentary and did not explore more sophisticated hypotheses that might have uncovered harm caused by exposure to pornography. One serious shortcoming was that the experimenters and the commission did not differentiate the types of sexually explicit material, such as material with and without a violent theme. The cautious phrasing of the 1970 commission's conclusion was thus appropriate given the research then available. In the years that followed, researchers conducted experiments that did distinguish among types of sexually explicit material. In light of the apparent increase in violent sexual material since the 1970 commission report, many studies focused on the harm caused by this material.

THE REPORT OF THE ATTORNEY GENERAL'S COMMISSION ON PORNOGRAPHY

In 1985, at the request of President Ronald Reagan, Attorney General William French Smith appointed another commission to study the effects of pornography on American society. (Despite being appointed by Smith, the commission became known in the popular press as the Meese Commission, after Attorney General Edwin Meese, who was in office when the commission reported.) Unlike the president's commission, the attorney general's commission distinguished among various types of pornography in assessing harm, dividing sexually explicit material into three categories: (1) sexually violent material, (2) nonviolent but degrading material, and (3) material that is neither violent nor degrading.

The commission defined "sexually violent material" as that "featuring actual or unmistakably simulated or unmistakably threatened violence presented in a sexually explicit fashion with a predominant focus on the sexually explicit violence."[5] This category included material with "sado-masochistic themes, with the standard accouterments of the genre, including whips, chains, [and] devices of torture"; it also included material depicting "a man making some sort of sexual advance to a woman, being rebuffed, and then raping the woman or in some other way forcing himself on the woman." Also subsumed in this category is more "mainstream" material, such as "slasher" films, that portrays sexual activity or sexually suggestive nudity coupled with extreme violence, such as disfigurement or murder.[6]

The commission found that "[i]ncreasingly, the most prevalent forms of pornography" contain depictions of violence.[7] In reaching this conclusion, the commission relied on a study by a Canadian commission that determined that 10 percent of the sexual acts depicted in text of mainstream sexually explicit magazines (*Playboy, Penthouse, Hustler,* and the like) involved "the use of force," including "anal penetration, bondage equipment, weapons, rape and murder."[8] The commission also referred to a study that analyzed the content of *Playboy* and

Penthouse cartoons and pictures from 1973 to 1977 and concluded that "[p]ictorial violent sexuality was found to have increased significantly" over this five-year period (although it was still a relatively small percentage of the total pictorial material, reaching about 5 percent in 1977).[9] According to another study the commission cited, the covers of hard-core pornographic magazines indicated that "bondage and domination" imagery had greatly increased since 1970.[10]

The category of nonviolent but degrading sexually explicit material is described as "depicting degradation, domination, subordination, or humiliation." Such material shows "people, usually women, in decidedly subordinate roles in their sexual practices that would to most people be considered humiliating."[11] The commission found that this category constitutes "somewhere between the predominant and overwhelming portion of what is currently standard fare heterosexual pornography" and that degradation is a "significant theme" in other sexually oriented material not explicit enough to be considered pornographic.[12] At another point in the report, the commission referred to the category of degrading material as "the largely predominant proportion of commercially available pornography."[13]

The third category of sexually explicit material that is neither violent nor degrading is, according to the commission, "in fact quite small in terms of currently available materials."[14]

With respect to the sexually violent material, the commission concluded that "the available evidence strongly supports the hypothesis that substantial exposure to sexually violent materials . . . bears a causal relationship to antisocial acts of sexual violence and, for some subgroups, possibly to unlawful acts of sexual violence."[15] In reaching this conclusion, the commission relied on a number of laboratory experiments conducted since the president's commission report in 1970 showing that "exposure to sexually violent materials [results in] an increase in the likelihood in aggression," specifically in "aggressive behavior towards women."[16]

Typical of the experiments on which the commission relied is the one conducted by Edward Donnerstein in 1980.[17] Male subjects were first angered by either female or male confederates of the experimenter and then exposed to one of three films: a sexually explicit but nonviolent film, a pornographic film depicting a rape, or a film that was neither sexually explicit nor violent. Following the exposure, the subjects were put in a position in which they could engage in aggressive behavior by (supposedly) administering electric shock as punishment to another person for failure correctly to perform a task in what the subject thought was a learning experiment.[18] As summarized by the commission, this study showed that "when the target of angered subjects was a male, there was no difference in aggressive behavior (measured by the shock intensity on an aggression machine) among males in the erotic and the aggressive-pornographic conditions. However, when the target was a female, aggressive behavior was higher [but] only in the aggressive-pornographic film condition."[19]

The commission acknowledged that scientific studies such as Donnerstein's suggested only that violent pornography caused increased levels of aggression, not that this elevated aggression led to actual acts of sexual violence. Relying primarily on their own "common sense," however, the members of the commission were willing to make the assumption that "increased aggressive behavior towards women is causally related, for an aggregate population, to increased sexual violence."[20] The commission was thus able to conclude "unanimously and confidently" that violent pornography is a cause of sexual violence.[21]

In bridging this gap between evidence of laboratory aggression and its finding of actual acts of sexual violence, the commission expressly stated that it considered certain types of evidence unreliable. For instance, the commission discounted testimony of sex offenders who claimed that pornography led them to commit sex crimes, noting that psychological research shows "the tendency of people to externalize their own problems by looking too easily for some external source beyond their own control."[22] Similarly, the commission viewed skeptically various types of "correlational" evidence, such as reports of law enforcement personnel that sex offenders disproportionately had large quantities of pornography in their homes, and even the more scientific studies that show a correlation between high consumption of pornography in certain regions of this country and a high rate of sex crimes. The commission noted that "[c]orrelational evidence suffers from its inability to establish a causal connection between the correlated phenomena [for] it is frequently the case that two phenomena are positively correlated precisely because they are both caused by some third phenomena [sic]." Thus the commission noted that some other factor, for example, "some sexual or emotional imbalance," might be responsible both for the excessive use of pornography and the urge to commit sex crimes.[23] Nonetheless, the commission found that although such correlational data cannot definitely establish causality, they provide nonetheless "some evidence" that a causal link might exist.[24]

Sexual violence was not, however, the only harm that the commission concluded violent pornography caused. Again relying on scientific research, the commission reported that "[t]he evidence is also strongly supportive of significant attitudinal changes on the part of those with substantial exposure to violent pornography."[25] The commission pointed to a 1980 study by Malamuth, Haber, and Feschbach in which subjects read a sexually explicit story from *Penthouse* magazine modified to create a violent and nonviolent version. According to the commission, the study found that males exposed to the violent version "perceived more favorably a rape depiction that was presented to subjects subsequently" and that "[s]ubjects were found to believe that a high percentage of men would rape if they knew they would not be punished and that many women would enjoy being victimized."[26]

In a 1981 experiment by Malamuth and Check, male and female subjects agreed to participate in a study ostensibly focusing on movie ratings. Some of the subjects saw two feature-length films containing sexual violence, *Swept Away* and *The Getaway*.[27] Other subjects watched a nonviolent movie. Several days after viewing this material, the subjects were given a sexual attitude survey in classes, but the subjects were not informed that there was any connection between this survey and the films they had viewed. As summarized in the commission report: "Results showed that exposure to sexual violence increased male subjects' acceptance of interpersonal violence against women. A similar trend, though statistically nonsignificant, was found for the acceptance of rape myths."[28]

In light of these and other studies, the commission concluded that:

substantial exposure to violent sexually explicit material leads to a greater acceptance of the "rape myth" in its broader sense—that women enjoy being coerced into sexual activity, that they enjoy being physically hurt in a sexual context, and that as a result a man who forces himself on a woman sexually is in fact merely acceding to the "real" wishes of the woman, regardless of the extent to which she seems to be resisting. . . . We [therefore] have little trouble concluding that this attitude is both pervasive and profoundly harmful, and that any stimulus reinforcing or increasing the incidence of this attitude is for that reason alone properly designated as harmful.[29]

The commission also found that scientific evidence is "strongly supportive" of the conclusion that "substantial exposure" to violent pornography causes its viewers to perceive victims of rape as "more responsible for the assault, as having suffered less injury, and as having been less degraded as a result of the experience" and that these viewers "are likely to see the rapist or other sexual offender as less responsible for the act and deserving of less stringent punishment."[30] Typical of the studies the commission cited is a 1985 experiment by Linz involving male college students who watched slasher films containing explicit violence in a sexual context (e.g., *Toolbox Murders*, which depicts a naked woman masturbating in a bathtub, then being stalked and killed by a masked man wielding a power tool). After viewing one film per day for five days, subjects were asked to participate in what they were told was a different study ("a pretest of a law school documentary" of a rape trial) and then completed a questionnaire about the victim. According to the commission, the study found that "[t]hose massively exposed to sexual violence judged the victim of the assault to be significantly less injured and evaluated her as less worthy than did the control group."[31]

In reporting its findings as to the harm of violent pornography, the commission emphasized "[t]wo vitally important features of the evidence." First, perpetuation of the rape myth and other harms "are more pronounced when the sexually violent materials depict women as experiencing arousal, orgasm, or other form of enjoyment as the ultimate result of the sexual assault."[32] The second point that the commission emphasized was that the harms it identified apparently "*do not vary with the extent of sexual explicitness so long as the violence is presented in an undeniably sexual context.*"[33] Indeed, the commission acknowledged that it is "unclear whether sexually violent material makes a substantially greater causal contribution to sexual violence itself than does material containing violence alone." But what was fairly certain to the commission was that "increasing the amount of violence after the threshold of connecting sex with violence is more related to increase in the incidence and severity of harmful consequences than is increasing the amount of sex." Thus in the commission's view, slasher films, which depict a great deal of violence in an "undeniably" sexual context but one that is far less explicit than is found in "truly pornographic" material, are more likely to produce the harms described by the commission than are "most of the materials available in 'adults only' pornographic outlets."[34]

With respect to sexually explicit material that is nonviolent but depicts "degradation, domination, subordination, or humiliation" (usually of women), the commission also found that "substantial exposure to materials of this type bears some causal relationship to the level of sexual violence, sexual coercion, or unwanted sexual aggression in the population so exposed."[35] Specifically, the commission found that "substantial exposure to material of this variety is likely to increase the extent to which those exposed will view rape or other forms of sexual violence as less serious than they otherwise would have, will view the victims of rape and other forms of sexual violence as significantly more responsible, and will view the offenders as significantly less responsible."[36] The commission, however, qualified its conclusion regarding this material with the caveat that "there is less evidence" of a causal link with antisocial behavior than is the case with violent pornography. The commission thus reached its decision about the harm caused by degrading pornography with "somewhat less confidence" than it did concerning violent pornography and acknowledged that its conclusion "requires more in the way of assumption than was the case with respect to violent material."[37] Again the commission relied on scientific studies in judging that degrading pornography caused attitudinal changes.

One such study was a 1985 experiment by Check, a Canadian researcher. Subjects were exposed to one of three types of sexually explicit films: (1) a film that contained sexual violence, (2) a nonviolent but degrading film, or (3) a film that was neither violent nor degrading. As the commission described it, the sexually violent film contained "[s]cenes of sexual intercourse which included a woman strapped to a table and being penetrated by a large plastic penis"; the degrading film included a scene with "a man masturbating into a woman's face while sitting on top of her"; and the film that was neither violent nor degrading contained "[s]ex activities leading up to intercourse between a man and a woman."[38]

According to the commission, the study showed that "those in the violent and in the degrading exposure condition reported significantly greater likelihood of engaging in [rape and coercive sex] compared to the control group" (those who did not watch any film). The commission noted, however, that these findings should be "viewed with caution" because of various methodological problems, such as the participants' being told the study was funded by a Canadian commission on pornography.[39] The attorney general's commission also relied on a 1982 study by Zillmann and Bryant, discussed in more detail below, that showed that degrading pornography leads to similar attitudinal changes.[40]

As it did with respect to its findings regarding violent pornography, the commission acknowledged that the scientific data indicated only that degrading pornography led to attitudinal changes, not that these changes actually led to antisocial acts. Once again, however, the commission was willing to make the assumption, based on "all the evidence," including their "own insights and experience" that "[o]ver a large enough sample a population that believes that many women like to be raped, that believes that sexual violence or sexual coercion is often desired or appropriate, and that believes that sex offenders are less responsible for their acts, will commit more acts of sexual violence or sexual coercion than would a population holding these beliefs to a lesser extent."[41]

The commission also found that "substantial exposure" to degrading pornography "bears some causal relationship to the incidence of various nonviolent forms of discrimination against or subordination of women in our society."[42] As the commission explained:

> To the extent these materials create or reinforce the view that women's function is disproportionately to satisfy the sexual needs of men, then the materials will have perva-

sive effects on the treatment of women in society far beyond the incidence of identifiable acts of rape or other sexual violence. We obviously cannot here explore fully all of the forms in which women are discriminated against in contemporary society. Nor can we explore all of the causes of that discrimination against women. But we feel confident in concluding that the view of women as available for sexual domination is one cause of that discrimination, and we feel confident as well in concluding that degrading material bears a causal relationship to the view that women ought to subordinate their own desires and being to the sexual satisfaction of men.[43]

As to sexually explicit material that is neither violent nor demeaning, the commission stated that it was "on the current state of the evidence persuaded that material of this type does not bear a causal relationship to rape and other acts of sexual violence."[44] In coming to this conclusion, the commission acknowledged that although many of the recent studies distinguish between violent and nonviolent fare, only a few further subdivide nonviolent material into degrading and nondegrading. As the commission's review of the research reveals, studies that lump all nonviolent pornography together have yielded conflicting results with respect to whether such material negatively affects men's attitudes toward sexual violence against women. "But," suggested the commission, "when the stimulus material . . . is considered there is some suggestion that the presence or absence of negative effects from non-violent material might turn on the non-violent material being considered 'degrading.'"[45]

A 1982 study by Zillmann and Bryant, for example, showed that subjects massively exposed to nonviolent pornography "exhibited greater sex callousness" than did a control group.[46] In contrast, a 1985 study by Linz as well as a 1970 study by Mosher produced "contrary evidence" about the effects of nonviolent pornography.[47] The commission attempted to explain this conflict by suggesting that the Zillmann and Bryant study involved demeaning pornography—films in which "women are portrayed as masochistic, subservient, socially nondiscriminating nymphomaniacs"—whereas the nonviolent pornography Linz and others used in their studies that did not produce negative attitude changes was not demeaning.[48] This hypothesis is supported by Check's investigation, discussed above, which explicitly differentiated between demeaning and nondemeaning pornography.

Although concluding that the evidence does not show a causal link between pornography that is neither violent nor demeaning and acts of sexual violence, the commission emphasized that this conclusion does not mean that there might not be effects associated with this material that some would consider harmful. For instance, the commission acknowledged arguments that this material might lead to the legitimization of sex acts that many members of society believe to be immoral; might promote sexual activity outside of committed relationships; would expose to public view activities that some believe should take place only in private; might lead to a decline in the moral tone of society; and might fall into the hands of children, for whom this material would be harmful. As to these questions, the commission candidly admitted that it could reach no agreement and that the differences among the members of the commission reflected the different attitudes in society at large on sexual matters.[49]

Drawing on its conclusion that exposure to sexually violent or demeaning pornography contributes to sexual violence, coercion, and gender discrimination and pointing to the lack of evidence that pornography that is neither violent nor demeaning leads to such consequences, the commission recommended that law enforcement prioritize its enforcement of existing obscenity laws. The commission urged that prosecution of legally obscene material (that is, material that meets the test set forth in *Miller v. California*, the landmark obscenity case discussed in Chapter 2) that contains violence "be placed at the top of both state and federal priorities in enforcing the obscenity laws."[50] Because the evidence of harm was not as strong with respect to pornography that is nonviolent but degrading, the commission was of the view that "if choices have to be made," prosecution of nonviolent but degrading obscenity should "receive slightly lower priority than sexually violent material."[51] As to legally obscene material that is neither violent nor degrading, the commission was "deeply divided." Some members urged that all legally obscene material be prosecuted with "equal vigor," whereas other members believed that materials in this category should "quite consciously be treated as a lower priority."[52] But no member recommended deregulation or even total lack of prosecution of nonviolent, nondegrading obscenity.[53]

Despite its conclusion that sexually violent or demeaning material is harmful, the commission did not urge prohibiting such material unless it is also legally obscene under current doctrine. Thus the commission expressly rejected the suggestion that it recommend a definition of obscenity broader than the *Miller* standard: "Even assuming a desire to restrict materials not currently subject to restriction under *Miller,* a desire that most of us do not share, we find a strategy of embarking on years of constitutional litigation with little likelihood of success to be highly counterproductive."[54] The commission accordingly concluded that law enforcement officials should respect the constitutional line the Court has drawn between obscene material and sexually explicit material protected by the First Amendment.[55]

But this recognition and acceptance of constitutional limitations on the government's power to regulate expression raised a problem: Much, if not most, of the violent and degrading material that scientific studies showed leads to violence or discrimination is not sexually explicit enough to be legally obscene. Indeed, the studies suggest that some of the most harmful material might be slasher films, which although graphically violent are relatively low in sexual explicitness and thus cannot be fairly described as pornographic. The commission recognized that "even the most stringent legal strategies within current or even in any way plausible constitutional limitations would likely address little more than only the tip of the iceberg" of materials that scientific studies showed are likely to promote violence or discrimination against women.[56]

The commission was thus faced with the problem of defending its recommendations to spend considerable resources to regulate material that is but "a thin slice of the full problem." The commission offered two reasons for its decision. First, it suggested that because legally obscene materials present their messages "in a form undiluted by any appeal to the intellect," it may be that such material bears a "causal relationship to the harms we have identified to a disproportionate degree." In addition, the commission observed that "law serves an important symbolic function" and that by forbidding even a small portion of the harmful material these laws will serve "as a model for the condemnatory attitudes and actions of private citizens" with respect to harmful material that the law cannot forbid.[57]

Criticisms of the Report
of the Attorney General's Commission

The report, including its findings about harm, has been widely criticized. The most thorough critique is a point-by-point rebuttal prepared by the American Civil Liberties Union, *Polluting the Censorship Debate: A Summary and Critique of the Final Report of the Attorney General's Commission on Pornography.*[58] This critique charges that rather than clarifying the issues, the commission's report has "polluted the debate over sexually explicit materials" by, among other things, "extrapolat[ing] from a few modest social science experiments a theory of causation of sexual violence from certain kinds of pornography."[59] According to the ACLU, the commission's report "launches a national crusade against dirty pictures" by recommending "a panorama of unconstitutional proposals."[60]

The ACLU's rebuttal begins with an attack on the mission of the commission, its composition, and the manner in which it conducted its hearings. First, the ACLU takes issue with a major presupposition of the commission's mandate—that pornography is a problem that needs to be curtailed. The ACLU notes that a principal charge of the commission was to make specific recommendations concerning "more effective ways in which the spread of pornography could be contained, consistent with constitutional guarantees." The ACLU charges that this mandate curtailed inquiry into the "possible values of permitting the unfettered distribution of sexually explicit material."[61] Next, the ACLU challenges the makeup of the commission, claiming that the members "were carefully selected to insure" an outcome that would support increased governmental efforts to suppress pornography. According to the ACLU, six members of the eleven-person commission, including its chairman, had previously "supported anti-pornography efforts," and two others "had staked out positions" that would support limits on the distribution of sexually explicit material. Only three members "had no clearly defined positions" regarding the issues facing the commission, and "[n]ot a single person was appointed to the Commission who was known to be skeptical about the evidence linking pornography to violence or to be concerned about the First Amendment implications of anti-pornography legislation."[62] In addition, the ACLU complains about lopsided witness lists, claiming that nearly 80 percent of the 208 witnesses urged tighter controls of sexually explicit materials.[63]

The ACLU is particularly critical of the commission's findings about the harm caused by violent and degrading pornography. As an initial matter, the ACLU takes issue with the conclusion that violent pornography is "[i]ncreasingly, the most prevalent form of pornography," a claim that the ACLU charges "cannot be substantiated by any study at all."[64] To the contrary, the ACLU points to a study that shows a *decrease* in the sexual violence depicted in *Playboy* during the late 1970s and 1980s, as well as to reports by producers of X-rated films that the level of violence in such films has declined since the 1970s. Indeed, according to the ACLU, a study conducted by the commission on the April 1986 issues of the top-selling mainstream "adult" magazines revealed so little violence (0.6 percent of the total imagery) that the commission "covered up these results" by not citing them in the final report. In addition, the ACLU faults the commission for including sadomasochistic material within the category of sexually violent pornography when there is "a whole body of literature, some of it known to the Commissioners, that suggests that much 'S/M' activity is both wholly consensual and non-violent."[65]

Turning to the commission's key conclusion that scientific evidence shows that substantial exposure to sexually violent material causes sexual violence, the ACLU claims that the commission "wildly overstates" the "tentative results of a limited number" of studies.[66] The ACLU emphasizes the "highly artificial setting of the laboratory" and stresses that aggression in the laboratory "is really only an analogy to actual aggression," since it is "allowed or encouraged by an experimenter with the guarantee that no punishment will ensue (even if the college students believed that they were actually shocking their partners, itself a dubious proposition)." The ACLU also notes the possibility that the studies were infected with "experimenter demands," since a film that shows violence may lead subjects "to assume that the experimenter approves of, or at least permits, violence in the context of the experiment." In addition, the ACLU objects that "unlike the real world of college males who are sexually aroused," the experiments did not give the subjects an opportunity to masturbate. Thus the ACLU questions whether "the turned-on males are pushing their shock buttons out of aggression" rather than "out of unrecompensed annoyance at arousal without relief." Finally, the ACLU maintains that both the aggression demonstrated in the laboratory as well as the rape-trial experiments revealing "desensitization" to sexual violence "show only temporary alteration in attitude" and not necessarily any real-life effect.[67]

The ACLU winds up its assessment of the commission's conclusions about scientific evidence in support of a link between sexually violent pornography and violence to women by warning that "[b]efore the regulation of printed or visual material can be justified by the 'evidence' of science, the evidence should be both clear and compelling." Calling the evidence upon which the commission relied "contradictory," "ambiguous," and of a sort from which causation could be only "tentatively extrapolated," the ACLU concludes that it is far from the type of evidence that could support regulation of speech.[68]

With respect to the commission's findings that harm similar to that said to be linked with violent pornography is caused by nonviolent but degrading material, the ACLU objects that "[v]irtually no scientific study has been done on this class of material isolated from other materials." Additionally, the ACLU rejects the commission's assertion that degrading material is the "largely predominant proportion" of commercial pornography, calling this claim "both unsubstantiated and largely not open to analysis because the category is so vaguely defined."[69]

The ACLU does not quarrel with the commission's finding (consistent with the 1970 commission's conclusion) that sexually explicit material that is neither violent nor degrading does not lead to acts of sexual violence. It does, however, chide the commission for refusing to give such material "a clean bill of health," noting the commission's concern that people will model sexual activity observed in the material, that the "commercialization of sex" is inherently wrong, and that the material might fall into the hands of children.[70]

The most salient and pervasive objection filed by the ACLU, however, transcends any particular criticism of the commission's use or interpretation of scientific data. Rather, the ACLU objects that "[m]ost of the research discussed here simply reaches the not surprising conclusion that exposure to particular ideas and images, can, temporarily at least, change perceptions and attitudes." But the ACLU points out, "[t]his is both the purpose and result of most speech, pornographic or otherwise."[71] The ACLU concludes its review of the commission's chapter on the harm of pornography by warning that "[t]he First Amendment will be nullified if attitude-shifting becomes the basis for suppressing speech, or if communication is prohibited when it is effective in transferring its viewpoints to its audience."[72]

The ACLU is an advocacy group committed to protecting First Amendment freedoms. It is to be expected that it would look charily upon scientific findings used to justify the continued and in some cases increased regulation of sexually explicit speech. Far more surprising and (on the surface, at least) devastating to the commission's findings about harm is criticism from scientists on whose work the commission relied. Even before the final report was published, Edward Donnerstein denounced as "bizarre" the commission's conclusion based on his studies that violent pornography causes violence toward women.[73] And soon after the report was published, two other scientists whose work the commission cited, Daniel Linz and Steven Penrod, joined Donnerstein in an article charging that "many of [the commission's] recommendations are incongruent with the research findings."[74]

These scientists level three main criticisms at the report. First, because much of the stimulus material found to have harmful effects was R rated (e.g., slasher films) and thus "would not be legally defined as obscene," they assert that it is "somewhat misleading to consider them as evidence for the general conclusion that 'pornography' is harmful." Accordingly, the commission's "ultimate focus on 'pornography' as a causal factor in sexually violent behavior" together with its recommendations for "tighter legal control of pornography" is "somewhat misplaced." Rather, "[t]o remain true to the specific stimuli used by the experimenters and to the findings of their experiments," these researchers believe that the commission should have focused more generally "on the potentially harmful effects of depictions of violence against women" whether or not they were sexually explicit.[75]

More centrally, Linz, Penrod, and Donnerstein criticize the commission's conclusion that violent pornography leads to violence against women, faulting the commission for failing to "exercise proper caution" in generalizing from results showing that violent pornography causes aggression against women in a laboratory setting to violent behavior outside the laboratory. The scientists had a number of "criticisms concerning external validity" applicable to laboratory experiments on violence (some of which have already been mentioned in the summary of the ACLU's rebuttal). Among the criticisms were that laboratory subjects do not perceive themselves as inflicting harm; sanctions against violence exist in the outside world but not in the laboratory; subjects are drawn from a narrow population base; the experimenters subtly influence subjects' behavior ("experimenter demand effect"); and there is no "acceptable operational definition of aggressive behavior."[76] Linz, Penrod, and Donnerstein thus conclude that "artificial measures of aggression" produced by the laboratory experiments "prohibit direct extrapolation of experimental findings to situations outside the laboratory" and charge the commission with being "unable or perhaps unwilling to acknowledge these limitations."[77]

Finally, these experimenters dispute the commission's conclusion that studies show that nonviolent but degrading material has effects similar to those of sexually violent material. With respect to these materials, they warn that the evidence is not only "tentative" but "also very inconsistent." They claim that only one study (Zillmann and Bryant) found that long-term exposure to degrading material influences perceptions of rape victims and claim further that later studies have failed to replicate these findings; that the commission "selectively" reported the results of this study by failing to acknowledge that although the study showed that exposure to degrading pornography resulted in more callous beliefs about rape, such exposure also resulted in a *decrease* in aggressive behavior; and that only one study (Check's), an experiment with serious methodological flaws, found an increase in subjects' reporting that they would force women to have sex.[78]

ASSESSING THE CONFLICTING CLAIMS
ABOUT THE EFFECTS OF PORNOGRAPHY

What are we to make of these conflicting claims about the experimental data concerning the harm of pornography? More specifically, how are those of us without a background in experimental psychology to assess the significance and validity of scientific studies or the criticisms of these studies? Fortunately, the situation is not as hopeless as it may seem, for despite the various points of contention, there seems to be a core area of agreement, tacit though it may be. In a recent review of the literature on the effects of pornography, Neil Malamuth, one of the most distinguished and least ideological of the investigators of the effects of pornography, reports that there is currently enough evidence to justify the "tentative conclusion" that violent pornography causes both aggressive behavior in the laboratory and at least short-term attitudinal changes.[79]

It does not necessarily follow from this conclusion, however, that violent pornography significantly contributes to sexual violence or discrimination in the real world. As Linz, Penrod, Donnerstein, and the ACLU point out, laboratory experiments that attempt to measure the effects of stimuli on human behavior or attitudes suffer from inherent limitations, including experimenter demand effect and an artificial context that give subjects license to engage in behavior that they might not engage in given real-world constraints. It should be noted, however, that some of the investigators attempted to obviate the problem of experimenter demand. One study, for instance, had subjects watch movies supposedly as part of a campus film program and then tested them as part of a survey administered in class to all students days later with no reference to the films they had seen.[80] In addition, attitudinal changes, as opposed to changes in behavior in the real world, cannot readily be explained by the artificial conditions of the laboratories.

Some objections leveled at the commission, such as a lack of a precise definition of "aggression," seem to be mere quibbles. Others seem to be just plain wrong—for instance, the ACLU's objection that the aggression might stem from frustration at the lack of opportunity to masturbate after being sexually aroused does not explain the greater aggression found when the stimulus material is sexually violent as compared to just sexually explicit. Still others are both inaccurate and unfair, such as Linz, Penrod, and Donnerstein's charge that the commission seemed "unable or perhaps unwilling to acknowledge" the limitations imposed by artificial laboratory conditions.[81] Although the commission may have unduly discounted these limitations, they did in fact acknowledge them.[82]

But the basic criticism that the artificial context of the laboratory imposes considerable limitations on the inferences about real-world behavior that can be drawn from the experiment results remains valid.[83] Despite these limitations, the commission concluded that "the available evidence strongly supports the hypothesis that substantial exposure to sexually violent materials . . . bears a causal relationship to antisocial acts of sexual violence," bridging the gap between the laboratory findings and real-world behavior primarily by "common sense."[84] Is this conclusion justified, or as the ACLU charges, does it "wildly overstate" the "tentative results of a limited number" of studies? In my view, neither the commission's conclusion nor the ACLU's criticism is completely justified. A fairer assessment of what we know about the relationship between pornography and harm might be something like this: Scientific studies have shown that exposure to violent pornography causes aggression towards women in the laboratory, as well as at least a temporary increase in sexual callousness as measured in laboratory and field experiments. These studies, in combination with other data, as well as common sense, raise the possibility that substantial exposure to violent pornography might contribute to violence against women in society at large.[85]

In a law review article published a year after the commission submitted its report, Frederick Schauer, the commission member who drafted the report's section on the effects of sexually violent pornography, explained that the scientific data provide "some evidence" of real-world effect, thus contributing "one or a few bricks" toward a wall of proof.[86] For Schauer, the "substantial" gap between "the scientific evidence and any conclusion about the ultimate question of causation" can be bridged by making "plausible" connections between the scientific evidence and the ultimate question, as well as between nonscientific evidence and the ultimate conclusion. Concretely (to continue with the masonry metaphor), this "plausible connection" is supplied in large part by the assumption that the "favorable depiction of x [leads to a greater] incidence of x," as is borne out by the success of advertising. Ultimately, however, Schauer concedes that even the total evidence of real-world causation is "very far from conclusive."[87]

Would that Schauer had presented these conclusions as moderately in the report. There is obviously a large difference between Schauer's later cautious assessment that the evidence is "very far from conclusive" and the report's bold remark that the evidence "strongly supports" the existence of a causal relationship between violent pornography and violence against women. Indeed, in quoting the report in his article Schauer omits the modifier "strongly" altogether.[88] A similar distancing from the report's conclusion can be seen in Schauer's "recast[ing]" the report as finding only that there is "sufficient evidence" for the proposition that "there would be more acts of sexual violence committed by a population every member of which had been extensively exposed to favorable depictions of sexual violence than there would be in a population no member of which had been exposed to favorable depictions of acts of sexual violence."[89]

As rephrased, the conclusion is fairly uncontroversial. In light of the effect on attitude and behavior that violent pornography produces in the laboratory, as well as our commonsense assumption that favorable depictions of behavior tend to increase the likelihood of its occurrence, it does seem reasonable to suppose that at least one person exposed to pornography depicting women enjoying sexual violence might have committed an act of sexual violence in the real world as a result of this exposure. But this reformulation gains its unassailability by avoiding what is by far the most important and controversial implication of the commission's report, namely, that violent pornography *significantly* contributes to the problem of violence against women in American society. In marked contrast to Schauer's subsequent far blander statements about causality, the commission's report asserts that "sexually explicit materials featuring violence . . . [are] on the whole harmful to society."[90]

Moreover, although in his article Schauer makes no claims about the amount of violent pornography consumed by the American public, the report attempts to support its implication that violent pornography is a major cause of violence against women by emphasizing the prevalence of such material. In the next section, I discuss the commission's claim that "increasingly, the most prevalent forms" of pornography depict violence. My point here is that we can gauge the degree to which the commission's report exaggerates the significance of the scientific data by noticing how much more modest and careful the inferences from these data become when Schauer writes as a scholar rather than as a commissioner.[91]

Where, then, does this leave us with respect to the crucial question of whether violent pornography significantly contributes to violence against women? The answer turns on such subsidiary questions as: How powerful a stimulus to action is violent pornography? Will substantial exposure cause even "normal" men to commit acts of sexual violence or only those in some "deviant" population predisposed to such violence?[92] If only a deviant population, how large a segment of the population is this? And just how readily available is this stimulus? These questions are of course relevant to estimating how many acts of sexual violence are caused by consumption of pornography each year. Is it a causal factor in 10,000 sexual assaults a year, in 1,000, or in fewer than ten? Similar questions are relevant to assessing whether pornography is an important factor in the ongoing problem of discrimination against women in the workplace and elsewhere in society.[93]

It is of course difficult to disagree with Schauer that, generally speaking, a favorable depiction of x tends to increase the likelihood of x. Nonetheless, his analogy to commercial advertising is inapt. Unlike favorable depictions of commercial products, which are reinforced by a generally consumeristic society, sexual violence is morally condemned, and many forms of sexual violence constitute serious crimes. Given the strong social constraints against sexual violence, violent pornography is less likely to lead normally inhibited people to act in accordance with the depiction than is commercial advertising. But the combination of the violent imagery with sexual arousal might be a more powerful stimulus to imitative action than is the typical media image. What is certain, however, is that truisms like "favorable depictions of x increase the likelihood of x" or the "common sense" of eleven commissioners does very little to inform the inquiry as to whether violent pornography is a significant cause of violence or discrimination against women in this country.

The Prevalence of Violent Pornography

The commission is on particularly shaky ground to the extent that it relies on the prevalence of violent pornography as supporting its conclusion that such material is an important cause of harm. The report's claim that violent pornography is becoming "the most prevalent" type of pornography is apparently based on four studies. The first is a 1983 Canadian study that found that 10 percent of the sexual imagery depicted in the text of mainstream sexually explicit magazines (*Playboy, Penthouse, Hustler, Gallery, Cheri, Forum, Oui, Club, Swank,* and *Genesis*) involved force. The second is a 1980 study by Malamuth and Spinner, which concluded that pictorial violence in *Playboy* and *Penthouse* "increased significantly" from 1973 through 1977, reaching about 5 percent in 1977. Third is a 1982 study by Dietz (one of the commissioners) and Evans that examined the covers of 1,760 heterosexual pornographic magazines sold in "adult entertainment" shops in the Forty-second Street district of New York City and determined that the most prevalent imagery (17 percent) depicted "bondage and domination." The fourth is a 1985 study of detective magazines by Dietz, Harry, and Hazelwood that found that the covers tended to combine erotic images with images of violence; 28 percent of the depictions involved "sadistic imagery," most often with women as victims, whereas 38 percent involved bondage, all of which showed bound females.[94]

Subsequent research, however, has cast doubt on the findings of some of these studies and thus on the commission's conclusion about the pervasiveness of violent pornography. For instance, a 1987 study by Scott and Cuvelier found, in stark contrast to Malamuth and Spinner, that the level of pictorial sexual violence in *Playboy* has never exceeded 1 percent and has been decreasing in recent years.[95] This finding is supported by the commission's own study (which it did not report) showing that only 0.6 percent of the imagery of the April 1986 issues of mainstream sexually explicit magazines depict "force, violence or weapons."[96] With respect to the amount of sexual violence depicted in mainstream "adult" magazines, there is obviously a large discrepancy between the Malamuth and Spinner and the Canadian study, on the one hand, and the Scott and Cuvelier (and the commission's own study), on the other. What accounts for this disparity is difficult to say (although different views as to what constitutes violence may explain some of it). But until there is some consensus on this issue, it is premature to conclude, at least with respect to mainstream magazines, that sexually violent pornography forms a significant part of the imagery, let alone is on the rise. Indeed, there is some suggestion that the level of sexual violence in these magazines (whatever level it attained) may have peaked in the early 1970s and decreased somewhat since then.[97]

What about the prevalence of violence in hard-core pornographic films and magazines? One problem with the Dietz and Evans study cited by the commission is that it focuses on "bondage and domination." To the extent that this material depicts *consensual* sadomasochistic activity, there are, as Schauer later notes, "powerful arguments for treating such consensual material as fundamentally different in kind." Although also noting the argument "that depictions of even consensual sado-masochistic activities represent an admixture of sex and violence that in today's world is hardly likely to be gender neutral in impact," Schauer concedes that the report should at least have explored the issue.[98]

A year after the commission issued its report, commissioner Park Dietz, together with Alan Sears, the executive director of the commission, published an analysis of the covers of 5,132 magazines, books, or films sold in "adult" bookstores.[99] (The data were collected in 1985–1986 by commission staff but had not been analyzed at the time the commission disbanded.) The study found that approximately 13 percent of all materials depicted violence. The figure was highest for books (20 percent) and lowest for films (8 percent), with magazines in the middle (12 percent). Once again, however, this figure included bondage, with no attempt to distinguish between consensual and nonconsensual bondage or otherwise to distinguish between consensual and nonconsensual activity that arguably should be considered violent only when someone inflicts it against another's will (spanking, for example). Some indication of how much of this 13 percent figure may be inflated by the inclusion of consensual activity is that bondage was depicted in approximately 10 percent of all the material examined. In contrast, only about 3 percent of all imagery involved the use of force (rape, whipping, spanking, and women fighting), not all of which is necessarily violent (e.g., sadomasochistic spanking or women mud wrestling). Moreover, only about 1 percent of the material showed the effects of violence (bruising, blood, piercing, and corpses). Still, approximately 5 percent of the material depicted "implements of violence (other than simple restraints), whether in use or not (whips, guns, knives, or other weapons, hoists or racks)."[100]

There is a twofold problem with classifying depictions of consensual bondage and certain other consensual sadomasochistic activities as violence. First, many people simply do not think of such activities as violent, and thus an assertion that 13 percent of all images found on the covers of hard-core pornography depicts violence is in some sense misleading. But more significant, these figures are dubious *to the extent that they are meant to connect with the scientific studies* showing that exposure to violent pornography causes aggressive behavior in the laboratory and thus to support the commission's conclusion that violent pornography is a significant cause of violence against women. The violent pornography shown to produce aggression in the laboratory usually involved highly nonconsensual activity such as rape. Thus if any figure from the Dietz and Sears study is relevant in this respect, it is not that approximately 13 percent of the images depicted "violence" in some broad sense but that only about 3 percent of all images involved the use of force.

Yet there are reasons to believe that somewhat more than 3 percent of the selections in adult bookstores contain violence similar to the stimulus material used in the laboratory. The Dietz and Sears study looked just at the covers of magazines and books and videotape cases. It may well be, however, that items that did not feature the use of force on the covers nonetheless contained one or more scenes involving rape or other forms of violence shown to cause short-term attitudinal changes and aggression in the laboratory.[101] Good candidates are those materials that showed weapons on the cover but not use of force.

As the disparate figures for magazines, films, and books reported by Dietz and Sears suggest, the level of sexual violence in hard-core pornography seems to depend on the medium. A 1990 study by Yang and Linz found that in hard-core pornographic films, about 40 percent of all behavioral sequences depicted sex, about 5 percent depicted sexual violence, and another 5 percent depicted nonsexual violence.[102] (An interesting finding of this study is that for R-rated films approximately 5 percent of the sequences were sexual, whereas nearly 35 percent contained violence, and only slightly more than 3 percent contained sexual violence.) Unlike Dietz and Sears, Yang and Linz analyzed the contents of the items and thus avoided the problem of judging a book (or a videocassette) by its cover. But as in the Dietz and Sears study, Yang and Linz's definition of violence apparently included all depictions of bondage, slapping, and spanking and thus may have included consensual activity.[103]

Similarly, an unpublished statistical analysis prepared by the Kinsey Institute of the content of hard-core pornographic films apparently defines violence so broadly as to encompass not only consensual sadomasochistic images that include "light bondage" but also "horseplay" that involves playful bites or slaps on the buttocks.[104] In reviewing this material, Slade reports that two of the surviving thirty-three "stag" films from the 1920s in the Kinsey collection depict some violence (6 percent), as do ten of the eighty-four films from the 1930s (12 percent), nine of the ninety-six films from the 1940s (9 percent), eighteen of 155 films from the 1950s (11.6 percent), and 17 percent of a "large sample" of films from the 1960s. But Slade believes that this sampling is "heavily skewed" toward the particularly violent English films by the selection of the collector who donated the movies to the institute.[105]

Slade reports that during the 1970s violence in hard-core pornography "probably never reached above 10 percent," although the violence became more graphic.[106] In addition, he finds that rape occurs in sixty-seven (or about 5 percent) of the 1,333 "examples" in the Kinsey collection.[107] In contrast, a 1976 study by Smith of the content of pornographic paperback novels between 1968 and 1974 found that violence became more prevalent after 1969 (leveling off in 1974), with about one-third of the sex portrayed in these novels involving force. Moreover, in this time period the number of rapes depicted doubled.[108]

Despite the commission's confident claim about the "increasing" prevalence of violent pornography, the truth is that we do not yet have a very firm grasp of just how prevalent this type of pornography is or whether it is increasing, remaining constant, or perhaps even decreasing, having reached peak levels some time ago. All that we can confidently say at this point is that neither the percentage of hard-core pornographic films that contain violence nor the percentage of images in such films is trivial. (If we need some tentative figure, the convergence of the few studies suggests roughly 10 percent for both measures, again with the caveat that

this figure includes depictions of consensual sadomasochistic activity.) With respect to mainstream soft-core publications, we do not even know whether the
amount of violence is minimal or substantial. Similarly, we do not know much
about the violent content of hard-core pornographic magazines other than the
suggestion of Dietz and Sears's study that the level of violence in these publications is somewhat higher than found in hard-core pornographic films. We have
somewhat more information about the violent content of pornographic novels, for
Smith's study supports the finding by Dietz and Sears that the level of sexual violence described in such works is quite high.

The amount of violent pornography consumed by the American public is an
important matter in need of more carefully focused, nonideologically driven research. Particularly helpful would be studies that clearly distinguish between different types of activity that could conceivably be characterized as violent and,
even more important, attempt to tie the frequency of violent scenes to those found
to cause attitudinal changes and aggressive behavior in the laboratory.[109]

To the ACLU, it apparently does not matter whether images depicting rape and
other types of violence comprise more than 10 percent or less than 1 percent of
pornography, for the organization characterizes both numbers as "small" and
thus apparently dismisses as insignificant even the larger numbers reported in
some studies. But this position disregards the massive quantity of pornography
that Americans consume each year. According to U.S. News and World Report, in
1996, "Americans spent more than $8 billion on hard-core videos, peep shows,
live sex acts, adult cable programming, sexual devices, computer porn, and sex
magazines—an amount much larger than Hollywood's domestic box office re-
ceipts and larger than all the revenues generated by rock and country music
recordings."[110] Between 1985 and 1992, the number of hard-core videos rented
each year rose from 75 million to 490 million; in 1996 nearly 8,000 new hard-core
videos were released through the approximately 25,000 video stores that deal in
hard-core films.[111] A recent survey of the Internet found that in 1997 pornography
accounted for 10 percent of the money earned in cyberspace (between $750 mil-
lion and $1 billion) and that there are approximately 34,000 pornographic Web
sites, which account for 2 percent of all publicly viewable sites.[112]

If in fact 10 percent or more of the billions of images viewed or read annually
by sexually aroused males do depict rape or similarly violent behavior, then in
light of the studies showing attitudinal and behavior changes in the laboratory as
a result of such stimuli, there is considerable cause for concern that pornography
might be a significant contributor to that complex matrix that causes violence and
discrimination against women. If instead such violent images constitute less than
1 percent of the images depicted in mainstream soft-core magazines and only 5
percent of the hard-core fare, then there is less reason for concern, although even
such small percentage rates would be troubling given the massive amount of
pornography consumed in this country.

The Difficulties of Assessing the Harm of "Degrading" Pornography

Because of the inherent problems in generalizing from laboratory experiments to
real-world behavior, as well as the lack of certainty about the amount and nature

of violent pornography, any confident conclusion that violent pornography is a significant cause of violence against women is premature. What has been shown is only a distinct possibility that such a causal connection exists. With respect to pornography that is nonviolent but depicts "degradation, domination, subordination, or humiliation," even this modest conclusion is unwarranted on the current state of the evidence.

To begin with, there is the perhaps insuperable problem of defining what is meant by "demeaning" pornography. The commission defines this category as that which "depicts people, usually women, in decidedly subordinate roles in their sexual practices that would to most people be considered humiliating."[113] It is an understatement to say that people's attitudes toward sex vary widely and that there is no societal consensus as to which sexual acts are degrading or humiliating. Upbringing, education, religion, and prior sexual experience all contribute to one's views of these matters. To some, anything other than missionary-style, heterosexual intercourse is demeaning to women; to certain radical feminists, precisely that activity is degrading to women. Some consider anal intercourse, "doggy-style" vaginal intercourse, and oral sex to be acts of degradation; others regard these as perfectly natural, healthy sex acts. Moreover, each viewer or reader will interpret a given pornographic description differently, making any consensus about whether the depiction is demeaning even more unlikely.

To be useful, a term or concept must have a shared core meaning. This is decidedly not the case with the term "demeaning" as applied to sexual acts, let alone portrayals of sexual activities. Indeed, it is not clear that the pornographic image often cited as the height of degradation—a man ejaculating on a woman—can garner such a consensus. Author Wendy McElroy suggests that such scenes can be interpreted as showing that the male actor was really turned on by sex, with the woman's response of spreading the ejaculate over her body as showing that she, too, was enthusiastically involved in the encounter.[114] Personally, I find the erstwhile (and to some extent still extant) *Playboy* iconography of woman-as-bunny or man's "playmate" more demeaning to women than some of the much more explicit pornographic depictions. (In contrast, Dietz has opined that *Playboy* centerfolds are not only "harmless" but "actually healthy in many respects.")[115] In this regard, it is interesting to note that apparently even the commission was unable to agree on a list of examples of degrading pornography.[116]

Although it found that there is "less evidence causally linking [demeaning] material with sexual aggression" than there is with respect to violent pornography, the commission nevertheless decided that "substantial exposure to [demeaning pornography] bears some causal relationship to the level of sexual violence, sexual coercion, or unwanted sexual aggression" as well as to "various non-violent forms of discrimination against or subordination of women in our society."[117] Yet the section of the report that surveys the scientific evidence states matters much more cautiously. Here the explanation that the demeaning nature of nonviolent pornography causes an increase in sexual callousness is characterized as a "very tentative" suggestion based on "speculat[ion]."[118] Of these quite different statements about the effects of demeaning pornography, the latter comes much closer to summarizing accurately what can fairly be inferred about the effects of "demeaning" pornography. Most of the experiments that tested for sexual callousness or aggressive behavior—if they differentiated between types of pornography at all—distinguished between violent and nonviolent material, not between degrading and nondegrading material. It was only in retrospect that scientists suggested this distinction as a way of explaining contradictory results produced in studies of nonviolent pornography.[119]

At the time the commission reported, only a single study (the 1985 study by Check discussed above) differentiated between degrading and nondegrading pornography and found that demeaning pornography produced greater sexual callousness.[120] But as Linz, Penrod, and Donnerstein correctly point out, there were several serious methodological flaws in this study. Even the commission acknowledged that the results of this study must be "viewed with caution."[121] The commission also relied on a 1982 study by Zillmann and Bryant that found that long-term exposure to even nonviolent pornography can cause sexual callousness. Although the study itself did not differentiate between degrading and nondegrading pornography, Check and Malamuth subsequently suggested that the material used in this study "dehumanized women" because it portrayed them as "hysterically euphoric in response to just about any sexual or pseudosexual stimulation, and as eager to accommodate seemingly any and every sexual request."[122]

Linz, Penrod, and Donnerstein charge that "later studies with both male and female subjects have not replicated [Zillmann and Bryant's] findings."[123] But they refer to only two contrary studies, and both are unpublished doctoral dissertations supervised by Donnerstein, one by Linz with male subjects and the other by Krafka with female subjects.[124] In another work not dedicated to rebutting the commission's findings, these scientists suggest that the differing results might be explained by the fact that the demeaning images in studies that did not produce an increase in sexual callousness were part of feature-length films that contained other images as well. In contrast, the studies that did produce increased sexual callousness were either made up of clips of degrading scenes taken from full-length movies (Check) or stag films with a high concentration of demeaning images (Zillmann and Bryant). They suggest that "it may not be frequency of exposure to images of female promiscuity that produce[d] the [sexual callousness], but rather the ratio of these images to other (not necessarily sexually related) images that might account for negative changes in attitudes about women."[125]

But even if the contrary evidence is not quite as devastating as Linz, Penrod, and Donnerstein suggest, their overall criticism of the commission's assessment of the effects of degrading pornography remains valid. At the time the commission reported, the scientific evidence was far too sparse and contradictory to support the claim that degrading pornography causes sexual violence. Nor have there been any significant studies since that time that would support such a conclusion.[126] The commission's conclusion about the effects of degrading pornography is a paragon of restraint, however, compared to its claims about the prevalence of such material. The commission asserts that demeaning pornography constitutes "somewhere between the predominant and overwhelming portion of what is currently standard fare heterosexual pornography" and that such material is "the largely predominant proportion of commercially available pornography."[127] But the commission cites not a single study or other source to back these claims, and there is in fact little support for them.

Soon after the commission disbanded, Dietz and Sears published a study analyzing the data collected by the commission staff in a survey of the content of the covers of pornographic material sold in "adult" bookstores.[128] In their section on "degrading and humiliating imagery," the authors begin by acknowledging that "[t]here is no standardized procedure for determining whether an image is degrading or humiliating" and that "the American public is divided over questions as to whether particular forms of sexual conduct" can be described as such. For instance, Dietz and Sears acknowledge that there is no societal consensus whether conduct commonly portrayed in pornography, including "fellatio, cunnilingus, anal intercourse, ejaculation onto the partner's face, or homosexual acts," is debasing.[129]

Since they recognize this lack of consensus, one might expect the authors to conclude that any attempt to determine what portion of the surveyed material constituted "degrading" pornography would be bootless. Undaunted, however, Dietz and Sears offer alternative classifications based on "traditional," "moderate," and "liberal" views of which pornographic depictions are degrading or humiliating. They assert that according to the traditional view, every item in the survey would be regarded as degrading or humiliating "because each item in the sample at minimum depicts a person as an object of purely sexual interest or exposes to public view portions of the body that are customarily concealed and does so for commercial gain."[130]

Moderates, according to Dietz and Sears, accept that certain depictions of nudity and sexual activity can occur without degradation or humiliation but find degrading or humiliating "all those sexual activities that are regarded as deviant or shameful according to traditional values." The authors "operationally" define "traditional values" as "the values that predominated in open discourse prior to the sexual revolution of the 1960's." Dietz and Sears contend that

> the sexually moderate generally view as degrading or humiliating not only sexual depictions of anorectal eroticism, urination or urine, bestiality, an anatomically normal man wearing female clothing, a person with breasts and a penis ("He/She"), leather, rubber, or latex, exaggerated shoes or boots, diapers or diapering, shaved pubic areas, childlike clothing, props or setting, or penetration by inanimate objects, . . . but also sexual depictions of pregnancy, engorged breasts with depiction of milk production, three or more persons engaged in sexual activity, a woman dealing with more than one penis, sex between two women, sex between two men, fellatio, or cunnilingus.[131]

Dietz and Sears conclude that "[a]t least 52.5 percent of the [surveyed] material" (58.3 percent of the magazines, 40.3 percent of the books, and 33.5 percent of the films) contain such images and thus would be considered degrading or humiliating by sexual moderates.

Sexual liberals, according to Dietz and Sears, are those "who have by and large accepted the changes in social behavior that accompanied the sexual revolution of the 1960's." The authors claim that even this group would find the following depictions degrading or humiliating:

> anorectal eroticism (which includes fisting, enemas, feces and defecation, and anal insertion of penis . . .), urine and urination, diapers and diapering, bestiality, a person with breasts and a penis, an anatomically normal man wearing female clothing,

leather fetish items, rubber or latex fetish items, exaggerated shoes or boots, childlike clothing, props or settings, shaved pubic areas or penetration by inanimate objects.[132]

Dietz and Sears find that "a minimum of 22.6 percent" of the surveyed material (24.6 percent of the magazines, 18.5 percent of the books, and 16.9 percent of the films) contained such depictions and thus "was degrading or humiliating according to the view of the sexual liberal."

There are several devastating problems with this attempt to quantify the amount of degrading or humiliating material found in "adult" bookstores. Rather than conducting a survey of self-proclaimed traditionalists, moderates, and liberals to discover their reactions to this material or even consulting data on Americans' attitudes to depictions of various sex acts, the authors simply declare what sexually traditional, moderate, and liberal views would consider demeaning or humiliating. Not only is this ipse dixit unsupported, but it is unsupportable, particularly when it comes to Dietz and Sears's assessment of what liberals find degrading or humiliating. The very essence of sexual liberalism is toleration of even the most "deviant" sexual practices as long as they occur between or among freely consenting adults. Although many sexual liberals might find a number of the items on Dietz and Sears's list unappealing or even disgusting and thus would not themselves care to engage in them, this does not mean that liberals would condemn these acts as demeaning or humiliating, at least not in all circumstances. Rather, whether most sexual liberals would consider depictions of anal sex, transvestitism; leather, rubber, latex, or shoe fetishism; shaved pubic regions; penetration by inanimate objects; or many others on the list demeaning depends enormously on context.

Dietz and Sears allude to context by referencing titles such as *Cornholed Blondes* or *Dildo Babies,* and perhaps sexual liberals, particularly those with a feminist bent, would find these and similar items demeaning to women. But to assume that sexual liberals would find various sexual practices per se "shameful" and thus humiliating or demeaning reveals a profound misunderstanding of sexual liberalism. More significant, the failure to consider context renders absurd such precise statements as "a minimum of 22.6% of the merchandise studied was degrading or humiliating according to the view of the sexual liberal."

Similar criticisms can be made of the assumptions about the opinions of moderates (and to a lesser extent even traditionalists). For one, Dietz and Sears seem to assume that every depiction that a moderate or a traditionalist would consider offensive or immoral they would also denounce as demeaning or humiliating. Although there is doubtless a large overlap here, I doubt it is complete, especially for the moderate.

I could go on pointing out flaws in this remarkable attempt to quantify the portion of material found in "adult" bookstores that is demeaning or humiliating, but I think I have said enough to show that these figures are basically meaningless except to confirm that there is extensive disagreement in society as to which pornographic images are degrading. Thus even if we were to accept the inflated figures that Dietz and Sears arbitrarily assign as the percentage of the material that liberals would find demeaning or humiliating, what their analysis most clearly shows is that with respect to nearly 80 percent of the material surveyed, there is widespread societal disagreement as to whether it is demeaning or humiliating.

More important, the figures proffered by Dietz and Sears would seem totally irrelevant to the inquiry into whether degrading pornography is a significant cause of violence or other antisocial behavior. Like its findings as to the prevalence of violent pornography, the commission's statement that degrading pornography is the "largely predominant" fare commercially available is obviously meant to be read together with its findings of negative effects in laboratory studies to suggest that such material significantly contributes to real-world harm to women. Dietz and Sears's study, which analyzes data the commission collected and explicitly refers to the commission's category of degrading and humiliating pornography, would seem to be an attempt to bolster the commission's "findings" about the prevalence of this type of pornography and thus the harm it causes.[133] If this is its implicit purpose, it fails utterly, for the study does not attempt to explain the relationship between the various classifications of demeaning or humiliating pornography that it employs and the stimulus material found to cause the increase in sexual callousness in laboratory experiments. Dietz and Sears leave unexplored whether the material that traditionalists, moderates, or liberals consider degrading causes these effects or whether, as is more likely the case, there is some other description that better fits the stimulus material used in the experiments. In speculating that the distinction between degrading and nondegrading material might explain the seemingly contradictory results of experiments with nonviolent pornography, Check and Malamuth do not, as do Dietz and Sears, focus on the types of sexual activities portrayed but rather on context. Thus these investigators note that a study that failed to produce negative effects depicted "more affection than is typical of much pornography," whereas the stimulus material in a study that did find an increase in sexual callousness "dehumanized" women by portraying them as "nondiscriminating," "hysterically euphoric" in response to sexual stimulation, and "eager to accommodate seemingly any and every sexual request."[134]

There is a certain irony, however, in impeaching the commission's conclusion that degrading pornography causes harm. One of the more "liberal" conclusions that this rather "conservative" commission reached was that pornography that is neither violent nor degrading "does not bear a causal relationship to rape and other acts of sexual violence." But if the inconsistent results of the studies examining the effects of nonviolent pornography cannot be explained by differentiating between demeaning and nondemeaning material, then we are left, for the time being at least, with no category of pornography that studies have consistently shown not to cause increased sexual callousness or aggression in the laboratory. In other words, precisely because the commission's conclusion that degrading pornography causes harm is overstated, so, too, is its conclusion about the harmlessness of pornography that is neither violent nor degrading. Of course, there may well be a category of nonviolent sexually explicit material that causes neither sexual callousness nor aggressive behavior in the laboratory. But until there is a well-substantiated explanation of why some experiments involving nonviolent pornography show negative effects whereas others do not, it is premature to conclude with certainty that pornography that is neither violent nor demeaning does not contribute to sexual violence or discrimination.

In summary, then, Linz, Penrod, and Donnerstein are correct in their basic criticism that the commission overstates the evidence that either violent or degrading pornography causes violence or other antisocial behavior. There are just too many crucial questions that need to be answered before anything approaching the certainty of the report's conclusions about the harms of pornography would be justified.[135]

Clouding the Debate: Mixing Science with Ideology

Although several attacks on the report leveled by Linz, Donnerstein, and Penrod are well founded, others seem driven more by ideological disagreement than concern for scientific accuracy. These scientists believe that the negative effects shown in the experiments do not justify the suppression of even legally obscene depictions of sexual violence. They advocate instead the classic free speech solution of "more speech," recommending mass audience educational interventions to counteract any ill effects of violent pornography and other violent depictions: "Since legal remedies . . . directed at suppressing pornography have the potential of cutting into every form of communication and any law devised to curb messages of violence against women could be used to suppress other messages of questionable interpretation, we call for a more informed public rather than for stricter laws."[136] Like any citizen, these scientists are free to express any view on matters of public policy. But scientists' political views should not lead them to make inaccurate or distorted claims about scientific data or even to make unfair or misleading criticisms of a government report with which they disagree. Unfortunately, in responding to the attorney general commission's report, Linz, Penrod, and Donnerstein have done just that.

For instance, these scientists fault the commission for focusing on violent depictions in a sexual context rather than on depictions of violence against women in general, implying that violent images rather than the sexual context are responsible for the results shown in the laboratory.[137] This criticism is both unfair and misleading. It is unfair because the commission's mandate was to examine "the nature, extent, and impact on society of pornography in the United States," not to determine the impact of all violent images on American society.[138] It is misleading because the studies on which the commission relied suggest that it is *the combination* of violent and sexual images rather than violent images alone that accounts for the degree of the effects measured in the experiments. Indeed, Donnerstein and Linz's own experiments have shown that "aggressive pornography" produced higher levels of aggression against women in the laboratory than did aggressive films without sexual content, a result that Linz, Penrod, and Donnerstein describe in another publication as consistent with other studies.[139] Judging from these and similar experiments, Malamuth concludes in a recent review of the literature that "exposure to messages in the context of pornography, where relatively high states of arousal and positive affect may occur, could have considerably stronger effects than exposure to the same messages in a neutral state of arousal or affect."[140]

Linz, Penrod, and Donnerstein's insistence that "violence against women need not occur in a pornographic or sexually explicit context to have a negative effect on viewer attitudes or behavior" is beside the point.[141] Since a number of experiments have shown that the presence of a sexual context increases the level of aggression demonstrated in the laboratory, the commission's and other researcher's focus on sexually oriented depictions of violence is not "misguided."[142] It may be true, as Linz, Penrod, and Donnerstein claim, that the depictions of nonsexualized violence are more readily available and thus a bigger problem. (A recent study found that in R-rated films sexual violence accounts for only about 3 percent of all behavior sequences, whereas nonsexual violence accounts for about 35 percent.)[143] But given the possibility that depictions of sexualized violence might have a particularly pernicious influence on viewers, the existence of a more widespread problem does not make focusing on the effects of depictions of sexualized violence inappropriate.

After criticizing the commission for having too narrow a focus, Linz, Penrod, and Donnerstein then complain that the commission's focus is too broad. They point out that much of the stimulus material shown to affect attitudes and cause aggression in the laboratory, for instance, the R-rated slasher films, was not nearly sexually explicit enough to be considered pornographic, let alone obscene.[144] They thus condemn as "misleading" the commission's reliance on these experiments "as evidence for the general conclusion that 'pornography' is harmful."[145] The charge is unfounded.

First, the commission did not make a blanket assertion that pornography has harmful effects, as this criticism implies. To the contrary, the commission limited its findings of harm to violent and demeaning pornography and expressly concluded that even the most sexually explicit material that is neither violent nor degrading does not cause sexual violence. More important, the commission emphasized that the negative consequences reported in the experiments "do not vary with the extent of sexual explicitness so long as the violence is presented in an undeniably sexual context" and speculated that slasher films "are likely to produce the consequences discussed here to a greater extent than most of the materials available in 'adults only' pornographic outlets."[146] Still, although not all of the stimulus material was obscene or even pornographic, much of it was.[147] And of course there is no reason to believe that the negative effects shown in violent films with mild sexual content would be *less* where the sex is more explicit. It was therefore perfectly reasonable for the commission to report that sexually violent pornography produced aggression in the laboratory setting as well as short-term attitude change.

The commission recommended that although violent obscenity is only the "tip of the iceberg" of the material that the studies suggest causes violence against women, violent obscenity should nonetheless be vigorously prosecuted for "symbolic" reasons, to serve "as a model for the condemnatory attitudes and actions of private citizens."[148] One can, of course, vigorously disagree with this proposed course of action, but given the report's express acknowledgment that it is not only obscene or pornographic material that has been shown experimentally to produce negative changes in behavior and attitudes, there is nothing "misleading" about the commission's conclusion that violent pornography has been shown to cause these results in the laboratory experiments.[149]

Finally, it should be noted that Linz and Donnerstein's condemnation of the commission for inadequate caution in generalizing from the laboratory to the real world, albeit valid, is also applicable to their own statements. In a 1984 *Psychology Today* article entitled "Sexual Violence in the Media: A Warning," Donnerstein and Linz declare that "[r]esearchers have shown . . . that exposure to even a few minutes of sexually violent pornography, such as rape and other forms of sexual violence against women, can lead to antisocial attitudes and behavior." "If a brief exposure to sexually violent pornography can have these effects," they ask, "what are the effects of exposure to hours of such material?"[150] And in a book published in 1983 Donnerstein summarizes the scientific evidence as revealing "a direct causal relationship between exposure to aggressive erotica and violence against women."[151]

The ACLU is an ideological rather than a scientific organization, and thus one would not expect scientific detachment in its critique of the report. Indeed, its strong civil libertarian perspective provides a fitting dialectic to the commission's conservative one. There is nothing inappropriate with an advocacy organization's having a distinct perspective on a matter of public concern, but this does not diminish the fact that the ACLU's commentary is every bit as tendentious, and in places even as misleading, as the report it criticizes. As noted, the commission unequivocally stated that it accepts the line drawn by the Supreme Court between sexually explicit speech that is protected by the First Amendment and that which is not. The commission expressly declined to recommend banning sexually explicit speech that is not obscene under *Miller*. Despite this clear statement, the ACLU's response reads as if the commission had called for the suppression of all pornographic material. For instance, the ACLU charges that "the intention of the Commission clearly is to eliminate virtually all sexually explicit material currently available."[152] Similarly, the ACLU accuses the commission of arguing that pornography should be banned based on research suggesting that men who consume pornography are less satisfied with the physical appearance of their wives.[153] Although the chapter of the commission's report summarizing the scientific studies on the effects of pornography does mention this research,[154] nowhere does the report suggest that these findings justify the legal suppression of pornography. The ACLU also charges that in accepting the Supreme Court's view that obscenity is not protected speech and in urging that such material be vigorously prosecuted, the commission fosters a "censorship mentality" that leads citizens to try to remove valuable but controversial literature from school libraries.[155]

As anyone who has received ACLU fund-raising letters is well aware, alarmist, slippery-slope arguments are typical of this organization. There is perhaps nothing inappropriate about such hyperbole from an advocacy organization. What is disturbing about the ACLU's response to the commission's report is its insouciance about the harm that pornography might cause women. Although the ACLU played a useful role in exposing the commission's exaggerated claims about harm, it goes too far in the other direction by denying the possibility of harm. Thus it claims that there is "*no* evidence to suggest that broad 'evils' like sex discrimination have any link to pornography at all."[156] The evidence is far from conclusive, but the laboratory studies showing increased aggression and negative attitudes toward women are *some* evidence. It is certainly appropriate for a civil liberties organization to argue that laboratory evidence of aggression and changed attitudes do not warrant suppression of speech. Indeed, it might even be appropriate for such an organization to argue that even if the evidence were conclusive that pornography led to acts of violence or discrimination through changed attitudes, suppression of the speech would still be unwarranted. But for an organization whose agenda includes women's rights to refuse to acknowledge that there is some evidence that pornography might contribute to women's inequality suggests that the ACLU does not have confidence in its own premise that even potentially harmful speech is entitled to constitutional protection.[157]

An accurate nonideological assessment of what the scientific studies show about the effects of pornography is presented in the *Report of the Surgeon General's Workshop on Pornography and Public Health*. Issued about the same time as the commission's report, this report concluded:

> In sum, these experiments should heighten concern that aggressive behavior toward women may be increased by viewing aggressive and sexually aggressive films, but presently this effect has only been seen in controlled and potentially artificial laboratory settings. . . . Pornography does have its effects; it is just not yet known how widespread or powerful they really are. There is a clear lack of extensive knowledge or unifying theory, and global statements about the effect of exposure to pornography have not yet been substantiated.[158]

Notes

Chapter One

1. Hustler Magazine v. Falwell, 485 U.S. 46 (1988).

2. 163 U.S. 537 (1896).

3. For instance, in *Plessy* the Court obfuscated the value choice it makes in upholding segregation by declaring that "in the nature of things [the Fourteenth Amendment] could not have been intended to abolish distinctions based on color, or to enforce social as distinguished from political equality, or a commingling of the two races upon terms unsatisfactory to either."

4. 347 U.S. 483 (1954).

5. See Loving v. Virginia, 388 U.S. 1 (1967).

6. See Adarand Constructors, Inc. v. Pena, 515 U.S. 200 (1995). Four members of the majority backtrack somewhat from the full implication of this holding by insisting that this scrutiny, unlike the scrutiny applied to racial classifications that disadvantage minorities, is not necessarily "fatal in fact." They note that the "unhappy persistence of both the practice and the lingering effects of racial discrimination against minority groups in this country is an unfortunate reality, and government is not disqualified from acting in response to it." In a separate opinion, however, Justice Scalia declared that "government can never have a 'compelling interest' in discriminating on the basis of race in order to 'make up' for past racial discrimination in the opposite direction. . . . [It is this] way of thinking that produced race slavery, race privilege and race hatred." Similarly, Justice Clarence Thomas stated that "there is a moral and constitutional equivalence between laws designed to subjugate a race and those that distribute benefits on the basis of race in order to foster some current notion of equality."

7. Bradwell v. State, 16 Wall. (83 U.S.) 130 (1872).

8. Goesaert v. Cleary, 335 U.S. 464 (1948).

9. Reed v. Reed, 404 U.S. 71 (1971).

10. Geduldig v. Aiello, 417 U.S. 484 (1974).

11. Personnel Administrator of Mass. v. Feeney, 442 U.S. 256 (1979).

12. John Stuart Mill, "On Liberty," in *On Liberty and Other Essays* 59 (John Gray, ed., 1991).

13. See State v. Mitchell, 485 N.W. 2d 807 (Wis. 1992); State v. Wyant, 597 N.E. 2d 450 (Ohio 1992). See also Susan Gellman, "Sticks and Stones Can Put You in Jail, But Can Words Increase Your Sentence?" 39 *U.C.L.A. L. Rev.* 333 (1991).

14. Wisconsin v. Mitchell, 508 U.S. 476 (1993).

15. R.A.V. v. City of St. Paul, 505 U.S. 377 (1992).

CHAPTER TWO

1. See Gerald Gunther and Kathleen Sullivan, *Constitutional Law* 1025–1029 (13th ed., 1997). See also Thomas Emerson, *The System of Freedom of Expression* 6–7 (1970).

2. Connick v. Myers, 461 U.S. 138 (1983). See also Stromberg v. California, 283 U.S. 359 (1931) ("The maintenance of the opportunity for free political discussion to the end that government may be responsive to the will of the people and that changes may be obtained by lawful means . . . is a fundamental principle of our constitutional system"); Landmark Communications, Inc. v. Virginia, 435 U.S. 829 (1978) ("Whatever differences may exist about the interpretations of the First Amendment, there is practically universal agreement that a major purpose of that Amendment was to protect the free discussion of governmental affairs").

3. Frederick Schauer, *Free Speech: A Philosophical Enquiry* 40 (1982). See also Larry Alexander, "Freedom of Speech," 2 *Encyclopedia of Applied Ethics* 299, 302 (1998).

4. E.g., Robert Bork, "Neutral Principles and Some First Amendment Problems," 47 *Ind. L. J.* 1 (1971).

5. As does Alexander Meikeljohn in "The First Amendment Is an Absolute," 1961 *Sup. Ct. Rev.* 245.

6. John Milton, "Areopagitica—A Speech for the Liberty of Unlicensed Printing" (1644) ("Let [Truth] and Falsehood grapple; who ever knew Truth put to the worst, in a free and open encounter?").

7. Abrams v. United States, 250 U.S. 616 (1919) (Holmes, J., dissenting).

8. Chaplinsky v. New Hampshire, 315 U.S. 568 (1942).

9. Kovacs v. Cooper, 336 U.S. 77 (1949) (Frankfurter, J., concurring).

10. Emerson, supra note 1 at 7. See also Police Dept. of Chicago v. Mosley, 408 U.S. 92 (1972) ("[t]o permit the continued building of our politics and culture, and to assure self-fulfillment for each individual, our people are guaranteed the right to express any thought, free from government censorship").

11. See, e.g., Red Lion Broadcasting v. FCC, 395 U.S. 367 (1969) ("It is the purpose of the First Amendment to preserve the uninhibited marketplace of ideas in which truth will ultimately prevail"); FCC v. Pacifica Foundation, 438 U.S. 726 ("government must remain neutral in the marketplace of ideas"); Simon & Schuster, Inc. v. Members of N.Y. St. Crime Board, 502 U.S. 105 (1991) ("the Government's ability to impose content-based burdens on speech raises the specter that the Government may effectively drive certain ideas or viewpoints from the marketplace"). As discussed in Chapter 6, the assertion that an unregulated marketplace of ideas leads to truth or progress has come under attack in recent years, particularly by radical critics.

12. See, e.g., Whitney v. California, 274 U.S. 357 (1927) (Brandeis, J. concurring) (free speech is valued "both as an end and as a means"); First National Bank of Boston v. Belloti, 435 U.S. 765 (1978) ("The individual's interest in self-expression is a concern of the First Amendment separate from the concern for open and informed discussion"). For an example of commentators who deny that free speech is an individual right, see Owen Fiss, *The Irony of Free Speech* 2–3 (1996).

13. Also telling is the Supreme Court's rejection of any broad, constitutionally protected autonomy right in areas of the law other than speech. See, e.g., Bowers v. Hardwick, 478 U.S. 186 (1986) (refusing to find consensual homosexual sodomy to be a fundamental right); Washington v. Glucksberg, 521 U.S. 702 (1997) (no fundamental right of terminally ill to physician-assisted suicide). In light of these cases, it would be anomalous to posit some broad, autonomy-based right to engage in speech. It would require, at minimum, an explanation of why speech as an activity is more essential to individual self-determination than sex or choosing when to end one's life. To be consistent with these cases, as well as the free speech decisions allowing many types of expression to be readily regulated, any broad autonomy interest in expression must be seen not as a fundamental right but as a "liberty interest." Although such an interest could be readily overridden, the state would at least have to show some legitimate reason for doing so. Such a justification-oriented approach is not only consistent with the Court's jurisprudence (for instance, the expressive conduct cases) but with Scanlon's autonomy-based theory (discussed in the subsequent paragraph in the text).

14. Perhaps an autonomy-based right to speak extends only to *self-regarding* speech, such as diary entries or singing in the shower or even viewing obscene material in the privacy of one's home. See Stanley v. Georgia, 394 U.S. 557 (1969). But see Osborne v. Ohio, 495 U.S. 103 (1990) (finding no constitutional right to view or possess child pornography even in the privacy of one's home).

15. Thomas Scanlon, "A Theory of Free Expression," 1 *Phil. & Pub. Aff.* 204, 215–216 (1972).

16. Ronald Dworkin, "The Coming Battles over Free Speech," *New York Review of Books,* June 11, 1992.

17. See, e.g., Marci Hamilton, "Art Speech," 49 *Vand. L. Rev.* 73, 99–100 (1996) ("[A]rt traditionally has been the target of totalitarian governments. For example, . . . China attempted to eradicate a panoply of art forms, the governments of Eastern Europe suppressed and marginalized art and artists, and Nazi Germany censored all art that would not assist Hitler's ideological goals"). As discussed in Chapter 3 at text accompanying notes 70 to 71, another reason that nonideational art is highly protected may be that art as a medium is vitally connected to political discourse.

18. Ronald Dworkin, "Women and Pornography," *New York Review of Books,* October 21, 1993.

19. Dworkin does not, however, limit his rationale to the protection of political speech. "The wrong is just as great," he insists, "when government forbids the expression of some social attitude or taste as when it censors explicitly political speech; citizens have as much right to contribute to the formation of the moral or aesthetic climate as they do to participate in politics." This extension makes his theory more controversial. It is one thing to argue that a right to equal participa-

tion in the political process is a precondition for the government's legitimately exercising power over individuals; it is quite another to argue that government may not legitimately exercise authority over individuals unless each individual has a right to contribute "to the formation of the moral or aesthetic climate." An obvious connection exists between individuals' ceding political authority to the government on the condition that they retain an equal right to participate in deciding how this political authority shall be exercised. The connection between ceding political power to the government and "the formation of the moral or aesthetic climate" is not so apparent.

20. 249 U.S. 47 (1919).

21. In the course of this opinion, Holmes also wrote what has come to be the most widely quoted phrase in any judicial opinion: "The most stringent protection of free speech would not protect a man in falsely shouting fire in a theatre and causing a panic." (Contrary to the popular rendition, Holmes says nothing about a "crowded" theater.)

22. Oliver Wendell Holmes Jr., *The Common Law* 1 (1881).

23. 249 U.S. 204 (1919).

24. 249 U.S. 211 (1919). Debs received nearly 1 million votes, or about 6 percent of all votes cast in the 1912 election. See Gunther and Sullivan, supra note 1 at 1038.

25. While serving his prison term, Debs received nearly 1 million votes in the 1920 presidential election. In 1921 his sentence was commuted by President Warren Harding. Ibid., 1038–1039.

26. 250 U.S. 616 (1919).

27. Masses Publishing Co. v. Patten, 244 Fed. 535 (S.D. N.Y. 1917).

28. Masses Publishing Co. v. Patten, 246 Fed. 24 (2d Cir. 1917).

29. In the meantime, however, Hand's most important contribution to free speech doctrine would be his influence on Holmes through private correspondence. Hand biographer Gerald Gunther believes that Hand's gentle prodding in letters to Holmes is primarily responsible for Holmes's marked change in attitude about free speech reflected in the *Abrams* dissent. See Gerald Gunther, *Learned Hand: The Man and the Judge* 161–166 (1994).

30. Letter from Learned Hand to Zechariah Chafee Jr., January 8, 1920, reprinted in Gerald Gunther, "Learned Hand and the Origins of Modern First Amendment Doctrine: Some Fragments of History," 27 *Stan. L. Rev.* 719, 766 (1975).

31. Letter from Learned Hand to Zechariah Chafee Jr., January 2, 1921, reprinted in Gunther, supra note 30 at 749.

32. Gunther and Sullivan, supra note 1 at 1035.

33. 268 U.S. 652 (1925).

34. Like the rest of the Bill of Rights, the First Amendment is a restriction on federal, not state, power. For decades, the Court had been using the Due Process Clause to strike down state laws that attempted to protect the health and safety of workers. In contrast to its approach in *Gitlow,* the Court in these cases gave very little deference to the findings of state legislatures. See, e.g., Lochner v. New York, 198 U.S. 45 (1905).

35. 274 U.S. 357 (1927).

36. Finding that Whitney had not adequately presented her constitutional arguments to the state courts, Brandeis agreed with the majority that the conviction must be affirmed.

37. Herndon v. Lowry, 301 U.S. 242 (1937).

38. 183 F. 2d 201 (2d Cir. 1950).

39. 341 U.S. 494 (1951).

40. Two justices, Hugo Black and William Douglas, dissented from the affirmance of the convictions, the latter commenting that in this country communists are "miserable merchants of unwanted ideas; their wares remain unsold."

41. Bond v. Floyd, 385 U.S. 116 (1966). Warren's approach in *Bond* builds on Justice John Harlan's opinion for the Court in Yates v. United States, 354 U.S. 298 (1957). In reversing Smith Act convictions of "lower echelon" leaders of the American Communist Party, Harlan distinguished between "abstract advocacy of forcible overthrow," which he held could not be suppressed, and "advocacy directed at promoting unlawful action," which could claim no immunity from punishment.

42. United States v. Spock, 416 F. 2d 165 (1st Cir. 1969).

43. Watts v. United States, 394 U.S. 705 (1969).

44. Brandenburg v. Ohio, 395 U.S. 444 (1969).

45. The opinion did not bear the name of any justice but was designated "per curiam," or "by the Court"; it is thought that the opinion had been drafted by Justice Abe Fortas before his resignation under a cloud of scandal.

46. Gunther, supra note 30 at 754.

47. 414 U.S. 105 (1973).

48. NAACP v. Claiborne Hardware, 458 U.S. 886 (1982).

49. Brandenburg v. Ohio (Douglas, J., concurring).

50. 315 U.S. 568 (1942).

51. See, e.g., Gooding v. Wilson, 405 U.S. 518 (1972); Rosenfeld v. New Jersey, 408 U.S. 901 (1972); Lewis v. New Orleans, 408 U.S. 913 (1972); Brown v. Oklahoma, 408 U.S. 914 (1972). In all of these cases, the Court found that the defendant was convicted under regulations that applied (or may have applied) to protected speech as well as fighting words. For more on the "overbreadth doctrine" see note 12 to Chapter 4.

52. Defamation comprises libel and slander. If the defamatory statement is in writing, it is libel; if made orally, slander. Although the Court in *Chaplinsky* referred just to libel, it no doubt meant to exclude slander from First Amendment protection as well.

53. 376 U.S. 254 (1964).

54. This "malice" requirement is somewhat of a misnomer in that it does not require that the defendant have ill will toward the plaintiff.

55. Valentine v. Chrestensen, 316 U.S. 52 (1942).

56. The abortion advertisement case was Bigelow v. Virginia, 421 U.S. 809 (1975). The lawyers' advertisement case was In re Primus, 436 U.S. 412 (1978).

57. *Virginia Pharmacy Board v. Virginia Citizens Consumer Council*, 425 U.S. 748 (1976), was the first case in which the Court held that ordinary commercial speech was entitled to some First Amendment protection. *Central Hudson Gas v. Public Service Commission*, 447 U.S. 557 (1980), announced the four-part test. The first part

of the test determines whether the speech is entitled to any First Amendment protection at all. If on the one hand the speech either proposes an illegal transaction or is misleading, the ban will be upheld without any further inquiry. If on the other hand the speech concerns a lawful activity and is not misleading, the second part of the test asks whether the government interest in regulating the speech is "substantial." If it is not, the regulation is unconstitutional. If the interest is "substantial," the regulation will be upheld as long as it "directly advances the government interest asserted" and is "not more extensive than is necessary to serve that interest." (Despite the use of the word "necessary" in the final step of the analysis, later decisions make clear that the fit between the ends of the regulation and the means of accomplishing it need not be perfect but only reasonable.)

58. Significantly, however, in a recent decision four justices (one shy of a majority) suggested that this fairly deferential test be applied only to regulations designed to protect a fair bargaining process (e.g., regulations protecting consumers from misleading advertising). In contrast, truthful, nonmisleading advertisements should in the view of these justices be afforded full First Amendment protection. See 44 Liquormart, Inc. v. Rhode Island, 517 U.S. 484 (1996).

59. 354 U.S. 476 (1957) (decided together with Alberts v. California).

60. For Dreiser, see Commonwealth v. Friede, 271 Mass. 318, 171 N.E. 472 (1930); for Lawrence, Commonwealth v. DeLacey, 271 Mass. 327, 171 N.E. 455 (1930); and for Miller, Besig v. United States, 208 F. 2d 142 (9th Cir. 1953).

61. For sex education, see United States v. Dennett, 39 F. 2d 564 (2d Cir. 1930). For *Life*, see People v. Larsen, 5 N.Y.S. 2d 55 (1938).

62. 413 U.S. 15 (1973).

63. Unlike the *Brandenburg* test, which requires an assessment of the harm alleged to be caused by each specific instance of the speech that the government seeks to punish, the obscenity test does not require a showing that the material in question is likely to cause harm. Similarly, the Court has avoided serious inquiry into whether as a class of speech obscene material causes harm and, if so, whether the harm is sufficient to warrant its prohibition. The Court has reasoned, somewhat circularly, that no such analysis is necessary because obscenity is outside the protection of the First Amendment.

64. See "Cincinnati's Trial Unanswered Question," *New York Times*, October 18, 1990, C17.

65. Skywalker Records, Inc. v. Navarro, 739 F. Supp. 578 (S.D. Fla. 1990).

66. Luke Records v. Navarro, 960 F. 2d 134 (11th Cir. 1992).

67. For a defense of the categorical exclusion approach in certain circumstances, see Frederick Schauer, "Codifying the First Amendment: New York v. Ferber," 1982 *Sup. Ct. Rev.* 285.

68. 458 U.S. 747 (1982).

CHAPTER THREE

1. On a sociological level, Marcel Duchamp's "sculpture" *The Fountain* shows how crucial the medium is to defining whether an act will be understood as expression. Displayed in a 1917 New York art exhibition, *The Fountain* was "notori-

ously nothing other than a men's urinal . . . transformed [into art] by force of its incorporation into the acknowledged medium of an art exhibition." Robert Post, "Recuperating the First Amendment," 47 *Stan. L. Rev.* 1249 (1995).

2. The nomenclature "unprotected" speech is not felicitous, for the First Amendment does impose some limitations on government's power to regulate such expression. In R.A.V. v. City of St. Paul, 505 U.S. 377 (1992), the Court held that although the state might ban the use of all "fighting words," it could not single out for special prohibition fighting words with a racial content.

3. 427 U.S. 50 (1976).

4. Justice Lewis Powell, who supplied the fifth vote for upholding the regulation in *Young*, wrote separately, stating that he was not "inclined to agree" with the plurality's position that "nonobscene, erotic material may be treated differently under First Amendment principles from other forms of protected expression." Rather, Powell found that "the governmental interest prompting the inclusion in the ordinance of adult establishments was wholly unrelated to any suppression of free expression" and that impact on any free speech interests was "incidental and minimal." This "secondary effects" rationale was adopted by a majority of the Court in Renton v. Playtime Theatres, 475 U.S. 41 (1986), discussed more fully in the text. That the Court has accepted the "secondary effects" rationale only with respect to sexually explicit but nonobscene speech supports the proposition that this speech is effectively treated by the Court as "lower-value" expression.

5. Commercial speech has also been referred to as occupying a "subordinate position in the scale of First Amendment values." See Ohralik v. Ohio State Bar Assn., 436 U.S. 447 (1978).

6. Spence v. Washington, 418 U.S. 405 (1974). Read literally, this test is too broad. Violent acts such as racially motivated lynchings or political assassinations are often intended to send specific messages that would be clearly understood. The Court has held, however, that violence can never be considered expressive conduct. Thus *Spence* should be read as stating a necessary but not a sufficient condition for communication as expressive conduct. Generalizing from the Court's exclusion of violence, I have suggested that any activity causing a harm obviously unrelated to expression is also ineligible for classification as expressive conduct. See James Weinstein, "Hate Crime and Punishment," 73 *Ore. L. Rev.* 345, 355 n. 45 (1994).

7. See, e.g., Texas v. Johnson, 491 U.S. 397 (1989). Finding that all the state's asserted interests in forbidding flag burning were related to the suppression of speech, the Court subjected the ban to "strict scrutiny." Because these interests were not sufficiently compelling, the Court held that the ban on flag burning as a form of political protest was unconstitutional.

8. See, e.g., United States v. O'Brien, 391 U.S. 367, in which the Court found (dubiously, in my view) that a federal law banning draft card burning was unrelated to the suppression of speech. Accordingly, the Court subjected the regulation to little scrutiny and easily upheld it.

9. Note, however, that the concern is with the government's *stated* rationale for the regulation, not the *actual* purpose (sometimes referred to as "motive") revealed by legislative history. See ibid.

10. See Wisconsin v. Mitchell, 508 U.S. 476 (1993).

11. Police Dept. of Chicago v. Mosley, 408 U.S. 92 (1972).

12. R.A.V. v. City of St. Paul, 505 U.S. 377 (1992).

13. Chaplinsky v. New Hampshire, 315 U.S. 568 (1942), quoting Cantwell v. Connecticut, 310 U.S. 296 (1940).

14. Regan v. Time, Inc., 468 U.S. 641 (1984).

15. See Turner Broadcasting System, Inc. v. FCC, 512 U.S. 622 (1994) (regulations justified by their "communicative impact" on the audience are content based).

16. See, e.g., Boos v. Barry 485 U.S. 312 (1988) (restrictions "justified without reference to the content of the regulated speech" are content neutral). Ordinarily, as in the examples given in the text, it is obvious from the face of the regulation whether or not the law regulates expression *because* of the message it conveys; sometimes, however, it is necessary to inquire into the regulation's justification. See, e.g., Texas v. Johnson, 491 U.S. 397 (1989); Renton v. Playtime Theatres, 475 U.S. 41 (1986).

17. Rosenberger v. Rector and Visitors of the Univ. of Virginia, 515 U.S. 819 (1995).

18. 360 U.S. 684 (1959).

19. Rosenberger v. Rector and Visitors of the Univ. of Virginia, 515 U.S. 819 (1995). In National Endowment for the Arts v. Finley, 524 U.S. 569 (1998), the majority of the Court found that a provision requiring the NEA to "tak[e] into consideration general standards of decency and respect for the diverse beliefs and values of the American public" not to be "the kind of directed viewpoint discrimination" that "will compromise First Amendment values"; three other justices (two of whom agreed with the majority that the restriction was valid) found the provision "unquestionably" and "quintessentially" viewpoint based.

20. 403 U.S. 15 (1971).

21. 491 U.S. 397 (1989).

22. Ibid. (Rehnquist, C. J., dissenting).

23. 512 U.S. 622 (1994).

24. 475 U.S. 41 (1986).

25. Ibid. (emphasis added).

26. Turner Broadcasting System, Inc. v. FCC, 512 U.S. 622 (1994).

27. Simon & Schuster, Inc. v. Members of New York State Crime Board, 502 U.S. 105 (1991).

28. See Carey v. Brown, 447 U.S. 455 (1980).

29. City of Ladue v. Gilleo, 512 U.S. 43 (1994) (O'Connor, J., concurring).

30. Geoffrey Stone, "Restrictions of Speech Because of Its Content: The Peculiar Case of Subject-Matter Restrictions," 46 *U. Chi. L. Rev.* 81, 107 (1978).

31. For a law regulating protests at abortion clinics, see the Freedom of Access to Clinic Entrances Act (FACE), 18 U.S.C. § 248, forbidding "physical obstruction" or "force or threat of force" that "intentionally injures, intimidates, or interferes . . . with any person because that person has been . . . obtaining or providing reproductive health services." The Mississippi law was upheld in Cameron v. Johnson, 390 U.S. 611 (1968).

32. See Cameron v. Johnson (upholding Mississippi regulation); Cheefer v. Reno, 55 F. 3d 1517 (11th Cir. 1995) (upholding FACE). As Robert Post has ob-

served, "the [Supreme] Court has shown little inclination to assess content neutrality in terms of the discriminatory 'effects' of a regulation." Post, supra note 1 at 1268.

33. See International Society for Krishna Consciousness, Inc. v. Lee, 505 U.S. 672 (1992).

34. Even as ardent a champion of rule-bound jurisprudence as Justice Scalia recognizes that because "[a]ll generalizations . . . are to some degree invalid . . . every rule of law has a few corners that do not quite fit." Antonin Scalia, "The Rule of Law as a Law of Rules," 56 U. Chi. L. Rev. 1175, 1177 (1989).

35. Boos v. Barry, 485 U.S. 312 (1988).

36. Gerald Gunther, "Foreword: In Search of Evolving Doctrine on a Changing Court: A Model for Newer Equal Protection," 86 Harv. L. Rev. 1, 8 (1972).

37. The only speech regulations to have survived "strict scrutiny" involve restrictions on expenditures or contributions to influence the political process. See, e.g., Buckley v. Valeo, 424 U.S. 1 (1976); Austin v. Michigan Chamber of Commerce, 494 U.S. 652 (1990). In Burson v. Freeman, 504 U.S. 191 (1992), the Court upheld a law prohibiting electioneering in the immediate vicinity of polling places. Although seven of the eight justices participating in the case applied strict scrutiny, only four of the five justices who voted to uphold the law applied that standard. (Justice Scalia voted to uphold the law but found strict scrutiny inappropriate because he thought the restricted area was not a public forum.)

38. Ward v. Rock Against Racism, 491 U.S. 781 (1989).

39. See Gerald Gunther and Kathleen Sullivan, Constitutional Law 1266 (13th ed., 1997). The Court has made clear that with respect to a content-neutral law, the "narrow tailoring" requirement does not mean that the regulation must be the "least restrictive or least intrusive" means of accomplishing the government's interest, as it does with respect to a content-based regulation. "Narrow tailoring" in this context means only that "the regulation promotes a substantial government interest that would be achieved less effectively absent the regulation." See Ward v. Rock Against Racism.

40. See James Weinstein, "Free Speech, Abortion Access, and the Problem of Judicial Viewpoint Discrimination," 29 U. C. Davis L. Rev. 471, 481–485 (1996).

41. See, e.g., Turner Broadcasting System, Inc. v. FCC, 512 U.S. 622 (1994) (finding a law requiring cable systems to devote one-third of their channels to the transmission of local broadcasts to be content neutral, despite the plainly content-based justification for the law, including the promotion of "educational and informational programming" and "local news and public affairs programming"). See also Regan v. Time, Inc., 468 U.S. 641 (1984) (finding content neutral a federal law requiring that photographs of U.S. currency be in black and white and either less than three-fourths or more than one and one-half the size of the actual currency).

42. See Regan v. Taxation with Representation, 461 U.S. 540 (1983). Cf. Gunther and Sullivan, supra note 39 at 1208 (classifying speaker-based restrictions as content based).

43. See City of Ladue v. Gilleo, 512 U.S. 43 (1994) (invalidating a near total ban on residential signs, including political messages placed by homeowners on their front lawns or in their windows). But see Members of City Council v. Taxpayers for Vincent, 466 U.S. 789 (1984) (upholding a Los Angeles ordinance that forbade

the posting of signs, including campaign posters, on publicly owned utility poles). The heightened scrutiny sometimes applicable to total medium bans is the legacy of early free speech cases. See Schneider v. State, 308 U.S. 147 (1939) (invalidating an ordinance banning the distribution of leaflets as a means of controlling litter); Martin v. Struthers, 319 U.S. 141 (1943) (invalidating a ban on the distribution of leaflets by ringing doorbells or otherwise summoning residents to the door). Although generally less speech-protective than modern doctrine, the free speech jurisprudence of the 1930s and 1940s was less formalistic and thus sometimes more attuned to the practical impact of speech regulation.

44. Regan v. Time, Inc., 468 U.S. 641 (1983).

45. Turner Broadcasting System, Inc. v. FCC, 512 U.S. 622 (1994).

46. See Perry Education Assn. v. Perry Local Educators' Assn., 460 U.S. 37 (1983) (establishing tripartite division of government property into traditional public fora; designated public fora, such as school board meetings; and nonpublic fora).

47. See Cornelius v. NAACP Legal Defense Fund, 473 U.S. 788 (1985).

48. Members of City Council v. Taxpayers for Vincent, 466 U.S. 789 (1984) (utility poles); United States v. Kokinda, 497 U.S. 720 (1990) (post office sidewalk).

49. International Society for Krishna Consciousness, Inc. v. Lee, 505 U.S. 672 (1992).

50. See, e.g., Connick v. Myers, 461 U.S. 138 (1983).

51. See National Endowment for the Arts v. Finley, 524 U.S. 569 (1998) (content-based judgments "are a consequence of the nature of art funding"). In *Finley* the Court upheld a provision of the NEA funding statute that required those awarding grants according to "artistic excellence and artistic merit" to "tak[e] into consideration general standards of decency and respect for the diverse beliefs and values of the American public." The majority found that this provision, as interpreted and enforced by the NEA, did not constitute the "kind of directed viewpoint discrimination" that poses "a realistic danger [to] First Amendment values."

52. See Regan v. Taxation with Representation, 461 U.S. 540 (1983).

53. See Rust v. Sullivan, 500 U.S. 173 (1991). See also *Finley*, (Souter, J., dissenting) ("if the Food and Drug Administration launches an advertising campaign on the subject of smoking, it may condemn the habit without also having to show a cowboy taking a puff on the opposite page"). Indeed, the only definite constitutional limitations on government-subsidized speech are in the realm of partisan politics. There is thus no doubt that Congress could not constitutionally fund only Republican candidates. See ibid. (Scalia, J., concurring). Accordingly, any limitation on the government's power to speak would seem to stem not from any commitment to the marketplace of ideas (which government propaganda can badly distort) but from the democratic self-governance rationale.

54. Gunther and Sullivan, supra note 39 at 1023. For a criticism of this position, see James Weinstein, "Casebook Review: Combining the Best of Gunther and Sullivan," 21 *Seattle L. Rev.* 907, 925–926 (1998).

55. See Dun & Bradstreet, Inc. v. Greenmoss Builders, Inc., 472 U.S. 749 (1985).

56. See Hustler Magazine v. Falwell, 485 U.S. 46 (1988).

57. See generally, Robert Post, "The Constitutional Concept of Public Discourse: Outrageous Opinion, Democratic Deliberation, and *Hustler Magazine v. Falwell*," 103 *Harv. L. Rev.* 603 (1990).

58. Admittedly, regulation of speech through tort liability might in some instances pass "strict scrutiny." For instance, there is a compelling state interest in allowing a child injured because of an explosion caused by faulty instructions in a chemistry set to recover, and such a remedy is undoubtedly narrowly tailored. The same, however, cannot be said about a suit for faulty instructions on rug cleaner that leads to some slight discoloration. Although the state certainly has a legitimate interest in allowing such recovery, it is hardly "compelling." More important, product liability cases such as these are usually not thought of as free speech cases, let alone ones triggering strict scrutiny.

59. Connick v. Myers, 461 U.S. 138 (1983).

60. Dun & Bradstreet, Inc. v. Greenmoss Builders, Inc., 472 U.S. 749 (1985).

61. Connick v. Myers (upholding dismissal by district attorney of a subordinate who circulated a "questionnaire" critical of the way he ran the office). (Note to music fans: The district attorney in this case is the father of Harry Connick Jr.)

62. Gertz v. Robert Welch, Inc., 418 U.S. 323 (1974). *Gertz* held that in defamation suits brought by private individuals concerning statements of public concern the First Amendment forbids the imposition of strict liability; thus the plaintiff must show that the defendant was at fault (e.g., negligent) in making the false statement. This is a significantly less onerous standard than the *New York Times* "malice" test, which requires the plaintiff to show that the defendant was reckless in making the defamatory remark or knew that it was false. *Gertz* also imposed First Amendment limitations on the recovery of damages.

63. "When the speech is of exclusively private concern and the plaintiff is a private figure as in *Dun & Bradstreet*, the constitutional requirements do not necessarily force any change in at least some of the features of the common-law landscape." Philadelphia Newspapers, Inc. v. Hepps, 475 U.S. 767 (1986). Thus in Dun & Bradstreet, Inc. v. Greenmoss Builders, Inc., 472 U.S. 749 (1985), a defamation suit involving a false credit report that damaged a corporation's reputation, the Court held that even *Gertz*'s limited protection did not apply.

64. Hustler Magazine v. Falwell, 485 U.S. 46 (1988).

65. In drawing the line between speech that is highly protected from content regulation and speech that is not, the Court most often uses the phrase "speech on matters of public concern" rather than the term "political speech." This usage, combined with the Court's continued reference to the marketplace of ideas as an underlying free speech value, suggests both that the term "on matters of public concern" encompasses more than political speech and that the underlying values advanced by the protection of this speech include more than just democratic self-governance.

66. Connick v. Myers, 461 U.S. 138 (1983).

67. Perry Education Assn. v. Perry Local Educators' Assn., 460 U.S. 37 (1983).

68. Which is not to say that in every case the occurrence of speech in a highly protected setting will automatically bestow added protection. For instance, I very much doubt that any First Amendment protection would attach just because two competitors communicated price information by holding up signs in a public fo-

rum or through a secret code in a published novel. The phenomenon I have described here is a strong tendency, not a rigid rule.

69. A similarly ad hoc determination is required in determining the degree of First Amendment protection afforded defamatory statements.

70. See Post, supra note 1 at 1253 (if "a medium [is] constitutionally protected by the First Amendment, each instance of the medium [will] also be protected"). It should be noted, however, that even among the highly protected media there are some differences in the degree of protection. For instance, the print media have been afforded greater immunity from content regulation than have the broadcast media. Compare Miami Herald v. Tornillo, 418 U.S. 241 (1974) (right-to-reply law applicable to newspapers held unconstitutional) with Red Lion Broadcasting v. FCC, 395 U.S. 367 (1969) (right-to-reply regulation upheld). Compare also Papish v. University of Missouri Curators, 410 U.S. 667 (1973) (holding that a university could not expel a student for violating "conventions of decency" by using the term "mother fucker" in a student newspaper) with FCC v. Pacifica Foundation, 438 U.S. 726 (1978) (upholding an FCC regulation prohibiting the broadcast of "indecent" material at times when children were likely to be in the audience). See also Times Film Corp. v. Chicago, 365 U.S. 43 (1961) (upholding licensing scheme for movies that would be plainly unconstitutional if applied to print media). Until recently there had been uncertainty whether the Internet would be afforded the extremely strong immunity from content regulation applicable to the print media or given the more qualified protection applicable to the broadcast media. In striking down a law regulating "indecent" speech on the Internet, the Court in Reno v. ACLU, 521 U.S. 844 (1997) held that there is "no basis for qualifying the level of First Amendment scrutiny that should be applied to this medium."

71. As the obscenity doctrine shows, the protection afforded expression just because it occurs in a setting dedicated to public discourse or a medium essential to such discourse is defeasible. Similarly, despite the highly protected status of the print media, publishers of a cookbook that negligently called for the use of poisonous mushrooms in a recipe would not be immune from civil liability. Still, because books are a highly protected medium of expression, such a lawsuit would be seen as raising more of a free speech concern than a suit against a drug company for negligently mislabeling medicine bottles.

72. In conceptualizing doctrinal rules as constructing a realm dedicated to public discourse in which content regulation is forbidden and other spheres in which content regulation is routinely permitted, I have been greatly influenced by Robert Post's insightful work in this area, much of which is collected in his *Constitutional Domains: Democracy, Community and Management* (1995). See also Robert Post, "Community and the First Amendment," 29 *Ariz. St. L. J.* 473 (1995). I do not, however, share Post's view that the rigorous protection afforded public discourse is entirely limited to public discourse. See James Weinstein, "A Brief Introduction to Free Speech Doctrine," 29 *Ariz. St. L. J.* 461, 470 (1995). For a criticism of Post's perspective and the usefulness of the concept of "public discourse," see Paul Bender, "Comment on Robert C. Post's 'Community and the First Amendment,'" 29 *Ariz. St. L. J.* 485 (1997). For a reply, see Robert Post, "Reply to Bender," 29 *Ariz. St. L. J.* 495 (1997).

73. Police Dept. of Chicago v. Mosley, 408 U.S. 92 (1972) (emphasis added).

74. In the murky middle are settings such as the private workplace, places not dedicated to the accomplishment of governmental functions but where the government nevertheless has strong regulatory interests to vindicate. In such places the absence of any overarching, pervasive government purpose forecloses the need for general governmental control of expression. In addition, although a setting such as the private workplace is not *primarily* dedicated to the discussion of matters of public concern, it is where most adults spend the majority of their waking lives, and thus for many it is an important forum for the exchange of ideas. Yet the existence of pressing regulatory interests unrelated to the suppression of ideas (e.g., preventing racial and gender discrimination) may justify specific instances of content-based speech regulation. In these "intermediate" places, the determination of whether speech will be afforded highly protected status will turn on more particularized considerations of both subject matter and context.

75. R.A.V. v. City of St. Paul, 505 U.S. 377 (1992).

76. Which is not to say that applications of these regulations cannot raise serious free speech questions. Both because the workplace is an important setting for the sharing of ideas on matters of public concern and because sexist and racist speech can be ideological, *application* of these antiharassment provisions can implicate free speech concerns far more than the application of laws to counter insider trading.

CHAPTER FOUR

1. Mari Matsuda, "Public Response to Racist Speech: Considering the Victim's Story," in *Words That Wound* 36 (Mari Matsuda, Charles Lawrence, Richard Delgado, and Kimberlè Crenshaw, eds., 1993).

2. Regina v. Zundel, [1987] 35 D.L.R. (4th) 338.

3. Regina v. Andrews, [1990] 3 SCR 970.

4. Dun & Bradstreet, Inc. v. Greenmoss Builders, Inc., 472 U.S. 749 (1985).

5. This is the approach taken by Judge Easterbrook, for instance, in striking down the viewpoint-oriented antipornography ordinance discussed later in the chapter.

6. Kathleen Sullivan, "Discrimination, Distribution and Free Speech," 37 *Ariz. L. Rev.* 439, 443 (1995).

7. Rosenberger v. Rector and Visitors of Univ. of Virginia, 515 U.S. 819 (1995).

8. See Kingsley International Pictures Corp. v. Regents, 360 U.S. 684 (1959) (New York's refusal to issue a movie license to *Lady Chatterley's Lover* on the grounds that it presented adultery in a morally favorable light "struck at the very heart of constitutionally protected liberty").

9. 395 U.S. 444 (1969).

10. Racist oratory whipping up a mob to lynch a black man is an example from the not-too-distant past. See also the incitement to racial violence at issue in *Wisconsin v. Mitchell,* discussed in the concluding section of this chapter.

11. If, however, the law proscribed only *racist* incitement, it would founder on *R.A.V.*'s antiselectivity principle. See Chapter 5, text accompanying notes 16 to 24.

12. See, e.g., Matsuda, supra note 1 at 25–26 (by "plant[ing] in our minds" ideas of "racial inferiority," hate speech "interfer[es] with our perception and interaction with the person next to us"). Because a general ban on hate speech would prohibit an enormous amount of speech that *Brandenburg* holds may not be outlawed, the Court would likely invalidate the law as "overbroad." Pursuant to the Court's overbreadth doctrine, laws that prohibit a "substantial" amount of protected speech are under certain circumstances invalid in their entirety. See, e.g., Reno v. ACLU, 521 U.S. 844 (1997).

13. Perry Education Assn. v. Perry Local Educators' Assn., 460 U.S. 37 (1983).

14. In R.A.V. v. City of St. Paul, 505 U.S. 377 (1992), the cross-burning case previously discussed, the Court found that the state had a compelling interest in "ensur[ing] the basic human rights of members of groups that have historically been subjected to discrimination." In addition, the Court stated that a law prohibiting use of certain racist symbols "can be said to promote" this interest. The Court nonetheless held the ordinance unconstitutional because the statute "plainly" was not necessary to achieve that end. The Court found that "precisely the same beneficial effect" could be achieved by banning all fighting words rather than singling out just racial ones. See also Bob Jones University, 461 U.S. 574 (1983) ("[T]he government has a fundamental, overriding interest in eradicating racial discrimination in education").

15. See generally Gerald Gunther and Kathleen Sullivan, *Constitutional Law* 1111–1112 (13th ed., 1997) (discussing arguments that bans on hate speech would not effectively reduce acts of illegal discrimination).

16. Reno v. ACLU, 521 U.S. 844 (1997). The narrow-tailoring requirement obviously overlaps considerably with the requirement that the restriction be "necessary" to achieving some compelling interest.

17. Indeed, it is doubtful that a general hate speech ban would survive even the intermediate level of scrutiny applicable to commercial speech. In 44 Liquormart, Inc. v. Rhode Island, 517 U.S. 484 (1996), the Court invalidated a prohibition on advertising the price of alcoholic beverages. The plurality found that the ban did not "directly advance" the interest in promoting temperance because the state "presented no evidence to suggest that its speech prohibition will significantly reduce market-wide consumption." Accordingly, the ban impermissibly rested on "speculation [and] conjecture." In addition, the plurality found the restriction "more extensive than necessary," pointing, inter alia, to "educational campaigns focused on the problems of excessive . . . drinking." The plurality concluded that "even under the less than strict standard that generally applies in commercial speech cases," the ban was unconstitutional. Four other justices agreed that the "fit" between the ban and the goal of reducing drinking was "not reasonable" in light of "other methods" by which the state could more directly accomplish this goal.

18. Matsuda, supra note 1 at 25.

19. 485 U.S. 46 (1988).

20. Texas v. Johnson, 491 U.S. 397 (1989). See also United States v. Eichman, 496 U.S. 310 (1990) ("We are aware that desecration of the flag is deeply offensive to many. But the same might be said, for example, of virulent ethnic and religious epithets").

21. 505 U.S. 377 (1992).

22. Years earlier the U.S. Court of Appeals invalidated a Skokie ordinance that banned the "dissemination of [material] . . . which [intentionally] promotes or incites hatred against persons by reason of their race, national origin, or religion." Collin v. Smith, 578 F. 2d 1197 (7th Cir. 1978). See also National Socialist Party v. Skokie, 432 U.S. 43 (1977) (vacating for lack of procedural safeguards an injunction prohibiting the National Socialist Party from parading in party uniform, displaying the swastika, or distributing anti-Semitic literature).

23. 343 U.S. 250 (1952).

24. See Milkovich v. Lorrain Journal Co., 497 U.S. 1 (1990).

25. In the unlikely event that the Court would still allow prosecutions for racial libel to be brought at all, the *New York Times* "malice" standard of reckless or knowing falsity would probably apply. At minimum, the state would have to show that the speaker was "at fault" (e.g., negligent) in making these false statements. Cf. Gertz v. Robert Welch, Inc. 418 U.S. 323 (1974) (in defamation suits concerning matters of public concern brought by private figures, states may not impose liability without fault).

26. Even if Beauharnais's empirical claims could be disentangled from his expression of political beliefs, the courtroom is not an appropriate forum to assess the empirical accuracy of theories asserting that traits of particular groups are biologically based rather than a product of the environment. The judicial system is simply not designed to deal with such imponderable questions.

27. Gertz v. Robert Welch, Inc., 418 U.S. 323 (1974). *New York Times* and its progeny perhaps leave room for narrow group defamation law. Thus it is possible that falsifiable statements (e.g., all Jews have congenital syphilis) made with "malice" (i.e., with knowing or reckless disregard for their truth) might be punishable. Still, in light of *R.A.V.*'s antiselectivity principle, any such group libel law might have to apply not just to defamation of racial or ethnic groups but to any collectivity with legally protected reputational interests.

28. See American Booksellers Assn., Inc. v. Hudnut, 598 F. Supp. 1316 (S.D. Ind. 1984).

29. American Booksellers Assn., Inc. v. Hudnut, 771 F. 2d 323 (7th Cir. 1985). The full text of the key provisions of the model ordinance (which is substantially the same as the Indianapolis law) appears in Chapter 5, text accompanying note 40.

30. 475 U.S. 1001. A "summary affirmance" (a practice developed by the Court in response to a now largely repealed jurisdictional statute that required the Court to review certain classes of cases) means that the Court agrees with the result reached by the lower court, although not necessarily with its reasoning. A summary affirmance is binding precedent on lower courts. Chief Justice Warren Burger and Justices Rehnquist and O'Connor dissented from this summary disposition, arguing that the Court should have given the case plenary consideration.

31. In Chapter 5, text accompanying notes 48 to 51, I discuss at length the objection that Judge Easterbrook's condemnation of this ordinance as viewpoint oriented was unjustified.

32. See, e.g., Jenkins v. Georgia, 418 U.S. 153 (1974) (film whose subject matter is sex and that contains some nudity but does not include exhibition of actors' genitals, lewd or otherwise, is not obscene). Judge Easterbrook's emphasis in the

Hudnut opinion that the ordinance regulates material that is not obscene under *Miller* suggests that the court thought the ordinance, in addition to being unconstitutionally viewpoint based, was unconstitutional because it was inconsistent with the Supreme Court's obscenity cases. This supports my suggestion above that courts may well find a general hate speech ban per se unconstitutional because it is inconsistent with the Supreme Court's incitement jurisprudence.

33. 521 U.S. 844 (1997).

34. That the Court uses strict scrutiny here is not contrary to either Judge Easterbrook's approach in *Hudnut* or my suggestion that the Court would probably find a broad hate speech ban unconstitutional per se. Unlike the Indianapolis ordinance or a general hate speech ban, this pornography restriction was not viewpoint based. Additionally, the law did not *ban* speech but merely tried, albeit in an overly intrusive way, to keep children from gaining access to it.

35. The Court also found the law to be unconstitutionally vague.

36. See Renton v. Playtime Theatres, Inc., 475 U.S. 41 (1986) and Young v. American Mini Theatres, Inc., 427 U.S. 50 (1976) (zoning of adult theaters); FCC v. Pacifica Foundation, 438 U.S. 726 (1978) (regulation of broadcast "indecency").

37. See Ginsberg v. New York, 390 U.S. 629 (1968). Cf. Reno v. ACLU, 521 U.S. 844 (1997) (invalidating law controlling Internet distribution of "indecent" material to children because the law unduly interfered with adults' access to such material).

38. See, e.g., Delph v. Dr. Pepper Bottling Co. of Paragould, Inc. 130 F. 3d 349 (8th Cir. 1997) (noting that the plaintiff in that case was "called some of the most offensive of racist epithets"). These cases, however, have been careful not to construe Title VII as outlawing "isolated" use of racial slurs but have found a violation only when the harassment has been "sufficiently severe or pervasive to alter the conditions of the victim's employment and create an abusive working environment." See Meritor Savings Bank v. Vinson, 477 U.S. 57 (1986).

39. See, e.g., Harris v. L & L Wings, Inc., 132 F. 3d 978 (4th Cir. 1997) (noting that pornography contributed to the sexually hostile environment that supported the award of punitive damages to a Title VII plaintiff); Carr v. Allison Gas Turbine Division, General Motors Corp., 32 F. 3d 1007 (7th Cir. 1994) (finding that employees' use of pornography to harass female coworker was evidence of Title VII violation); Burns v. McGregor Electronic Industries, Inc., 989 F. 2d 959 (8th Cir. 1993) ("The EEOC agrees that a 'workplace in which sexual slurs, displays of "girlie" pictures, and other offensive conduct can constitute a hostile work environment even if many people deem it to be harmless or insignificant'"—citing *EEOC Compliance Manual* [CCH], s. 614, para. 3114[C][1], at 3274 [1990]); Ellison v. Brady, 924 F. 2d 872 (9th Cir. 1991) (noting, in dicta, that presence of pornography can be sufficient to show hostile work environment under Title VII); Stair v. Lehigh Valley Carpenters Local Union 600, 1993 WL 235491 (E.D.Pa.) ("The intent to discriminate on the basis of sex in cases involving pornographic materials is 'implicit,' and courts should recognize this as a matter of course"); Wise v. New York City Police Dept., 928 F. Supp. 355 (S.D.N.Y. 1996) ("A jury could reasonably conclude that given the alleged omnipresence of pornography in the Precinct and Wise's alleged repeated complaints about sexually harassing inci-

dents, [the supervisor] had actual or constructive notice of the sexual harassment, and that his failure to remedy it demonstrated deliberate indifference"); Blakely v. Continental Airlines, Inc., 992 F. Supp. 731 (D. New Jersey 1998) (noting that for three years Title VII plaintiff was subjected to pornography in the workplace, including "vile and disgusting pornography directed at her" that resulted in compensable psychological harm). But see Rabidue v. Osceola Refining Co., 805 F. 2d 611 (6th Cir. 1986) ("The sexually oriented poster displays had a de minimis effect on the plaintiff's work environment when considered in the context of a society that condones and publicly features and commercially exploits open displays of written and pictorial erotica at the newsstands, on prime-time television, at the cinema, and in other public places"). *Rabidue*'s view, however, has been questioned by later Sixth Circuit decisions. See, e.g., Yates v. Avco Corp., 819 F. 2d 630 (6th Cir. 1987) (adopting *Rabidue* dissenter's opinion that sexual harassment should be considered from the perspective of the victim).

40. Andrews v. City of Philadelphia, 895 F. 2d 1469 (3rd Cir. 1990).

41. See, e.g., Kingsley Brown, "Title VII as Censorship: Hostile Environment Harassment and the First Amendment," 52 *Ohio St. L. Rev.* 481 (1991).

42. See Eugene Volokh, "What Speech Does 'Hostile Work Environment' Harassment Law Restrict?" 85 *Geo. L. J.* 627 (1997).

43. R.A.V. v. City of St. Paul, 505 U.S. 377 (1992).

44. See, e.g., Doe v. University of Michigan, 721 F. Supp. 852 (E.D. Mich. 1989); UWM Post, Inc. v. Board of Regents of the University of Wisconsin, 774 F. Supp. 1163 (E.D. Wis. 1991). See also Alan Kors and Harvey Silvergate, *The Shadow University* (1998).

45. As the University of Michigan did pursuant to the code struck down in the *Doe* case cited in note 44.

46. In suggesting that campus hate speech restrictions might constitutionally be effectuated through a code aimed at racial discrimination, I am not suggesting that such restrictions are necessarily a good idea. For my views on this matter, see James Weinstein, "A Constitutional Roadmap to the Regulation of Campus Hate Speech," 38 *Wayne L. Rev.* 163 (1991).

47. 508 U.S. 476 (1993).

48. *Wisconsin v. Mitchell* also suggests that despite *R.A.V.*'s antiselectivity principle it may still be possible effectively to punish unprotected speech with racist content more harshly than other subcategories of unprotected speech. A little-discussed fact about the *Mitchell* decision is that although the underlying crime in that case was aggravated battery, Mitchell never laid a hand on the victim. Rather, Mitchell committed the battery by inciting his companions to attack the victim. The predicate crime in *Mitchell* (battery) was, however, one that is only rarely committed by speech. But what if a hate crime statute were applied to enhance the penalty for a speech crime, such as incitement to violence or use of fighting words? Such an application would seem to fit squarely within *R.A.V.*'s caveat that a "subcategory of a proscribable class of speech can be swept up incidentally within the reach of a statute directed at conduct rather than speech." For a more detailed discussion of this possibility, see James Weinstein, "Hate Crime and Punishment: A Comment on *Wisconsin v. Mitchell*," 73 *Ore. L. Rev.* 345, 369–373 (1994).

Chapter Five

1. Richard Delgado and David Yun, "Pressure Valves and Bloodied Chickens: An Analysis of Paternalistic Objections to Hate Speech Regulation," 82 *Calif. L. Rev.* 871, 883 (1994).

2. Mari Matsuda, "Public Response to Racist Speech: Considering the Victim's Story," in *Words That Wound* 34 (Mari Matsuda, Charles Lawrence, Richard Delgado, and Kimberlè Crenshaw, eds., 1993).

3. See In re Primus, 436 U.S. 412 (1978).

4. See New York Times v. Sullivan, 376 U.S. 254 (1964); Gertz v. Robert Welch, 418 U.S. 323 (1974). See also the discussion of defamation in Chapter 2.

5. Watts v. United States, 394 U.S. 705 (1969).

6. New York Times Co. v. United States, 403 U.S. 713 (1971).

7. See, e.g., NAACP v. Claiborne Hardware Co., 458 U.S. 886 (1982).

8. See Janice Oakes, "Copyright and the First Amendment: Where Lies the Public Interest?" 59 *Tul. L. Rev.* 135, 140 n. 35 (1984). See also Campbell v. Acuff-Rose Music, Inc., 510 U.S. 569 (1994) (finding parody eligible for fair use defense even if the parody is commercial in character).

9. See, e.g., Bethel School District No. 403 v. Fraser, 478 U.S. 675 (1986) (upholding against First Amendment challenge punishment of high school student for delivering lewd speech at a school assembly).

10. See Lewis v. New Orleans, 408 U.S. 913 (1972) (Powell, J., concurring) (constitutional protection may extend to fighting words "addressed to a police officer trained to exercise a higher degree of restraint than the average citizen").

11. The regulation that comes closest to a regulation of public discourse is the restriction on "proemployer propaganda during union elections" mentioned by Matsuda. See Matsuda, supra note 2 at 34. The widely criticized exception is discussed in note 48 below.

12. See Louis Henkin, "Morals and the Constitution: The Sin of Obscenity," 63 *Colum. L. Rev.* 391 (1963).

13. Charles Lawrence, "If He Hollers Let Him Go: Regulating Racist Speech On Campus," in *Words That Wound,* supra note 2 at 57.

14. See, e.g., Stephen Gard, "Fighting Words as Free Speech," 58 *Wash. U. L. Q.* 531 (1980).

15. 505 U.S. 377 (1992).

16. Northern Securities v. United States, 193 U.S. 197 (1904) (Holmes, J., dissenting).

17. 505 U.S. 377 (1992).

18. The need for the number of exceptions created in the opinion does, however, tend to cast doubt on the validity of the basic rule announced in that decision.

19. Chaplinsky v. New Hampshire, 315 U.S. 568 (1942).

20. Kunz v. New York, 340 U.S. 290 (1951) (Jackson, J., dissenting).

21. As an alternative to the overbreadth rationale invoked by the concurring justices, the Court could have disposed of the case by expressly holding that the city's *justification* for the ordinance was unconstitutional, a rationale that seems to

be implicitly at work in Scalia's opinion. See James Weinstein, "Casebook Review: Combining the Best of Gunther and Sullivan," 21 *Seattle L. Rev.* 907, 919 (1998).

22. Catharine MacKinnon, *Only Words* 33 (1993).

23. Scalia's reference to "disfavored subjects" was not to cross burning but to the topic discrimination worked by the ordinance. Indeed, one of the major flaws in Scalia's *R.A.V.* opinion is that the cross burning that gave rise to prosecution plays no role in what Justice White aptly characterized as an "arid, doctrinaire" analysis of the ordinance.

24. *R.A.V.*'s holding subjecting content-based regulation of unprotected speech to strict scrutiny may not stand the test of time. It was supported by only five justices, and subsequent events have proved Justice White correct that the majority's broad pronouncements about content-oriented regulations of unprotected classes of speech have served mainly to "confuse the lower courts." See Alan Brownstein, "Rules of Engagement for Cultural Wars: Regulating Conduct, Unprotected Speech, and Protected Expression in Anti-Abortion Protests," 29 *U. C. Davis L. Rev.* 553, 565–584 (1996).

25. MacKinnon, supra note 22 at 12.

26. Ibid. at 12–14.

27. Ibid. at 17.

28. Ibid. at 15.

29. Ibid. at 18.

30. Ibid.

31. Owen Fiss, *The Irony of Free Speech* 14 (1996).

32. See Frederick Schauer, *Free Speech: A Philosophical Enquiry* 181 (1982).

33. MacKinnon agrees that "[p]ornography contains ideas, like any other social practice" but insists that "the way it works is not as a thought or through ideas as such." Rather, it is "constructing and performative" rather than "referential or connotative." MacKinnon, supra note 22 at 21.

34. My own view is that because pornography's primary purpose and function is sexual arousal rather than artistic expression or social commentary, there is an interesting sense in which it is more "actlike" than most expression (although perhaps no more so than slapstick comedy or horror films, which are similarly designed to trigger physiological reactions).

35. 413 U.S. 15 (1973).

36. See Chapter 4, text accompanying notes 36 to 37.

37. The term "speech act" has a technical meaning in the philosophical literature. In his seminal work *How to Do Things with Words* (2nd ed., 1962), philosopher J. L. Austin observed that under certain circumstances the very utterance of words can constitute action (e.g., the minister at a wedding saying, "I now pronounce you husband and wife"), a phenomenon that he referred to as the "illocutionary" aspect of language. Whether MacKinnon means to argue that pornography is a speech act in this technical sense is unclear. See MacKinnon, supra note 22 at 121 n. 31 ("Austin is less an authority for my particular development of 'doing things with words' and more a foundational exploration of the view in language theory that some speech can be action"). For an interesting although in my view unpersuasive attempt to argue that pornography is a speech act in the Austinian sense,

see Rae Langton, "Speech Acts and Unspeakable Acts," 22 *Philosophy & Pub. Affairs* 293 (1993).

38. MacKinnon, supra note 22 at 16.

39. MacKinnon also argues that pornography is a speech act in that women are harmed in its production and that it silences women's speech. See MacKinnon, supra note 22 at 9, 15. I discuss the silencing rationale for suppressing pornography and the harm-in-production rationale in Chapters 7 and 9.

40. In this definition the use of "men, children, or transsexuals in the place of women" is also considered pornography. MacKinnon, supra note 22 at 121 n. 32.

41. See Chapter 4, text accompanying notes 29 to 30.

42. MacKinnon, "Pornography, Civil Rights and Speech," 20 *Harv. C.R.-C.L. L. Rev.* 1, 21 (1985).

43. See United States v. One Book Entitled "Ulysses," 72 F.2d 705 (2d Cir. 1934); Yudkin v. Maryland, 182 A. 2d 798 (1962).

44. Miller v. California, 413 U.S. 15 (1973).

45. See Chapter 2, text accompanying notes 64 to 66.

46. American Booksellers, Inc. v. Hudnut, 771 F. 2d 323 (7th Cir. 1985).

47. Kingsley International Pictures Corp. v. Regents, 360 U.S. 684 (1959).

48. Cass Sunstein, *Democracy and the Problem of Free Speech* 223 (1993). The "controls on what employers may say during a union election" refers to NLRB v. Gissel Packing Co., 395 U.S. 575 (1969). In this case the Supreme Court affirmed a National Labor Relations Board ruling that an employer's statement that the plant would probably have to be shut down if the union were elected was an unfair labor practice because it constituted a threat of retaliatory action rather than a "demonstrably probable" prediction of economic consequences. Unlike the other speech regulations cited by Sunstein, the restriction upheld in *Gissel* does raise the specter of illegitimate government purpose, namely, favoring unions in a labor dispute. This suspicion is raised partly because of the lack of clear standards for determining whether speech in this context constitutes a threat or a prediction. Such suspicion is also created because, like the topic of women and their sexuality, union elections are inextricably linked to broader political ideologies. The *Gissel* decision has been widely criticized. See, e.g., Mark Rapaport, "Bargaining Orders Since *Gissel Packing*: Time to Blow the Whistle on *Gissel?*" 1972 *Wis. L. Rev.* 1170; Julius Getman, "Labor Law and Free Speech: The Curious Policy of Limited Expression," 43 *Md. L. Rev.* 4 (1984).

49. Ronald Dworkin, "Women and Pornography," *New York Review of Books,* October 21, 1993. Dworkin is wide of the mark, however, when he asserts that these "dirty films are watched by a small minority." See the Appendix, text accompanying notes 94 to 112.

50. Regina v. Butler, [1992] 89 D.L.R. (4th) 577.

51. See Renton v. Playtime Theatres, Inc., 475 U.S. 41 (1986) (Brennan, J., dissenting).

52. Advertisements of casino gambling are the least palpably harmful type of speech on Sunstein's list. Nonetheless, bans on such advertisements are still far less suspicious from a First Amendment perspective than the Indianapolis ordinance. There is no reason to suspect that bans on gambling advertisements are motivated by anything other than a paternalistic desire to protect people from los-

ing money they cannot afford to lose or perhaps by the more traditional belief that gambling is immoral. In particular, there is no reason to believe that when government bans advertisement of gambling it is doing so because the speech portrays a worldview with which the government disagrees or finds offensive. Whether government should constitutionally be able to regulate activity on paternalistic or moral grounds is an interesting issue but one that does not directly involve the First Amendment.

Of course not everything on Sunstein's list is necessarily constitutional under current doctrine. A recent decision by the Supreme Court puts in doubt the ability of the government to ban truthful, nonmisleading advertising of products, services, or activities, which, even though demonstrably harmful, the government has chosen not to prohibit. See 44 Liquormart, Inc. v. Rhode Island, 521 U.S. 484 (1996).

53. See Matsuda, supra note 2 at 37 (equality rights violated by hate speech are of "constitutional dimension"). See also MacKinnon, supra note 22 at 106 ("When equality is recognized as a constitutional value and mandate, the idea that some people are inferior to others on the basis of group membership is authoritatively rejected as the basis of policy. . . . [Consequently], social inferiority cannot be imposed through any means, including expressive ones"); ibid. at 71 (the Reconstruction amendments, i.e., the Thirteenth, Fourteenth, and Fifteenth Amendments ratified after the Civil War, may "demand reconstruction of the speech right itself").

54. "[T]he alternative to regulating racist speech is infringement of the claims of Blacks to liberty and equal protection. The best way to constitutionally protect these competing interests is to balance them directly." Lawrence, supra note 13 at 64. See also ibid. at 86 (arguing that "[w]e must weigh carefully and critically the competing constitutional values expressed in the first and fourteenth amendments").

55. "Issues at the equality-speech interface are not framed as problems of balance between two cherished constitutional goals . . . but as whether the right to free speech is infringed acceptably or unacceptably." MacKinnon, supra note 22 at 73.

56. The Bill of Rights, the first ten amendments to the Constitution, begins with the words "*Congress* shall make no law" and limits only the federal government. See Barron v. Baltimore, 7 Pet. (32 U.S.) 243 (1833). Similarly, the Fourteenth Amendment, which starts, "*No State* shall," constrains only state governments. See Shelley v. Kraemer, 334 U.S. 1 (1948) ("[the fourteenth] amendment erects no shield against merely private conduct, however discriminatory or wrongful"). In contrast, the Thirteenth Amendment's prohibition against slavery and involuntary servitude contains no reference to government and thus applies to private as well as governmental action. See United States v. Kozminski, 487 U.S. 931 (1988). Aside from the prohibition against slavery and involuntary servitude, the only other individual right protected by the Constitution against private interference is the unenumerated right to interstate travel. See United States v. Guest, 383 U.S. 745 (1966).

57. E.g., Lawrence, supra note 13 at 62–63.

58. Charles Black, "The Supreme Court, 1966 Term—Foreword: 'State Action,' Equal Protection, and California's Proposition 14," 81 *Harv. L. Rev.* (1967).

Similarly, Tribe comments: "[D]espite the precedents, and despite the vocabulary, the Supreme Court has not succeeded in developing a body of state action 'doctrine,' a set of rules for determining whether governmental or private actors are to be deemed responsible for an asserted constitutional violation." Laurence Tribe, *American Constitutional Law* 1690 (2nd ed., 1989). Tribe continues: "Chaos, however, may itself be a form of order. If the usual premise is reversed—if the state action cases are assumed *not* to reveal any general rule, and if the inquiry is redirected to consider *why* this anarchy prevails—it is possible to construct an 'anti-doctrine,' an analytical framework which, in explaining why various cases differ from one another, paradoxically provides a structure for the solution of state action problems." Ibid. at 1691.

59. Shelley v. Kraemer, 334 U.S. 1 (1948); Burton v. Wilmington Parking Authority, 365 U.S. 715 (1961).

60. Jackson v. Metropolitan Edison Co., 419 U.S. 345 (1974). See also Moose Lodge No. 107 v. Irvis, 407 U.S. 163 (1972) (holding that racial discrimination by private social club is not state action despite state conferred liquor license).

61. Tribe, supra note 58 at 1691.

62. See, e.g., San Francisco Arts and Athletics v. USOC, 483 U.S. 522 (1987) (5–4 decision holding that the refusal by private organization to allow organizers of gay athletic event to use the word "Olympic" was not governmental action despite congressional grant of exclusive licensing power to organization).

63. It will not do to argue, as some have, that racist speech in a public park is state action because the speaker is using public property. Such "public" speech is essential to democratic self-government, and characterizing it as state action would obliterate any meaningful distinction between private and state action in free speech.

64. R.A.V. v. City of St. Paul, 505 U.S. 377 (1992); Bob Jones University v. United States, 461 U.S. 574 (1983).

65. The Due Process Clause of the Fourteenth Amendment prohibits state government from depriving "any person of life, liberty or property without due process of law."

66. See, e.g., Brownstein, supra note 24 at 1215; Leslie Jacobs, "Nonviolent Abortion Clinic Protests: Reevaluating Some Current Assumptions About the Proper Scope of Government Regulations," 70 *Tul. L. Rev.* 1359, 1429, 1433 (1996); *Brief Amicus Curiae of the American Civil Liberties Union et al.*, in Schenck v. Pro-Choice Network, 519 U.S. 537 (1997) ("the fact that the medical service at issue has specific constitutional protection adds weight to the reasons supporting the injunction [against harassing protests at abortion clinics]"). See also Robyn E. Blumner, "ACLU Backs Free Speech for All—Except Pro-Lifers," *Wall Street Journal*, February 10, 1999, A22 (former executive director of Florida ACLU complains that ACLU's viewing cases of antiabortion speech as a "clash between two constitutional rights" has "tended to get in the way" of the ACLU's commitment to supporting the First Amendment rights of antiabortion demonstrators).

67. For instance, a conflict between the Free Speech Clause and the Establishment Clause can arise when religious speakers are denied a generally available speech subsidy. See Rosenberger v. Rector and Visitors of the Univ. of Va., 515 U.S. 819 (1995). See also Burson v. Freeman, 504 U.S. 191 (1992) (because gov-

ernment has affirmative duty "to protect the integrity and reliability" of the election process, regulation of private speech at a polling place to prevent "intimidation and fraud" presents a conflict between the constitutional right of free speech and the constitutional right to vote); Sheppard v. Maxwell, 384 U.S. 333 (1966) (because government has an affirmative obligation to assure that a criminal defendant receives a fair trial, widespread publicity generated by the press about a criminal defendant can violate the constitutional right to due process). For more on the distinction between true and spurious conflicts of constitutional rights, see James Weinstein, "Free Speech, Abortion Access, and the Problem of Judicial Viewpoint Discrimination," 29 *U. C. Davis L. Rev.* 471, 492–502 (1996).

68. Fiss, supra note 31 at 11.

69. See, e.g., Yates v. United States, 354 U.S. 298 (1957); United States v. Robel, 389 U.S. 258 (1967); Communist Party v. Catherwood, 367 U.S. 389 (1961).

70. See Weinstein, supra note 67 at 477. See also Eugene Volokh, "Freedom of Speech and the Constitutional Tension Method," 3 *U. Chi. Roundtable* 223 (1996).

71. MacKinnon, supra note 22 at 86.

72. Texas v. Johnson, 491 U.S. 397 (1989) (Rehnquist, C. J., dissenting).

73. Stanley Fish, *There's No Such Thing as Free Speech* 113 (1994).

74. Ibid. at 102.

75. Brandenburg v. Ohio, 395 U.S. 444 (1969) (Douglas, J., concurring) (emphasis added).

CHAPTER SIX

1. Ronald Dworkin, "Women and Pornography," *New York Review of Books,* October 21, 1993.

2. Police Dept. of Chicago v. Mosley, 408 U.S. 92 (1972), quoting Alexander Meiklejohn, *Political Freedom: The Constitutional Powers of the People* 27 (1948).

3. See, e.g., Richard Delgado and David Yun, "Pressure Valves and Bloodied Chickens: An Analysis of Paternalistic Objections to Hate Speech Regulation," 82 *Cal. L. Rev.* 871, 881–882 (1994).

4. The motif of the damsel in distress, common through the 1980s, seems to have been less prevalent in the 1990s.

5. There are, of course, contrary media depictions of strong, independent women even on television commercials. Still, moms in charge of laundry, dinner, and children predominate.

6. Richard Delgado and Jean Stefancic, "Images of the Outsider in American Law and Culture: Can Free Expression Remedy Systemic Social Ills?" 77 *Cornell L. Rev.* 1259, 1262–1275 (1992).

7. See Richard Delgado, "Campus Antiracism Rules: Constitutional Narratives in Collision," 85 *Nw. L. Rev.* 343 (1991); Delgado and Yun, supra note 3.

8. Unlike violent pornography, however, gender stereotyping in television shows and mainstream films has not been linked to violence against women. The fear that certain types of pornography cause violence would therefore be a reason for arguing for its suppression but not for urging a similar ban on gender stereotyping on television and in movies.

9. 424 U.S. 1 (1976).

10. See, e.g., Joel Gora, "Campaign Finance Reform: Still Searching Today for a Better Way," 6 *J. L. & Pol'y* 137 (1997).

11. See Adam Winkler, "Beyond Belloti," 32 *Loy. L.A. L. Rev.* 133 (1998).

12. Mark Tushnet, "An Essay on Rights," 62 *Tex. L. Rev.* 1363, 1387 (1984).

13. Red Lion Broadcasting v. FCC, 395 U.S. 367 (1969). But see Miami Herald v. Tornillo, 418 US. 241 (1974) (holding unconstitutional a Florida right-to-reply law applicable to newspapers). Cf. Columbia Broadcasting Systems, Inc. v. Democratic National Committee, 412 U.S. 94 (1973) (First Amendment does not provide the Democratic National Committee and antiwar group a constitutional right to place paid political advertisements on television). For a discussion on the crucial distinction between reading the Constitution to *permit* a speech regulation designed to increase equality in the marketplace of ideas and interpreting it to *require* such a regulation, see James Weinstein, "Taking Liberties with the First Amendment," 17 *L. & Phil.* 160, 174 (1998), reviewing Owen Fiss's *Irony of Free Speech* (1996).

14. Metro Broadcasting v. FCC, 497 U.S. 547 (1990). As a matter of equal protection law, however, the validity of the program upheld in *Metro Broadcasting* has been put in doubt by Adarand Constructors, Inc. v. Pena, 515 U.S. 520 (1995).

15. See James Weinstein, "Free Speech, Abortion Access, and the Problem of Judicial Viewpoint Discrimination," 29 *U. C. Davis L. Rev.* 471, 519 n. 163 (1996).

16. See Alan Brownstein, "Rules of Engagement for Cultural Wars: Regulating Conduct, Unprotected Speech, and Protected Expression in Anti-Abortion Protests—Section II," 29 *U. C. Davis L. Rev.* 1163, 1208–1209 (1996); Alan Brownstein and Stephen M. Hankins, "Pruning Pruneyard: Limited Free Speech Rights Under State Constitutions on the Property of Private Medical Clinics Providing Abortion Services," 24 *U. C. Davis L. Rev.* 1073 (1991).

17. See Lloyd Corp., Ltd. v. Tanner, 407 U.S. 551 (1972); Hudgens v. NLRB, 424 U.S. 507 (1976). But cf. PruneYard Shopping Center v. Robins, 447 U.S. 74 (1980) (free speech provision of California constitution providing speakers right of access to privately owned shopping centers does not constitute taking of property without just compensation in violation of the Fifth Amendment or a violation of the shopping center owner's First Amendment rights).

18. See, e.g., Delgado and Stefancic, supra note 6 at 1279 ("Racism forms part of the dominant narrative, the group of received understandings and basic principles that form the baseline from which we reason").

19. I am grateful to Larry Alexander for suggesting this idea to me.

20. Although often mistakenly believed to derive from "nigger," the term "niggardly" is etymologically distinct from this slur.

21. See Pam Belluck, "Avowed Racist Barred from Practicing Law," *New York Times*, February 10, 1999, A12. Several years ago there were calls for the resignation of a university president who, in arguing *in favor* of affirmative action, made a statement that some interpreted as suggesting that blacks have less inherent academic aptitude than whites. He apologized, explaining that the remark was a slip of the tongue and was "an absolute contradiction of everything I believe, of everything I stand for and of everything I have done throughout my life." He kept his job, but the protest continued. See Calvin Baker, "Tulane Graduates Boycott Speech by Rutgers Chief," *New Orleans Times-Picayune*, May 21, 1995, B1.

22. See Department of Defense, Directive no. 1325.6 (October 1, 1996).

23. See, e.g., Amy Gage, "Woman Boss? Not Here, Please," *San Diego Union,* June 10, 1996, D1.

24. Wisconsin v. Mitchell, 508 U.S. 476 (1993).

25. 163 U.S. 537 (1896) ("in the nature of things [the Fourteenth Amendment] could not have been intended to abolish distinctions based on color, or to enforce social as distinguished from political equality").

26. R.A.V. v. City of St. Paul, 505 U.S. 377 (1992); Wisconsin v. Mitchell, 508 U.S. 476 (1993).

27. R.A.V. v. City of St. Paul.

28. See, e.g., Charles Lawrence, "If He Hollers Let Him Go: Regulating Racist Speech On Campus," in *Words That Wound* 77–78 (Mari Matsuda, Charles Lawrence, Richard Delgado, and Kimberlè Crenshaw, eds., 1993) ("the idea of racial inferiority of nonwhites infects, skews, and disables the operation of the market"). See also Catharine MacKinnon, *Toward a Feminist Theory of the State* 206 (1989); Cedric Powell, "The Mythological Marketplace of Ideas, *R.A.V., Mitchell,* and Beyond," 12 *Harv. BlackLetter J.* 1, 1 (1995).

29. Richard Benjamin, "The Bizarre Classroom of Dr. Leonard Jeffries," *J. of Blacks in Higher Education* 91, 95 (Winter 1993–1994) (describing Jeffries's theories concerning the "melanin" factor, which makes whites "cold, materialistic 'ice people'" and blacks "warm, humanistic 'sun people'"). See also Jeffries v. Harleston, 21 F. 3d 1238 (2nd Cir. 1994), vacated, 516 U.S. 862 (1995), opinion substituted, 52 F. 3d 9 (1995) (lawsuit arising out of Jeffries's termination as chairman of Black Studies Department of City College of New York for anti-Semitic remarks made during an off-campus speech).

30. Delgado and Stefancic, supra note 6 at 1260.

31. Ibid. at 1276.

32. Ibid. at 1281–1282.

33. By the 1830s (and probably earlier), there was a growing recognition in the United States, even in the South, that slavery was morally wrong. See generally, Robert Cover, *Justice Accused* 33–82 (1975). See also Michael Curtis, "The Curious History of Attempts to Suppress Antislavery Speech, Press and Petition in 1835–37," 89 *Nw. L. Rev.* 785, 800 (1995). This moral recognition was sufficient to lead to abolition in those parts of the United States where slavery was not a significant part of the economic system, nor African Americans a large part of the population. Such was not the case, however, in the South, with its vested economic interest in slavery and its fears about the results of emancipation.

34. My source for all of the facts and quotations in this and the next paragraph is Curtis, supra note 33 at 803–859.

35. United States v. Schwimmer, 279 U.S. 644 (1929) (Holmes, J., dissenting).

36. Delgado and Stefancic, supra note 6 at 1284–1285 (emphasis added). These authors cite no cases for this remarkable proposition. Rather, their sole authority is an article by Charles Lawrence that they claim shows that "courts construed First Amendment law narrowly, so as to uphold convictions of *peaceful* protestors." Ibid. at 1285 n. 191 (emphasis added), citing Charles Lawrence, "If He Hollers Let Him Go: Regulating Racist Speech on Campus," 1990 *Duke L. J.* 431, 466–467. But Lawrence says something quite different: "In examining the first

amendment cases coming out of the civil rights protests of the 1960s one observes that although *the Court went to some length to reverse convictions in peaceful protests* designed to achieve conformity with *Brown* [*v. Board of Education*], they generally denied review to those cases in which there was evidence of disruption or violence—particularly in those cases where the disruption seemed to emanate from the protestors." Lawrence, ibid. at 467 n. 130 (emphasis added). (As we shall see, to the extent that "disruption" includes sit-ins at privately owned segregated facilities, even this more modest claim is inaccurate.) See also ibid. at 466 ("We are aware that the struggle for racial equality has relied heavily on the persuasion of peaceful protest protected by the first amendment, but experience also teaches us that our petitions often go unanswered until they disrupt business as usual").

37. My discussion of the civil rights cases draws heavily on Harry Kalven Jr.'s classic work, *The Negro and the First Amendment* (1966).

38. 340 U.S. 315 (1951).

39. 372 U.S. 229 (1963).

40. 379 U.S. 536 (1965).

41. 394 U.S. 111 (1969).

42. 394 U.S. 576 (1969).

43. Four justices who generally were among the most speech-protective on the Court at that time—Warren, Black, White, and Fortas—expressed the view in that case that flag burning was *not* protected speech.

44. 368 U.S. 157 (1961).

45. 373 U.S. 244 (1963).

46. 378 U.S. 130 (1964).

47. 378 U.S. 347 (1964).

48. 385 U.S. 39 (1966).

49. 388 U.S. 307 (1967). See also Cameron v. Johnson, 390 U.S. 611 (1968) (rejecting a challenge by civil rights activists to Mississippi ordinance prohibiting picketing and mass demonstrations that "obstruct or unreasonably interfere" with ingress or egress to public buildings).

50. 382 U.S. 87 (1965).

51. The Court arguably overextended free speech principles in Brown v. Louisiana, 383 U.S. 131 (1966), which reversed breach-of-peace convictions of civil rights activists for holding a silent demonstration, including a sit-in, to protest unconstitutional segregation of a small parish library. A plurality opinion by Justice Fortas, joined by Chief Justice Warren and Justice Douglas, found a First Amendment right to demonstrate in public libraries, at least so long as the demonstration was not disruptive. (Justice White concurred in the reversal of the conviction on the grounds that the protestors were asked to leave the library not because of their protest activities, which were not significantly different from normal library use, but because they were black. Justice Brennan invoked the overbreadth of the breach-of-peace statute to reverse the convictions.) In dissent, Justice Black described the plurality's holding as "completely new doctrine," insisting that the First Amendment "does not guarantee to any person the right to use someone else's property, even that owned by the government and dedicated to other purposes, as a stage to express dissident ideas."

52. *TV Guide,* June 29–July 5, 1996, 14, lists these images as among "the 100 most memorable moments in TV history." "First, attack dogs were set loose on the protestors, then the marchers were blasted with fire hoses shooting water at 100 p.s.i., enough force to knock bark off trees. The evening news programs on all three networks showed extensive footage of the appalling police response. The broadcasts awakened the nation to the barbarity being committed in the name of racial segregation and added considerable impetus to the civil rights movement."

53. Chaplinsky v. New Hampshire, 315 U.S. 568 (1942); Beauharnais v. Illinois, 343 U.S. 250 (1952).

54. 376 U.S. 254 (1964).

55. Robin Barnes, "The Reality and Ideology of First Amendment Jurisprudence: Giving Aid and Comfort to Racial Terrorists," in *Freeing the First Amendment* 257 (David Allen and Robert Jensen, eds., 1995).

56. Whether the rule announced in that case went too far in protecting free speech at the cost of reputational interests, as some now argue, or did not go far enough, as others maintain, is a much-debated issue.

57. See, e.g., Catharine MacKinnon, *Only Words* 79 (1993) (*"Sullivan* used support for civil rights to make it easier for newspapers to publish defamatory falsehoods without being sued.").

58. Kalven, supra note 37 at 67.

59. 174 F. Supp. 351 (E.D. Ark. 1959).

60. Lerner v. Casey, 357 U.S. 468 (1958).

61. 371 U.S. 415 (1963).

62. Kalven, supra note 37 at 69.

63. 278 U.S. 63 (1928).

64. 377 U.S. 288 (1964).

65. Kalven calls the Court's efforts to distinguish *Bryant* "surprisingly inept." Kalven, supra note 37 at 94.

66. 364 U.S. 480 (1960).

67. 372 U.S. 539 (1963).

68. 360 U.S. 109 (1959).

69. 360 U.S. 72 (1959). See also Braden v. United States, 365 U.S. 431 (1961) (rejecting First Amendment challenge to conviction for refusing to answer questions about Communist Party activity posed by the House Committee on Un-American Activities); Wilkinson v. United States, 365 U.S. 399 (1961) (upholding power of Congress to require witnesses to answer questions pertinent to its investigation of Communist activities).

70. 458 U.S. 886 (1992).

71. See, e.g., MacKinnon, supra note 57 at 41; Mari Matsuda, "Public Response to Racist Speech: Considering the Victim's Story," in *Words That Wound* 47 (Mari Matsuda, Charles Lawrence, Richard Delgado, and Kimberlè Crenshaw, eds., 1993); Lawrence, supra note 28 at 86.

72. See, e.g., Romer v. Evans, 517 U.S. 620 (1996) (state constitutional provision prohibiting state and local governments from passing laws forbidding discrimination on the basis of sexual orientation violates the Equal Protection Clause of the Fourteenth Amendment).

73. See Lawrence, supra note 28 at 83.

74. See Charles Calleros, "Reconciliation of Civil Rights and Civil Liberties After *R.A.V. v. City of St. Paul*: Free Speech, Antiharassment Policies, Multicultural Education, and Political Correctness at Arizona State University," *Utah L. Rev.* 1205, 1215–1219, 1220–1231 (1992).

75. See Gerald Gunther, "Good Speech-Bad Speech," 24 *Stanford Lawyer* 7 (Spring 1990).

76. Police Dept. of Chicago v. Mosley, 408 U.S. 92 (1972) (emphasis added).

77. 491 U.S. 397 (1989).

78. United States v. Eichman, 496 U.S. 310 (1990). Marshall joined Brennan's opinion in both flag-burning cases.

79. Linmark Associates, Inc. v. Township of Willingboro, 431 U.S. 85 (1977). Brennan joined this opinion.

80. See Paris Adult Theatre I v. Slaton, 413 U.S. 49 (1973) (Brennan, J., joined by Stewart and Marshall, JJ., dissenting). Marshall was the author of the Court's decision in Stanley v. Georgia, 394 U.S. 557 (1969) that held that despite the obscenity exception it was unconstitutional for the state to prosecute people for possession of obscene material in their homes.

81. Hudnut v. American Booksellers Assn. Inc., 475 U.S. 1001 (1986).

82. See, e.g., Nan Hunter and Sylvia Law, *Brief Amici Curiae of Feminist Anti-Censorship Task Force,* in American Booksellers Assn. v. Hudnut, reprinted in 21 *U. Mich. J. L. Ref.* 69 (1988); Nadine Strossen, *Defending Pornography* (1995).

83. "[Those] who operate . . . universities [and] major corporations . . . benefit, and on a subconscious level they know they benefit, from a certain amount of low-grade racism in the environment. If an occasional bigot or redneck calls one of us a nigger or spick one night late as we're on our way home from the library, that is all to the good. . . . This kind of behavior keeps non-white people on edge, a little off balance." Richard Delgado, "Address to State Historical Society," Madison, Wisconsin (April 24, 1989), quoted in Lawrence, supra note 28 at 82. See also Lawrence, ibid. ("[T]hose of us who abhor racist speech but insist that it cannot be regulated may be, perhaps unwittingly, benefitting from the presence of 'a certain amount of low grade racism' in the environment").

84. For instance, Mari Matsuda writes that she "admire[s] the courage and conviction" of "Jewish civil libertarians who have eloquently, and at great personal cost, argued for the free speech rights of Nazis and Klan members." Although she disagrees with this view, she recognizes that it does not come from insensitivity to the harms of hate speech but from the belief that "the right of protest [is] essential for the protection of minorities." Mari Matsuda, "Public Response to Racist Speech: Considering the Victim's Story," 87 *Mich. L. Rev.* 2320, 2326 (1989).

85. Colin Diver, "Of Water Buffaloes and Newspaper Heists," 29 *Penn Law Journal* 23 (1993).

Chapter Seven

1. Mari Matsuda, "Public Response to Racist Speech: Considering the Victim's Story," 87 *Mich. L. Rev.* 2320, 2336 (1989).

2. Ibid. at n. 84 (emphasis added).

3. Ibid.

4. Ibid.

5. MacKinnon reports that despite "an extensive literature search," she was unable to find any "laboratory or experimental research on racist hate literature parallel to that on the effects of pornography." Catharine MacKinnon, *Only Words* 134 n. 53 (1993).

6. Matsuda, supra note 1 at 2337 n. 88.

7. See 347 U.S. 483 (1954).

8. Even if it could be shown that racist propaganda is a significant cause of psychic injury or self-hatred, the further question would arise whether these injuries justify suppression of public discourse. The answer depends on one's views on the purpose of free speech protection. On the view that the core free speech value is respecting the right of each citizen to participate in the shaping of our politics, institutions, and culture, then prevention of these harms may not be sufficient grounds for suppressing racist propaganda.

9. Matsuda, supra note 1 at 2339.

10. Matsuda cites an unpublished paper and one of the sources it cites, with an additional reference to a study on media violence.

11. According to a recent estimate, there are now more than 1,000 hate speech sites online. See note 31 below. (In comparison, a recent study found there are approximately 34,000 pornographic sites. See the Appendix, note 112 and accompanying text.)

12. See the Appendix.

13. Cass Sunstein, *Democracy and the Problem of Free Speech* 217 (1993). See also Attorney General's Commission on Pornography, *Final Report* 299–351 (1986); *In Harm's Way: The Pornography Civil Rights Hearings* (Catharine MacKinnon and Andrea Dworkin, eds., 1997); Richard Delgado and Jean Stefancic, "Pornography and Harm to Women: 'No Empirical Evidence'?" 53 *Ohio St. L. J.* 1037 (1992).

14. See Edward Mulvey and Jeffrey Haugaard, *Report of the Surgeon General's Workshop on Pornography and Public Health* 34–35 (1986) (emphasis added). For a survey of the studies on the effects of the pornography, see Neil Malamuth, "Pornography's Impact on Male Adolescents," 4 *Adolescent Medicine: State of the Art Reviews* 563, 566–571 (1993) (reporting that there is currently enough evidence to justify the "tentative conclusion" that violent pornography causes both aggressive behavior *in the laboratory* and at least *short-term* attitudinal changes) (emphasis added). See also Daniel Linz and Neil Malamuth, *Pornography* (1993); *Pornography: Research Advances and Policy Considerations* (Dolf Zillmann and Jennings Bryant, eds., 1989); Edward Donnerstein, Daniel Linz, and Steven Penrod, *The Question of Pornography* (1987).

15. Matsuda, supra note 1 at 2339.

16. MacKinnon, supra note 5 at 11.

17. See, e.g., *Words That Wound* 7 (Mari Matsuda, Charles Lawrence, Richard Delgado, and Kimberlè Crenshaw, eds., 1993); Andrew Chin, "Making the World Wide Web Safe for Democracy: A Medium-Specific First Amendment Analysis," 19 *Hastings Comm. & Ent. L. J.* 309, 344 (1997); Marianne Wesson, "Sex, Lies and Videotape: The Pornographer as Censor," 66 *Wash. L. Rev.* 913, 934 (1991).

18. Owen Fiss, *The Irony of Free Speech* 16 (1996).

19. Indeed, Fiss's use of the passive voice to distance himself from this argument ("[i]t has been asserted that" and "[t]his silencing dynamic has also been attributed") suggests that even he may doubt its validity. See ibid.

20. Like so many who write on the subject of hate speech, Fiss does not distinguish face-to-face or otherwise personally directed racist speech from racist speech that is part of public discourse. Thus at times he refers to silencing by a person who "hurls racial epithets" (see, e.g., Fiss, supra note 18 at 17), whereas at other times he seems to be using the term "hate speech" in its more general sense to include all public expression of racist ideas.

21. Ibid. at 17–18.

22. Ibid. at 21 (emphasis added).

23. MacKinnon, supra note 5 at 9–10.

24. Attorney General's Commission Report, supra note 13 at 865–866.

25. Ibid. at 888.

26. Ibid. at 888–889. In an investigation of the pornography industry, Wendy McElroy found "no evidence that women are coerced into performing pornographic acts." Although she heard "rumors of women who had been pressured into performing sexual acts," none of the performers she interviewed reported having been so coerced. Rather, she saw "overwhelming evidence of informed consent." Wendy McElroy, *XXX: A Woman's Right to Pornography* 39 (1995).

27. MacKinnon, supra note 5 at 76 ("Americans are taught this view by about the fourth grade and continue to absorb it through osmosis from everything around them for the rest of their lives").

28. Forty-five states have laws banning obscenity. See Robert Jacobs, "Dirty Words, Dirty Thoughts and Censorship: Obscenity Law and Non-Pictorial Works," 21 *Sw. U. L. Rev.* 155, 171–172 nn. 110–112 (collecting state obscenity laws) (1992).

29. For a discussion of the ineffectiveness of current obscenity laws, see Bruce Taylor, "Hard-Core Pornography: A Proposal for a Per Se Rule," 21 *U. Mich. J. L. Ref.* 255 (1987/1988).

30. Nadine Strossen, *Defending Pornography: Free Speech, Sex, and the Fight for Women's Rights* 161–178 (1995).

31. Karen Kaplan, "Growth of Hate Sites," *Los Angeles Times*, December 7, 1998, C3 (reporting that according to the director of the Museum of Tolerance, the number of hate sites have increased from one in 1991 to more than 1,000 in 1998). As reported on National Public Radio "Morning Edition," March 6, 1998, a recent study by the Southern Poverty Law Center found 163 online hate groups. Available on Westlaw at 1998 WL 3306607. A directory of hate speech sites can be found at http://www.bcpl.lib.md.us/~rfrankli/hatedir.htm/.

32. See *Report to the Minister of Justice of the Special Committee on Hate Propaganda in Canada* 59 (1966).

33. See Frances D'Souza, introduction to *Striking a Balance: Hate Speech, Freedom of Expression and Non-Discrimination* vii (Sandra Coliver, ed., 1991).

34. In defending the hate speech ordinance in *R.A.V. v. City of St. Paul*, 505 U.S. 377 (1992), the city argued that the selective ban on racist fighting words was in-

tended to "communicate to minority groups that group hatred . . . is not condoned by the majority."

CHAPTER EIGHT

1. See Regina v. Butler, [1992] 89 D.L.R. (4th) 449.

2. See United States v. One Book Entitled *Ulysses,* 72 F. 2d 705 (2d Cir. 1934); Besig v. United States, 208 F. 2d 142 (9th Cir. 1953).

3. *Striking a Balance: Hate Speech, Freedom of Expression and Non-Discrimination* 141–142 (Sandra Coliver, ed., 1991). Members of the racist group were also found guilty of violating the law, but because they were also convicted of other crimes they ended up receiving no supplemental sentence for violation of the hate speech law. In 1992 Denmark amended the law to immunize such reporting on racist groups. For further discussion of this case, see Stephanine Farrior, "Molding the Matrix: The Historical and Theoretical Foundations of International Law Concerning Hate Speech," 14 *Berkeley J. Intl. L.* 1, 68–69 (1996).

4. See Venkat Eswaran, "Advocacy of National, Racial and Religious Hatred: The Indian Experience," in *Striking a Balance,* supra note 3 at 179.

5. See American Booksellers Assn., Inc. v. Hudnut, 771 F. 2d 323 (7th Cir. 1985).

6. See Skywalker Records, Inc. v. Navarro, 739 F. Supp. 578 (S.D. Fla. 1990), *rev'd,* Luke Records, Inc. v. Navarro, 960 F. 2d 134 (11th Cir. 1992).

7. Kimberlè Crenshaw, "Beyond Racism and Misogyny: Black Feminism and 2 Live Crew," in *Words That Wound* 122, 124 (Mari Matsuda, Charles Lawrence, Richard Delgado, and Kimberlè Crenshaw, eds., 1993).

8. See Joshua Schoffman, "Legislation Against Racist Incitement in Israel: A 1992 Appraisal," in *Striking a Balance,* supra note 3 at 192.

9. See Geoffrey Bindman, "Incitement to Racial Hatred in the United Kingdom: Have We Got the Law We Need?" in *Striking a Balance,* supra note 3 at 259.

10. Ibid. at 260.

11. See Joanna Oyediran, "The United Kingdom's Compliance with Article 4 of the International Convention on the Elimination of All Forms of Racial Discrimination," in *Striking a Balance,* supra note 3 at 251.

12. Ibid. at 252.

13. See Regina v. Keegstra, [1990] 3 SCR 697; Regina v. Andrews, [1990] 3 SCR 870 ; Canada (Human Rights Commission) v. Taylor, [1990] 3 SCR 892.

14. R. v. Hoaglin (1907), 12 C.C.C. 226 (N.W.T.S.C.); R. v. Carrier (1951), 104 C.C.C. 75 (Que. K.B.); R. v. Kirby (1970) 1 C.C.C. (2d) 286 (Que. C.A.).

15. R. v. Buzzanga and Durocher, [1979] 49 C.C.C. (2d) 369. With the exception of the case involving the disgruntled American, all of these convictions were overturned on appeal. See John Manwaring, "Legal Regulation of Hate Propaganda in Canada," in *Striking a Balance,* supra note 3 at 109.

16. "Language as Violence v. Freedom of Expression: Canadian and American Perspectives on Group Defamation," 37 *Buffalo L. Rev.* 337, 341 (1989) (comments of Alan Borovoy).

17. See Sandra Coliver, "Hate Speech Laws: Do They Work?" in *Striking a Balance,* supra note 3 at 365.

18. See R.A.V. v. City of St. Paul, 505 U.S. 377 (1992); Collin v. Smith, 578 F. 2d 1197 (7th Cir. 1978).

19. Catherine Itzin, "Legislating Against Pornography Without Censorship," in *Pornography* 408–409 (C. Itzin, ed., 1992).

20. Catherine Itzin, "A Legal Definition of Pornography," in *Pornography,* supra note 19 at 452.

21. [1992] 89 D.L.R. (4th) 499.

22. See Nadine Strossen, *Defending Pornography: Free Speech, Sex, and the Fight for Women's Rights* 229–244 (1995).

23. It is true that in Canada and Germany Holocaust deniers have been criminally prosecuted without any attempt to apply the relevant laws to serious academic works. But it is structurally ensured prosecutorial restraint rather than anything in the broadly worded substantive provisions of these laws that is probably responsible for this lack of abuse. In contrast, the broad prohibition on the spreading of false statements, pursuant to which Canada recently convicted a notorious Holocaust denier (see Regina v. Zundel, [1987] 35 D.L.R. (4th) 338, or the prohibition on "attacks on human dignity," which Germany uses to prosecute Holocaust deniers (see Rainer Hofmann, "Incitement to National and Racial Hatred: The Legal Situation in Germany," in *Striking a Balance,* supra note 3 at 162–180), would positively invite abuse in the hands of local prosecutors in the United States. The problem of Holocaust denial could, however, be addressed by a specific prohibition of this calumny, such as the 1990 French law that expressly makes denial of the Nazi genocide against the Jews a crime. But such a law would leave the rest of the universe of racist pseudoscience and pseudohistory untouched.

24. See Bindman, supra note 9 at 258, 260–262.

25. See Coliver, supra note 17 at 367.

26. See McClesky v. Kemp, 481 U.S. 279 (1987).

27. Cf. Richard Delgado and Jean Stefancic, *Must We Defend Nazis?* 101 (1997) ("The likelihood that officials in the United States would turn hate-speech laws into weapons against minorities seems remote"). More consistent with the deeper radical critique, Matsuda seeks to avoid the problem by limiting the reach of the law to hate speech directed at a member of a "historically oppressed group." Mari Matsuda, "Public Response to Racist Speech: Considering the Victim's Story," in *Words That Wound* 36 (Mari Matsuda, Charles Lawrence, Richard Delgado, and Kimberlè Crenshaw, eds., 1993). Aside from the problem of determining what qualifies as an historically oppressed group, this qualification would make enactment of Matsuda's proposal unlikely in most communities.

28. "[T]here is no agreement or feminist code as to what images are distasteful or even sexist." Statement of Feminists for Free Expression, quoted in Nat Hentoff, "Pornography War Among Feminists," *Washington Post,* April 4, 1992, A23.

29. Strossen, supra note 22, between pp. 160 and 161.

30. Ibid. at 158–159, quoting Andrea Dworkin, *Ice and Fire* (1987).

31. See Albert Nerenberg, "Fear Not, Brave Canadian: Customs Stands on Guard for Thee," *Montreal Gazette,* January 22, 1993.

32. The key terms of the obscenity standard currently in force in the United States—"appeal to the prurient interest," "patently offensive" depictions of sex-

ual activity, and lacking "serious literary, artistic, political or scientific value"—also are quite vague. What makes this standard workable is the Court's insistence that the material must consist of extremely graphic description of "ultimate sexual acts." Thus it is possible for prosecutors, judges, and juries to have a template of the forbidden material in mind (a film graphically showing people having sexual intercourse). And even if it contains some hard-core depictions, material is still not legally obscene if "taken as a whole" it does not "appeal to the prurient interest" in sex or has "serious literary, artistic, political or scientific value." Although it takes a certain degree of subjectivity to decide whether material is explicit enough to qualify as obscene, this is hard science compared to determining whether a depiction is "demeaning" or "dehumanizing" or "subordinating."

33. See Roger Errera, "In Defense of Civility: Racial Incitement and Group Libel in French Law," in *Striking a Balance,* supra note 3 at 155.

34. Bindman, supra note 9 at 259.

35. See National Socialist Party v. Skokie, 432 U.S. 43 (1977); Collin v. Smith, 578 F. 2d 1197 (7th Cir. 1978).

36. See Gerald Gunther and Kathleen Sullivan, *Constitutional Law* 1113 (13th ed., 1997).

37. See Philadelphia Newspapers, Inc. v. Hepps, 475 U.S. 767 (1986).

38. See, e.g., *Speaking Freely: The Case Against Speech Codes* v (Mark Holzer, ed., 1994), dedicating the book to a number of defendants in important free speech cases, including Joseph Beauharnais, the racist convicted of group libel in Beauharnais v. Illinois, 343 U.S. 250 (1952), discussed in Chapter 4.

39. Strossen, supra note 22 at 161–168.

40. Kathleen Sullivan, "The First Amendment Wars" (review of several books), *New Republic,* September 28, 1992, 35.

41. Quoted in Strossen, supra note 22 at 162.

42. See Gordon Allport, *The Nature of Prejudice* 467–473 (1954).

43. See Strossen, supra note 22 at 260–261 (1995) ("there may well be an inverse causal relationship between exposure to sexually explicit materials and misogynistic violence or discrimination").

44. See Chapter 7, text accompanying notes 13 to 14, and the Appendix.

45. For instance, in criticizing Stanford's hate speech code, former assistant secretary of state and presidential candidate Alan Keyes charged that it was "insulting" to be told that "white folks have the moral character to shrug off insults, and I do not." Quoted in Nadine Strossen, "Regulating Racist Speech on Campus: A Modest Proposal?" 1990 *Duke L. J.* 484, 486.

46. See Nan Hunter and Sylvia Law, *Brief Amici Curiae of Feminist Anti-Censorship Taskforce,* in American Booksellers Assn. v. Hudnut, reprinted in 21 *U. Mich. J. L. Ref.* 69, 122 (1988) (laws suppressing pornography on the grounds that it is demeaning to women "reinforce and perpetuate central sexist stereotypes; they weaken, rather than enhance, women's struggles to free themselves of archaic notions of gender roles").

47. Matsuda's proposal is a rare example of a law that bans only hate speech against minorities. See note 27 above.

48. Coliver, supra note 17 at 368.

Chapter Nine

1. Texas v. Johnson, 491 U.S. 397 (1989) (Rehnquist, C. J., dissenting).

2. See, e.g., Stanley Fish, *There's No Such Thing as Free Speech* 102 (1994).

3. Thus, even though he favors bans on racist propaganda, Fiss acknowledges that hate speech is part of public discourse. See Owen Fiss, *The Irony of Free Speech* 14 (1996).

4. Debs v. United States, 249 U.S. 211 (1919).

5. See, e.g., Masses Publishing Co. v. Patten, 246 Fed. 24 (2d Cir. 1917) (speech is not protected by the First Amendment if "the natural and reasonable effect of what is said is to encourage resistance to a law, and the words are used in an endeavor to persuade to resistance"). Indeed, the clear-and-present-danger test in the World War I era was supposed to supply greater protection to speech than the harmful-tendency standard. See Gerald Gunther and Kathleen Sullivan, *Constitutional Law* 1035, 1044 (13th ed., 1997). As applied, however, especially during the red scare of the 1920s, the clear-and-present-danger test was tantamount to a harmful-tendency test.

6. Cf. Kingsley International Pictures Corp. v. Regents, 360 U.S. 684 (1959) (invalidating a state motion picture licensing law banning films that portrayed "acts of sexual immorality . . . [or] which expressly or impliedly present[ed] such acts as desirable, acceptable, or proper patterns of behavior").

7. Fiss, supra note 3 at 14.

8. See, e.g., Catharine MacKinnon, *Only Words* 76 (1993); Jean Stefancic and Richard Delgado, "A Shifting Balance: Freedom of Expression and Hate Speech Restriction," 78 *Iowa L. Rev.* 737, 742 (1993).

9. See also Henry Hyde and George Fishman, "The Collegiate Speech Protection Act of 1991: A Response to the New Intolerance in the Academy," 37 *Wayne L. Rev.* 1469, 1489 (1991).

10. Planned Parenthood v. Casey, 505 U.S. 833 (1992). For further discussion of the distinction between slippery slopes and dangerously broad principles, see James Weinstein, "An American's View of the Canadian Hate Speech Decisions," in *Free Expression: Essays in Law and Philosophy* 208–209 (W. J. Waluchow, ed., 1994).

11. Fiss, supra note 3 at 21.

12. Ibid.

13. Cf. ibid. at 14 ("Pornography is . . . most certainly part of the discourse by which the public understands itself and the world it confronts. A similar point can be made about hate speech.").

14. Ibid. at 21. Fiss's claim that hate speech silences through "diminish[ing] victims' sense of worth" and pornography does so by making women "feel as though they have nothing to contribute to public discussions" (ibid. at 16) would also seem to implicate the persuasive power of public discourse.

15. In Chapter 7 I discuss whether hate speech and pornography do in fact silence minorities and women.

16. Later in this chapter I address the substantial objection that whatever might be said about hate speech, pornography is neither part of the expression by which we govern ourselves nor a contributor to the marketplace of ideas.

17. United States v. Schwimmer, 279 U.S. 644 (1929) (Holmes, J., dissenting).

18. See, e.g., MacKinnon, supra note 8 at 75–77, 82.

19. Fiss, supra note 3 at 11. Similarly, MacKinnon criticizes the Supreme Court for its "studied inability [in its free speech decisions] to tell the difference between oppressor," such as the Ku Klux Klan, whose speech promotes inequality, and "oppressed," such as civil rights leaders, whose speech furthers equality. Such "piously evenhanded treatment" that "passes for principled neutrality" is to MacKinnon entirely inappropriate in "a country that is supposedly not constitutionally neutral on the subject." MacKinnon, supra note 8 at 86.

20. Fiss, supra note 3 at 37.

21. Cass Sunstein, *Democracy and the Problem of Free Speech* 216–217 (1993). These harms are discussed in Chapter 7.

22. Ibid.

23. Those who argue for a ban on pornography based on the harms in production frequently invoke New York v. Ferber, 458 U.S. 747 (1982). *Ferber* upheld a ban on the distribution of "child pornography," that is, films or photographs depicting children actually engaged in sex acts. The Court emphasized that the distribution of such material is "intrinsically related to the sexual abuse of children" and found that "the distribution network for child pornography must be closed if the production of material which requires the sexual exploitation of children is to be effectively controlled." *Ferber*, however, does not supply a helpful analogy for the suppression of pornography made with adult actors and models. By definition, *every* production of child pornography entails harm—sexual exploitation of a minor. The same cannot be said of pornography production that involves adults. Thus Sunstein concedes that "most women who participate [in the making of pornography] are not so abused." Cass Sunstein, "Words, Conduct, Caste," 60 *U. Chi. L. Rev.* 795, 809–810 (1993).

24. Cf. Food Lion, Inc. v. Capital Cities/ABC, Inc., 984 F. Supp. 923 (M.D.N. Car. 1997) (television network reporters held liable for fraud and trespass in connection with investigative report on supermarket chain).

25. Cf. MacKinnon, supra note 8 at 39 ("Putting the pornographers in the posture of the excluded underdog, like communists, plays on the deep free speech tradition against laws that restrict criticizing the government. Need it be said, women are not the government?").

26. See, e.g., Andrea Dworkin, *Pornography: Men Possessing Women* 55 (1979) ("Violence is male; the male is the penis. . . . What the penis can do it must do forcibly for a man to be a man"); Catharine MacKinnon, *Toward a Feminist Theory of the State* 138 (1989) ("[W]hat men want is: women bound, women battered, women tortured, women humiliated, women degraded . . . women killed").

27. Masses Publishing Co. v. Patten, 244 Fed. 535 (S.D. N.Y. 1917).

28. See Chapter 2, text accompanying notes 15 to 19.

29. 403 U.S. 15 (1971); 491 U.S. 397 (1989).

30. See John Stuart Mill, *On Liberty and Other Essays* 60–61 (John Gray, ed., 1991).

31. "As I would not be a slave, so I would not be a master. This expresses my idea of democracy. Whatever differs from this, to the extent of the difference, is no democracy." Abraham Lincoln, quoted in *Lincoln on Democracy* 122 (Mario Cuomo, ed., 1991).

32. Gitlow v. New York, 268 U.S. 652 (1925) (Holmes, J., dissenting).

33. It could be objected that in agreeing to a constitution that specifies certain rights, the majority has agreed in advance to limit its power but has not agreed to limit its power to institute a new form of government. This objection seems to go to the *legitimacy* of stopping a majority from instituting a nondemocratic government, not to its consistency with liberal theory.

The conclusion that it is consistent with democracy to prevent the majority from eradicating democracy does not depend on the view that the deepest value of a liberal democracy is the assurance of equal concern and respect. If the new regime would suppress speech critical of it or its policies, preventing it from taking power would promote the interest in assuring that the government respect each individual's rational capacities. Even on a libertarian view focusing on the protection of individual autonomy, it would be consistent to stop the majority from instituting a regime in which all liberties, including the right to property and the right to be let alone, would exist only at the forbearance of the dictator.

34. In affirming the convictions of high-ranking members of the American Communist Party for advocating the overthrow of the United States in violation of the Smith Act, Justice Frankfurter acknowledged that "public interest is not wanting in granting freedom to speak their minds even to those who advocate the overthrow of the Government by force. For, as the evidence in this case abundantly illustrates, coupled with such advocacy is criticism of defects in our society." Dennis v. United States, 341 U.S. 494 (1951) (Frankfurter, J., concurring).

35. These arguments do not undermine the premise that it is not inconsistent with liberal democracy actually to stop the institution of a totalitarian regime. Liberalism may be at once sufficiently skeptical to envision the possibility that its basic premises are wrong and therefore allow democracy to be challenged in the realm of ideas and at the same time sufficiently sure of itself that it will prevent the actual institution of an antidemocratic regime even if the majority wants such a change.

36. Aside from the possibility of actual misapplication of this rationale to speech that is not in fact antidemocratic, the very existence of such a principle for stripping speech of constitutional protection will chill radical critique. As Justice Frankfurter wrote in affirming the convictions of high-ranking communists for advocating overthrow of the U.S. government: "Suppressing advocates of overthrow inevitably will also silence critics who do not advocate overthrow but fear that their criticism may be so construed. It is self-delusion to think that we can punish [these defendants] for their advocacy without adding to the risks run by loyal citizens who honestly believe in some of the reforms these defendants advance. . . . [I]t is a sobering fact that in sustaining the convictions before us we can hardly escape restriction on the interchange of ideas." Dennis v. United States, 341 U.S. 494 (1951) (Frankfurter, J., concurring).

37. "[I]n suppressing totalitarian movements a democratic society is not acting to protect the status quo, but the very same interests which freedom of speech itself seeks to secure—the possibility of peaceful progress under freedom. . . . [O]ne type of constitutional change in the constitutional system is excluded—a change that would endanger its democratic character." Carl Auerbach, "The

Communist Control Act of 1954: A Proposed Legal-Political Theory of Free Speech," 23 *U. Chi. L. Rev.* 173, 188, 194 (1956).

38. Sunstein, supra note 23 at 795, 797, 807–808. Sunstein makes essentially the same argument in *Democracy,* supra note 21 at 15. There is, unfortunately, a studied vagueness about just what "forms of pornography" Sunstein thinks lie sufficiently "far from the center of First Amendment concern" that they should be deemed low-value speech. It is clear, however, that he means to include much more than the hard-core material suppressible as obscene under current doctrine.

39. Sunstein suggests that even nonviolent pornography contributes to the inequality of women "through its place in the sexual subordination or objectification of women." He restricts his discussion to violent pornography, however, both because such material is in his view "an especially important ingredient in sexual inequality" and because any broader regulation would raise "some trickier First Amendment difficulties." *Democracy,* supra note 21 at 212–213.

40. Ibid. at 125, 152.

41. Ibid. at 158.

42. Ibid. at 135.

43. Ibid. at 152–153.

44. Ibid. at 150.

45. Ibid. at 155.

46. Ibid. at 158. Thus Sunstein would forbid government to regulate any expression based on "(1) its own disagreement with the ideas that have been expressed, (2) its perception of the government's (as opposed to the public's) self-interest, (3) its fear that people will be persuaded or influenced by ideas, and (4) its desire to ensure that people are not offended by the ideas that speech contains." Ibid. at 155.

47. See Sunstein, "Words," supra note 23 at 807. See also *Democracy,* supra note 21 at 215.

48. And as discussed in Chapter 2, when there is reason for suspicion, such as where the conspiracy or threat is of a political nature or where the private libel is on a matter of public concern, rigorous First Amendment protection is applicable to "smoke out" such illegitimate governmental purpose.

49. See Marci Hamilton, "Art Speech," 49 *Vand. L. Rev.* 73, 97–101 (1996).

50. See Members of City Council v. Taxpayers for Vincent, 466 U.S. 789 (1984) (upholding ban on posting signs on utility poles on the aesthetic grounds of avoiding "visual clutter").

51. In the 1950s the White Citizens Councils condemned rock 'n' roll as "sexualistic, unmoralistic and [as] bring[ing] people of both races together." See Tony Scherman, "Little Richard's Big Noise," *Legacy* 56 (supplement to 46 *American Heritage Magazine,* February/March 1995). See also Linda Martin and Kerry Segrave, *Anti-Rock: The Opposition to Rock 'n' Roll* (1988).

Sunstein claims that there is no reason to be more suspicious that government is acting for some illegitimate reason when it regulates "nonpolitical" art and literature than when it regulates "anything else." *Democracy,* supra note 21 at 135. He points out, for instance, that "[m]any forms of regulation are attempts to stop marketplace competition, favored by self-interested groups and operating at the expense of the public at large." But even on the dubious assumption that the typical economic regulation is as likely to be illegitimately motivated as is the typical attempt to suppress nondeliberative art or literature, Sunstein's argument is beside the point. Whatever their evil, illegitimate economic regulations do not usually threaten basic free speech values. There are, moreover, several reasons that U.S. courts more vigilantly guard against illegitimate speech regulation than against illegitimate economic legislation. For one, the Constitution expressly limits the government's power to regulate speech but contains no analogous provision for economic liberties. In addition, illegitimate speech regulations implicate democracy in ways that illegitimately motivated economic regulations do not. See generally, John Ely, *Democracy and Distrust* (1980).

52. See note 46 above.

53. See, e.g., Paris Adult Theatres I v. Slaton, 413 U.S. 49 (1973) ("The sum of experience . . . affords an ample basis for legislatures to conclude that a sensitive, key relationship of human existence, central to family life, community welfare, and the development of human personality, can be debased and distorted by crass commercial exploitation of sex"). As this quotation shows, bans on obscenity allowed under current doctrine also raise suspicions that such bans are motivated by impermissible concerns. This recognition, however, would seem to argue against, not for, expansion of the category of sexually explicit speech that may be banned consistent with the First Amendment.

54. Ibid. at 220.

55. It should also be noted that current doctrine tries to mitigate any cost associated with the overprotection of pornography by allowing sexually explicit but nonobscene speech to be regulated in ways that other speech in highly protected media may not. As discussed in Chapter 4, theaters and bookstores specializing in sexually explicit but nonobscene materials may be subject to special zoning regulations; the sale to minors of even soft-core pornographic magazines such as *Playboy* may be outlawed; and over-the-air broadcasters may be forbidden from airing sexually explicit material at times when children are likely to be in the audience. In the same vein, the U.S. Court of Appeals in 1997 upheld a ban of the sale of sexually explicit material on military bases. See General Media Communications, Inc. v. Cohen, 131 F. 3d 273 (2nd Cir. 1997).

CHAPTER TEN

1. Owen Fiss, *The Irony of Free Speech* 4 (1996).

2. As discussed in the Appendix, note 136, there is evidence that counterspeech may not be an effective means of preventing the negative attitudes toward women that certain forms of pornography may produce. Thus government propaganda in this area might be better aimed at persuading men not to use this pornography in the first place.

3. Mari Matsuda, "Public Response to Racist Speech," in *Words That Wound* 50 (Mari Matsuda, Charles Lawrence, Richard Delgado, and Kimberlè Crenshaw, eds., 1993).

4. See Chapter 2, text accompanying note 16.

CHAPTER ELEVEN

1. See Henry Hyde and George Fishman, "The Collegiate Speech Protection Act of 1991: A Response to the New Intolerance in the Academy," 37 *Wayne L. Rev.* 1469, 1473 (1991).

2. See James Weinstein, "A Constitutional Roadmap to the Regulation of Campus Hate Speech," 38 *Wayne L. Rev.* 163, 242 n. 223 (1991) (documenting this and other misrepresentations by Hyde and Fishman).

3. See Richard Delgado, "Campus Antiracism Rules: Constitutional Narratives in Collision," 85 *Nw. L. Rev.* 343, 357 (1991).

APPENDIX

1. See Attorney General's Commission on Pornography, *Final Report*, July 1986, part 2 at 326 (hereafter, "1986 Report").

2. Barry Lynn, *Polluting the Censorship Debate: A Summary and Critique of the Final Report of the Attorney General's Commission on Pornography* (ACLU public policy report, 1986) at 70 (hereafter, "ACLU Critique").

3. Diana Russell, "Pornography and Rape: A Causal Model," 9 *Political Psychology* 41, 71 (1988); Ronald Dworkin, "The Coming Battles over Free Speech," *New York Review of Books*, June 11, 1992.

4. *Report of the Commission on Obscenity and Pornography* (1970) at 286–287.

5. 1986 Report, supra note 1 at 323.

6. Ibid. at 324.

7. Ibid. at 323.

8. Ibid. at 1402.

9. Ibid. at 1402–1403.

10. Ibid. at 1404.

11. Ibid. at 331.

12. Ibid. at 334–335.

13. Ibid. at 331–332.

14. Ibid. at 335.

15. Ibid. at 326.

16. Ibid. at 324.

17. Curiously, although in reaching its conclusions the commission relied extensively on studies such as Donnerstein's, the chapter that reports findings about harm (chapter 5 of part 2) sedulously avoids citations to individual studies. Frederick Schauer, the author of this chapter, later explained that the exclusion of specific citations was a compromise to avoid references to particular studies that he found "methodologically dubious." See Frederick Schauer, "Causation Theory and Causes of Sexual Violence," *Am. B. Found. Res. J.* 737, 764 n. 58 (1987). The various studies the commission used are summarized and analyzed in a separate section, chapter 3 of part 4 of the report, entitled "Social and Behavioral Science Research Analysis."

18. 1986 Report, supra note 1 at 983–984. See also Edward Donnerstein, Daniel Linz, and Steven Penrod, *The Question of Pornography* 94 (1987).

19. 1986 Report, supra note 1 at 984.

20. Ibid. at 325.

21. Ibid. at 326.

22. Ibid. at 313.

23. Ibid. at 317.

24. Ibid.

25. Ibid. at 326–327.

26. Ibid. at 981. The report inaccurately implies that those exposed to violent pornography expressed a greater willingness to engage in rape if they knew they would not be caught than those exposed to the nonviolent version. In fact, there was no difference in the responses of the two groups. See Neil Malamuth, Scott Haber, and Seymour Feshbach, "Testing Hypotheses Regarding Rape: Exposure to Sexual Violence, Sex Differences and the 'Normality' of Rapists," 14 *J. of Research in Personality* 121–137 (1980). See also Donnerstein, Linz, and Penrod, supra note 18 at 101.

27. Cf. Neil Malamuth and Edward Donnerstein, *Pornography and Sexual Aggression* 33 (1984), describing films as portraying "sexual aggression and suggest that such aggression may have positive consequences."

28. 1986 Report, supra note 1 at 983.

29. Ibid. at 327.

30. Ibid.

31. Ibid. at 987. The report's description of the results of the experiment is not entirely accurate. The study found that subjects exposed to the slasher films "showed a tendency to be less sympathetic to the victim of rape portrayed in the trial [and] were less able to empathize with rape victims in general when compared to the no-exposure control group." Contrary to an early experiment by Linz, Donnerstein, and Penrod, however, "no effects were observed for judgments of injury." Nor did exposure to the films "affect the other objectification, endorsement of force, and posttrial measures." See Daniel Linz, Edward Donnerstein, and Steven Penrod, "Effects of Long-Term Exposure to Violent and Sexually Degrading Depictions of Women," 55 *J. of Personality & Soc. Psychol.* 758 (1988). The authors hypothesize that because in this experiment the mock jurors were presented with a picture of the injured victim, whereas in the previous experiment they were not, "little doubt [was left] that the victim was harmed," thus "wash[ing] out" the effects of the prior film. Ibid. at 766. As discussed later in the Appendix, this experiment also investigated the effects of highly explicit "degrading" pornography and found that this stimulus did not produce the attitudinal effects reported in previous experiments.

32. 1986 Report, supra note 1 at 328. For this conclusion, the commission apparently relied on studies such as the 1980 experiment by Malamuth, Heim, and Feschbach. See 1986 Report at 981.

33. Ibid. at 328 (emphasis in the original).

34. Ibid. at 329.

35. Ibid. at 333–334.

36. Ibid.

37. Ibid. at 332.

38. Ibid. at 1001.

39. Ibid. at 1002.

40. Ibid. The commission also discussed a 1985 study by Senn in which female subjects were exposed to "erotica" (described as "mutually pleasurable sexual expression between two individuals presented as equal in power"), "nonviolent dehumanizing pornography" (described as "having no explicit violence but portraying acts of [female] submission"), and explicitly violent pornography. The commission reported that in this study, "[b]oth violent and nonviolent [degrading] pornography resulted in greater anxiety, depression and anger than erotica and both were also reliably differentiated from the latter on a number of affective dimensions, with 'erotica' consistently rated more positively." Ibid. at 1002–1003.

41. Ibid. at 333.

42. Ibid. at 334.

43. Ibid. at 334.

44. Ibid. at 337.

45. Ibid. at 330.

46. Ibid. at 997. "Sex callousness" was measured by agreement with such statements as "A woman doesn't mean 'no' until she slaps you." See Donnerstein, Linz, and Penrod, supra note 18 at 75–76.

47. 1986 Report, supra note 1 at 1006, 998.

48. Ibid. at 330 n. 46. See also 1006–1007.

49. Ibid. at 338–347.

50. Ibid. at 377.

51. Ibid.

52. Ibid. at 380.

53. Ibid. See also 354–358.

54. Ibid. at 366.

55. Ibid. at 403.

56. Ibid. at 361.

57. Ibid. at 362–363. The commission reached the following conclusions about harm to the performers in pornographic films: "(1) that [the performers] are normally young, previously abused, and financially strapped; (2) that on the job they find exploitive economic arrangements, extremely poor working conditions, serious health hazards, strong temptations to drug use, and little chance of career advancement; and (3) that in their personal lives they will often suffer substantial injuries to relationships, reputation and self-image." Ibid. at 888.

58. ACLU Critique, supra note 2.

59. Ibid. at 2.

60. Ibid. at 3.

61. Ibid. at 5–6.

62. Ibid. at 14.

63. Ibid. at 7.

64. Ibid. at 68.

65. Ibid. at 69. See also 41–42.

66. Ibid. at 70.

67. Ibid. at 85–87.

68. Ibid. at 70.

69. Ibid. at 71–72.

70. Ibid. at 73.

71. Ibid. at 83.

72. Ibid. at 88.

73. Daniel Goleman, "Researchers Dispute Pornography Report on Its Use of Data," *N.Y. Times,* May 17, 1986, A1.

74. Daniel Linz, Steve Penrod, and Edward Donnerstein, "The Attorney General's Commission on Pornography: The Gaps Between 'Findings' and Facts," 1987 *Am. B. Found. Res. J.,* 713, 713.

75. Ibid. at 721.

76. Ibid. at 722.

77. Ibid. at 714.

78. Ibid. at 723–725.

79. See Neil Malamuth, "Pornography's Impact on Male Adolescents," 4 *Adolescent Medicine: State of the Art Reviews* 563, 566–571 (1993). Malamuth notes, however, that primarily because of differing ideological predispositions, there is a "lack of a broad-based consensus among researchers about the effects of pornography" and that even this tentative conclusion is "not shared by all researchers." Ibid. at 566. Nonetheless, with respect to aggression and sexual callousness caused by violence presented in a sexual (although not necessarily pornographic) context, the findings have been remarkably consistent. For example, a recent experiment essentially replicated the findings of the 1981 study by Malamuth and Check. See, e.g., Monica Weisz and Christopher Earls, "The Effects of Exposure to Filmed Violence and Attitudes Towards Rape," 10 *J. of Interpersonal Violence* 71 (1995). The one outlier is a study by Fisher and Grenier, which found that violent pornography "had no effect on attitudes towards women, acceptance of women as managers, acceptance of interpersonal violence, or rape myth acceptance." See William Fisher and Azy Barak, "Pornography, Erotica, and Behavior: More Questions Than Answers," 14 *Intl. J. of Law & Psychiatry* 65, 76 (1991), describing what was then an unpublished study of a 1987 experiment. The study was not published until 1994. See William Fisher and Guy Grenier, "Violent Pornography, Antiwoman Thoughts, and Antiwoman Acts: In Search of Reliable Effects," 31 *J. of Sex Research* 23 (1994). As is suggested by the lengthy delay in publication, there were some serious problems with this study. See Neil Malamuth, "Sexually Violent Media, Thought Patterns and Antisocial Behavior," in 2 *Public Comm. & Behavior* 159, 184–185 (1989).

80. See 1986 Report, supra note 1 at 983 (discussing 1981 experiment by Malamuth and Check and their efforts to deal with the experimenter demand effect).

81. Linz et al., supra note 74 at 714.

82. See 1986 Report at 1007–1021 (addressing "the problem of the ability to generalize the results outside the laboratory," among other methodological problems).

83. Obvious ethical constraints prevent scientists from exposing subjects to pornography and then seeing if they commit acts of sexual violence against women in the real world. Indeed, scientists who conducted experiments that produced aggressive behavior in the laboratory or changed attitudes were careful to debrief their subjects after the experiments in order to reduce the chances of a real-world spillover effect. See, e.g., 1986 Report, supra note 1 at 988; Paul Pollard, "Pornography and Sexual Aggression," *Current Psychology* 210–211 (Fall 1995).

These same considerations prevent laboratory experiments testing for long-term effects of exposure to pornography. For a recent study suggesting that the negative attitude changes caused by violent pornography may be short-term only, see Charles Mullin and Daniel Linz, "Desensitization and Resensitization to Violence Against Women: Effects of Exposure to Sexually Violent Films on Judgments of Domestic Violence Victims," 69 *J. of Personality & Social Psychol.* 449 (subjects tested three days after exposure to slasher films exhibited less sympathy for victims of domestic violence and found the victims to be less injured than did those in the no-exposure group; those tested five and seven days after exposure, however, were indistinguishable from the no-exposure group). For an article suggesting how aggression produced in laboratory experiments can inform us about the causes of real-world violence, see Brad Bushman and Craig Anderson, "Methodology in the Study of Aggression: Integrating Experimental and Nonexperimental Findings," in *Human Aggression: Theories, Research and Implications for Social Policy* (Russell Green and Edward Donnerstein, eds., 1998).

84. 1986 Report, supra note 1 at 325–326.

85. Other data might include correlational data. For a recent review of this data, see Robert Bauserman, "Sexual Aggression and Pornography: A Review of Correlational Research," 18 *Basic & Applied Social Psychol.* 405 (1996).

86. Schauer, supra note 17 at 764–765.

87. Ibid. at 766–767.

88. See ibid. at 737.

89. Ibid. at 763.

90. 1986 Report, supra note 1 at 329.

91. Other than the reference to Schauer's omission of the modifier "strongly" in his quotation of the report, my discussion of the discrepancy between the report and Schauer's article is not meant as a criticism of Schauer. In drafting the report, Schauer was in the unenviable position of trying to produce a consensus statement of eleven individuals, many of whom had very different views about pornography.

92. As reported by Malamuth, a recent study showed that "for the population as a whole, information about pornography usage did not add a great deal of predictive value" about whether men in the study were likely to be sexually aggressive. But "significant predictive value" was found "for those men who had earlier been identified as at highest risk for committing sexual aggression." Malamuth, "Pornography's Impact," supra note 79 at 570. Although cause and effect cannot be inferred from this correlational study, it is interesting to note that it is consistent with earlier experimental research, from which cause and effect can be inferred, showing that "men scoring relatively high in pretest measures of risk characteristics (e.g., self-reported attraction to sexual aggression) showed the most pronounced effects of exposure to sexually violent and highly degrading pornography." Ibid. at 571.

93. Malamuth believes that the available data are consistent with some "interactive models" suggesting that certain types of pornography may, in combination with several other risk factors, contribute to sexual aggression in the real world. Such models take into consideration factors such as (1) the content of the message portrayed by the pornography, e.g., "an eroticized rape depiction with a positive

outcome as contrasted to an equally sexually explicit depiction showing mutually-consenting sex"; (2) the characteristics of the audience, e.g., "a man with high 'hostile masculinity' or attraction to sexual aggression as contrasted with a man who has particularly egalitarian feelings and attitudes towards women"; and (3) the context of the exposure, e.g., "a social climate encouraging aggression and discrimination against women versus a social climate emphasizing gender equality and respect for women's rights." Correspondence with author, December 1998. See also Malamuth, "Pornography's Impact on Male Adolescents," supra note 79 at 569 ("one of the problems in the literature has been the use of oversimplistic models, including the lack of sufficient consideration of the role of individual and cultural differences as moderators of media influences"); Neil Malamuth and Eldad Malamuth, "Integrating Multiple Levels of Scientific Analysis and the Confluence Model of Sexual Coercers," 39 *Jurimetrics* 57 (1999).

94. 1986 Report, supra note 1 at 1406.

95. Joseph Scott and Steven Cuvelier, "Violence in *Playboy* Magazine: A Longitudinal Analysis," 16 *Archives of Sexual Behavior* 279 (1987). See also Fisher and Barak, supra note 79 at 70–71 (1991).

96. ACLU Critique, supra note 2 at 41–42, 69. Similarly, a 1985 study of 430 sexually explicit magazines found that 1.4 percent of the content depicted violence or domination. See Charles Winick, "A Content Analysis of Sexually Explicit Magazines Sold in Adult Bookstores," 21 *J. of Sex Research* 206 (1985). This is consistent with a study by the Canadian government that found that 1.2 percent of the photographs and 3.7 percent of the text in eleven of the top-selling sex magazines depicted force or violence. See Committee on Sexual Offense Against Children and Youths, *Report of the Committee on Sexual Offenses Against Children and Youths* (1984). In contrast, a 1988 study sampling X-rated videos found that although only 6 percent of the explicit sex scenes involved rape, 51 percent of the videos portrayed at least one rape and most sexually explicit scenes portrayed male dominance. Gloria Cowan, Carol Lee, Daniella Levy, and Debra Snyder, "Dominance and Inequality in X-Rated Videocassettes," 12 *Psychol. of Women Quarterly* 299 (1988).

97. See Marcia Pally, *Sex and Sensibility* 32–33 (1994). In response to the Malamuth and Spinner study showing a high level of violence in the magazine, the editor of *Playboy* informed Malamuth that he would issue a directive "requesting that the [*Playboy*] staff attend to and screen out violent images and messages." See Daniel Linz, Edward Donnerstein, and Steven Penrod, "The Findings and Recommendations of the Attorney General's Commission on Pornography: Do the Psychological Facts Fit the Political Fury?" 42 *American Psychologist* 946, 948 n. 1 (1987).

98. Schauer, supra note 17 at 740 n. 13.

99. Park Dietz and Alan Sears, "Pornography and Obscenity Sold in 'Adult Bookstores': A Survey of 5132 Books, Magazines, and Films in Four American Cities," 21 *U. Mich. J. L. Ref.* 7 (1988).

100. Ibid. at 24, 38–39.

101. Cf. Dietz and Sears, supra note 99 at 13 ("Of the 105 works examined internally after the cover imagery had been classified, all but two contained imagery that was more sexually explicit or deviant than the cover").

102. Ni Yang and Daniel Linz, "Movie Ratings and the Content of Adult Videos: The Sex-Violence Ratio," 40 *J. of Comm.* 28, 34 (1990).

103. Ibid. at 33.

104. Joseph Slade, "Violence in the Hard-Core Pornographic Film: A Historical Survey," 34 *J. of Comm.* 148, 158–159, 162 (1984).

105. Ibid. at 159–161.

106. Ibid. at 161.

107. Ibid. at 155. (It is not clear whether the numbers Slade cites refer to films or scenes involving graphic sex.)

108. Donald Smith, "The Social Content of Pornography," 26 *J. of Comm.* 16 (1976).

109. For instance, the available research suggests that violent pornography showing women "ultimately deriving physical pleasure" is far more likely to foster aggressive attitudes in male viewers than equally violent depictions showing victims "abhorring the experience." See Malamuth, "Pornography's Impact," supra note 79 at 566–567.

110. Eric Schlosser, "The Business of Pornography," *U.S. News and World Report,* February 10, 1997. The inclusion of "sexual devices" within pornography statistics is curious, for such fare would seem to be a distinct commodity. Perhaps they are included because they are commonly sold in outlets for pornographic material.

111. When the Attorney General's Commission on Pornography reported in 1986, it found that Americans spent $2 billion a year on hard-core pornographic films displayed in "peep show" booths (1986 Report, supra note 1 at 1477); that 13 percent of videos consumed by the public were "adult" (ibid. at 1388); that over 10 million issues of mainstream soft-core pornographic magazines were sold each month (ibid. at 1411); and that thousands of new titles of pornographic paperback novels were produced each year (ibid. at 1451). In 1994 the *Wall Street Journal* reported that nearly half a billion pornographic videotapes were rented or sold each year. See John Wilke, "Porn Broker: A Publicly Held Firm Turns X-Rated Videos into a Hot Business," *Wall Street Journal,* July 11, 1994, A1.

112. See Neil Munro, "Porn Comes in One Color: Green," *National Journal,* January 9, 1999.

113. 1986 Report, supra note 1 at 331.

114. Wendy McElroy, *XXX: A Woman's Right to Pornography* 135–136 (1995).

115. Pally, supra note 97 at 27 (citing T. Ferraro, "Playboy Redux and Christie Hefner," UPI, November 23, 1986).

116. See ACLU Critique, supra note 2 at 71–72, discussing how the final report did not contain examples of "degrading" material that had appeared in earlier drafts, apparently because of "[t]he failure of the Commissioners to agree on the contents of this . . . category." Malamuth believes that "[d]elineating what is degrading or dehumanizing may be feasible, [although] considerable 'gray' areas where differentiation is not reliable will probably remain." Malamuth, "Pornography's Impact," supra note 79 at 572. Malamuth cites a 1990 study by Senn and Radtke in which five Canadian undergraduate women were asked to categorize various material taken from *Playboy, Penthouse,* and *Hustler* magazines and two books as "erotica," "nonviolent pornography," or "violent pornography." The students agreed on about 75

percent of the stimuli but disagreed considerably on about 25 percent. "Erotica" was defined as "images that have as their focus the depiction of mutually pleasurable sexual expression between people who have enough power to be there by positive choice [and that] have no sexist or violent connotations and portray equal power dynamics individually as well as between the model(s) and the camera/photographer." "Nonviolent pornography" was defined as "images that have no explicitly violent content but may imply acts of submission or violence by the positioning of the models or the use of props. They may also imply unequal power relationships by differential dress, costuming, positioning, or by setting up the viewer as voyeur." (Malamuth explains that this category is "similar to that labeled as degrading or dehumanizing by other researchers.") "Violent pornography" was defined as "images that portray explicit violence of varying degrees perpetrated against one individual by another." See Charlene Senn and Lorraine Radtke, "Women's Evaluations of and Affective Reactions to Mainstream Violent Pornography, Nonviolent Pornography and Erotica," 5 *Violence & Victims* 143, 144 (1990).

With all due respect to Malamuth, 75 percent agreement by five female undergraduates (who, for all we know from the experiment, share similar backgrounds) would not seem to be persuasive evidence that it is possible to achieve consensus about what sexually explicit material is "demeaning." For a more recent attempt to distinguish degrading from nondegrading sexually explicit material involving twenty-six undergraduates, see Laura Jansma, Daniel Linz, Anthony Mulac, and Dorothy Imrich, "Men's Interaction with Women After Viewing Sexually Explicit Films: Does Degradation Make a Difference?" 64 *Communications Monographs* 1 (March 1997). As I emphasize in the text, however, what would seem most important with respect to identifying any harmful effects of pornography is not whether subjects can agree on what is demeaning but identifying certain material that although not explicitly violent nonetheless produces effects similar to violent pornography. The study by Jansma et al. reports that "[t]o date, no study has similarly attempted to define objectively and distinguish operationally sexually explicit *degrading* pornography from sexually explicit, *non-degrading* stimulus material to allow valid comparisons between these categories and others." Ibid. at 5.

117. 1986 Report, supra note 1 at 332–334.

118. Ibid. at 1006–1007.

119. Ibid.

120. The report discussed a 1985 study by Senn that similarly differentiated among "erotica," "nonviolent dehumanizing pornography," and "violent pornography." Both the violent and dehumanizing pornography produced greater depression, anxiety, and anger in the subjects—all of whom were women—than did the erotica. See 1986 Report, supra note 1 at 1002–1003.

121. Ibid. at 1002.

122. Ibid. at 1006. See 330 and n. 46.

123. Linz et al., supra note 74 at 723.

124. Ibid. at 723 n. 20. Linz subsequently published an article based on this dissertation. See Linz, Donnerstein, and Penrod, supra note 31. Krafka's findings have just recently been published. See Carol Krafka, Daniel Linz, Edward Donnerstein, and Steven Penrod, "Women's Reactions to Sexually Aggressive Mass Media Depictions," 3 *Violence Against Women* 149 (1997). The Linz study

found that exposure to degrading pornography did not increase "rape myth acceptance, belief in women as sexual objects, endorsement of force in sexual relations, [or] conservative sex roles." Nor when the subjects were tested after being shown what was presented to them as a documentary for law school use was there any effect on "assessments of the victim, defendant, verdict or sentence." Linz et al., supra note 31 at 766–767. Krafka's study revealed similar results for female subjects. See Donnerstein, Linz, and Penrod, supra note 18 at 79–80. As discussed above in the text accompanying note 31, both studies did, however, reveal attitude changes from R-rated slasher films.

125. Donnerstein, Linz, and Penrod, supra note 18 at 80. In addition, it is not at all clear that either study prospectively identified the sexually explicit material as degrading to women. Rather, like most of the other studies cited as evidence of the effects of demeaning pornography, it seems to have designated the stimulus material in this way retrospectively. Nor is it in fact clear that the films were in fact demeaning to women. Thus the study describes the films (*Debbie Does Dallas, Health Spa, The Other Side of Julie, Indecent Exposure,* and *Fantasy*) as "not overtly violent but . . . sexually explicit and *arguably* depict[ing] women as sexually degraded objects." Linz, Penrod, and Donnerstein, supra note 74 at 759 (emphasis added). According to the investigators, however, the sexually explicit scenes in these films were similar to those used in Check's study. Donnerstein et al., supra note 18 at 79.

126. Indeed, a 1997 study reports that several recent experiments failed to show that demeaning pornography causes sex callousness or aggressive behavior toward women in the laboratory. See Jansma et al., supra note 116 at 1–2. This study did, however, find that demeaning pornography might have other negative consequences. The study found that "sex-typed" men (i.e., those who scored high on stereotypical masculine traits and low on stereotypical feminine traits according to the Bem Sex Role Inventory) exposed to demeaning pornography were more likely to evaluate women with whom they interacted shortly thereafter as less intellectually capable, as compared to sex-typed men exposed to a nondegrading sexually explicit film or a film not containing sexual content. Ibid. at 17. As to non-sex-typed men, the study found that neither type of sexually explicit film was more likely to cause subjects to rate women as less intellectually capable than the nonsexual film.

127. 1986 Report, supra note 1 at 334–335, 331–332.

128. Dietz and Sears, supra note 99.

129. Ibid. at 30 and n. 52.

130. Ibid. at 30. Despite the recent feminist attack on pornography as demeaning to women, Dietz and Sears do not offer a classification based on a feminist perspective. Rather, they assume that "leading feminist thinkers on this topic" would "on independent grounds" arrive "at standards of degradation or humiliation that correspond closely to the standards of traditionalists." "Despite seemingly profound differences in other attitudes," the authors explain, "both the traditionalists and these feminists agree that the commercialized exploitation of people as sex objects is degrading and humiliating." Ibid. at 30 n. 53. Obviously, the feminists that Dietz and Sears have in mind are radical feminists such as MacKinnon and Andrea Dworkin rather than liberal feminists, whose views on this subject are likely to dif-

fer sharply from both the traditionalists and radical feminists. See, e.g., Nadine Strossen, *Defending Pornography* (1995); Nan Hunter and Sylvia Law, *Brief Amici Curiae of Feminist Anti-Censorship Taskforce,* in American Booksellers Assn. v. Hudnut, reprinted in 21 *U. Mich. J. Law Ref.* 69 (1988). In addition, there may not be as much overlap as Dietz and Sears suppose between conservative and radical feminist views concerning what sexually explicit material is degrading. For instance, conservatives would likely find degrading the examples of Andrea Dworkin's sexually explicit descriptions quoted in Chapter 8, text accompanying note 30.

131. Dietz and Sears, supra note 99 at 31.

132. Ibid. at 32–33.

133. The commission's category included in addition to materials depicting degradation and humiliation those that portrayed domination and subordination. Dietz and Sears's study, however, does not include material that depicts domination and subordination because the data collected were not coded to record such content. Ibid. at 30 n. 51.

134. See 1986 Report, supra note 1 at 1006.

135. In this regard it is interesting to note that a study commissioned by the Canadian Department of Justice concluded that "there is no persuasive evidence that the viewing of pornography . . . causes the average adult to harm others." See Working Papers on Pornography and Prostitution, Report 13 (1984). Similarly, the Williams Committee "unhesitatingly reject[ed] the suggestion that the available statistical information for England and Wales lends any support to the argument that pornography acts as a stimulus to the commission of sexual violence." *Obscenity and Film Censorship* 80 (Bernard Williams, ed., 1980).

136. Linz et al., supra note 74 at 730–731. Malamuth notes that such a counterspeech strategy may not be effective because "recent research indicates that once developed, attitudes such as beliefs in rape myths may be difficult to change. In fact, some people who already hold such beliefs to a relatively high degree may evidence boomerang effects; that is attempts to change negative attitudes may have the opposite effect of strengthening them." Malamuth, "Pornography's Impact on Male Adolescents," supra note 79 at 573.

137. Linz, Penrod, and Donnerstein, supra note 74 at 721.

138. 1986 Report, supra note 1 at 215.

139. Edward Donnerstein, Leonard Berkowitz, and Daniel Linz, "Role of Aggressive and Sexual Images in Violent Pornography," manuscript discussed in Donnerstein, Linz, and Penrod, supra note 18 at 110. See also Linz, Penrod, and Donnerstein, supra note 74 at 720, describing the results of this experiment. The authors do, however, also cite a 1974 study by Berkowitz that showed that subjects who viewed a violence-only film exhibited more "callous rape attitudes" and reported greater "likelihood of raping or using force" than subjects who viewed films that combined sex and violence. Ibid.

140. Malamuth, "Pornography's Impact on Male Adolescents," supra note 79 at 571.

141. Donnerstein, Linz, and Penrod, supra note 18 at 112.

142. Ibid.

143. Yang and Linz, supra note 102 at 34.

144. Linz, Penrod, and Donnerstein, supra note 74 at 721.

145. Ibid.

146. 1986 Report, supra note 1 at 328–329. Indeed, the commission acknowledges that it is "unclear whether sexually violent material makes a substantially greater causal contribution to sexual violence itself than does material containing violence alone." Ibid. at 328.

147. See, e.g., the experiment by Donnerstein described in the text accompanying notes 17 to 19 above.

148. 1986 Report, supra note 1 at 363.

149. There is, however, the following inconsistency in the report: At one place the commission suggests that legally obscene, sexually violent material may be more harmful than less sexually graphic material because such material presents its message "undiluted by any appeal to the intellect." Ibid. at 362. In another part of the report, however, the commission notes that graphically violent but not particularly sexually explicit slasher films are more harmful than most hard-core violent pornography. Ibid. at 328–329.

150. Edward Donnerstein and Daniel Linz, "Sexual Violence in the Media: A Warning," 14–15 *Psychology Today,* January 1984.

151. Edward Donnerstein, "Erotica and Human Aggression," in *Aggression: Theoretical and Empirical Reviews* 127, 151 (Russell Green and Edward Donnerstein, eds., 1983).

152. ACLU Critique, supra note 2 at 75.

153. Ibid. at 87.

154. 1986 Report, supra note 1 at 1000.

155. ACLU Critique, supra note 2 at 38.

156. Ibid. at 90 (emphasis added).

157. Such tendentiousness in assessing the harms of pornography is not limited to the commission, free speech organizations, and scientists. In arguing for the constitutional protection of pornography, philosopher Ronald Dworkin refers to the 1970 report as a "prestigious" study that denies that such a causal link exists and to the "infamous" Meese Commission as finding such a link. "Women and Pornography," *New York Review of Books,* October 21, 1993.

158. Edward Mulvey and Jeffrey Haugaard, *Report of the Surgeon General's Workshop on Pornography and Public Health* 34–35 (Office of the Surgeon General, U.S. Public Health Service, 1986).

Index